The Dilemma
of Freight Transport
Regulation

Studies in the Regulation of Economic Activity

The Dilemma of Freight Transport Regulation

ANN F. FRIEDLAENDER

A background paper prepared for a conference of experts at the Brookings Institution, together with a summary of the conference discussion.

The Brookings Institution Washington, D.C.

© 1969 by
THE BROOKINGS INSTITUTION
1775 Massachusetts Avenue, N.W., Washington, D.C. 20036

Second printing July 1970

ISBN 0-8157-2936-7

Library of Congress Catalog Card Number 69-18820

THE BROOKINGS INSTITUTION is an independent organization devoted to nonpartisan research, education, and publication in economics, government, foreign policy, and the social sciences generally. Its principal purposes are to aid in the development of sound public policies and to promote public understanding of issues of national importance.

The Institution was founded on December 8, 1927, to merge the activities of the Institute for Government Research, founded in 1916, the Institute of Economics, founded in 1922, and the Robert Brookings Graduate School of Economics and Government, founded in 1924.

The general administration of the Institution is the responsibility of a self-perpetuating Board of Trustees. The trustees are likewise charged with maintaining the independence of the staff and fostering the most favorable conditions for creative research and education. The immediate direction of the policies, program, and staff of the Institution is vested in the President, assisted by an advisory council chosen from the staff of the Institution.

In publishing a study, the Institution presents it as a competent treatment of a subject worthy of public consideration. The interpretations and conclusions in such publications are those of the author or authors and do not purport to represent the views of the other staff members, officers, or trustees of the Brookings Institution.

Foreword

PRESIDENT KENNEDY'S transportation message of 1962 marked the first time that the desirability of substantially reducing transport regulation had received official sanction. While earlier government studies had questioned specific aspects of the regulatory process, the Kennedy message explicitly called for "greater reliance on the forces of competition and less reliance on the restraints of regulation," and stated that "less Federal regulation and subsidization is in the long run a prime prerequisite of a healthy intercity transportation network."

Existing government practices and policies received a sweeping indictment in the Kennedy message. In particular, the following inefficiencies and inequities were singled out: the dulling of managerial initiative; the inability of carriers to divest themselves of traffic that fails to cover costs; the inability of carriers to make full use of their capacity by soliciting business or adjusting rates if such action would adversely affect other carriers; the substitution of cost-increasing service competition for cost-reducing rate competition; the unequal extent of regulation with respect to bulk and agricultural commodities; the unequal treatment of different carriers arising from government investments and user charges; and, finally, the decline of the common carrier relative to private and exempt carriage.

To correct these undesirable consequences of current government policies, the Kennedy message called for an end to minimum rate regulation on bulk and agricultural commodities, consistent policies of taxation and user charges, and other measures that would place reliance on "unsubsidized privately owned facilities, operating under the incentives of private profit and the checks of competition" to achieve the goals of an efficient, dynamic, and responsive transportation system.

As it challenged regulatory practices that have existed for some seventy-five years and as it threatened interests that have depended on these practices, the Kennedy message met with considerable opposition. Consequently, the bills incorporating the recommendations of the message were narrowly defeated in committee in 1963. Nevertheless, interest in a major overhaul of transport regulatory policy has not diminished, and a large group of transportation experts seems to feel that major changes in transportation policy are needed. The creation of a Department of Transportation in 1966 provides a new focus for the development of executive branch policy toward regulation.

Because of the divergence in views concerning the proper nature and extent of transport regulation, the Brookings Institution decided to undertake a study that would discuss systematically the implications of maintaining the current regulatory policies or of adopting alternatives. To this end, the Institution asked Professor Ann F. Friedlaender of Boston College to prepare a background paper for a conference of experts on issues in freight transportation policy that was held at Brookings on December 14 and 15, 1967. This volume, which presents Mrs. Friedlaender's paper supplemented by her summary of the conference discussion, attempts to evaluate the costs and benefits of various transportation policies. It may thus contribute to future discussions of transport policy by professional economists, industry experts, and the general public.

Although all conference participants influenced the final version of this study, Mrs. Friedlaender would like especially to thank Robert A. Nelson, James R. Nelson, John R. Meyer, Merton J. Peck, and Edwin T. Haefele for the time they generously gave in discussions and in commenting on the various drafts of the manuscript. Joseph A. Pechman and William M. Capron provided helpful comments throughout. Discussions with Gordon Murray, Ernest Weiss, Edward Margolin, and A. Scheffer Lang provided important insights that helped shape the formulation of the major issues facing transport regulatory policy. H. Michael Mann, William Hughes, Lester B. Lave, George W. Wilson, Dennis C. Mueller, Holland Hunter, E. Cary Brown, George H. Borts, and Aaron Gellman commented incisively on various sections of the manuscript. Robert Cohn, Edward J. Ford, and Roy Van Til provided research assistance. Mrs. Eileen Smith typed each draft of the manuscript.

The author is also grateful to the following Brookings staff members: Evelyn P. Fisher, who carefully checked the statistical material for consistency and accuracy, Evelyn Breck, who edited the manuscript, and Helen B. Eisenhart, who prepared the index.

The project was financed under a grant by the Sloan Foundation. The views expressed in this study are those of the author and are not presented as the views of the staff members, officers, or trustees of the Brookings Institution or the Sloan Foundation.

KERMIT GORDON
President

July 1969
Washington, D.C.

Contents

TEXT TABLES

CHAPTER ONE

The Problem

FREIGHT TRANSPORTATION has long been a problem sector in the United States economy, and four major government studies and messages on transportation since 1955 have made clear that the present is no exception.[1] Although their specific recommendations differed, all the reports criticized the working of the transport system and dealt with a common list of problems, including the erosion of the position of the common carriers by nonregulated and exempt carriers; the inefficiencies created by value-of-service pricing, which makes it profitable for trucks to carry goods that could go more cheaply by rail; the widespread excess capacity in virtually all transportation modes; and the lack of technical change and rationalization in transport. The encompassing nature of this list testifies eloquently to the inadequacies of present policies.

Disagreement over the desirability of alternative policies is almost as striking as the consensus on the nature of the problems. On one side are the Interstate Commerce Commission (ICC), truckers, and barge operators, favoring continued and extended regulation; on the other are the last two administrations and the railroads, favoring less regulation and

1. These are the Weeks Report to the President, *Revision of Federal Transportation Policy,* Report to the President by the Presidential Advisory Committee on Transport Policy and Organization (1955); the Mueller Report, U.S. Department of Commerce, *Federal Transportation Policy and Program* (March 1960); Special Study Group on Transportation Policies in the United States, *National Transportation Policy,* Preliminary Draft of a Report Prepared for the Senate Committee on Interstate and Foreign Commerce (1961), cited hereafter as Doyle Report; and "Transportation System of Our Nation," Message from the President to Congress, April 5, 1962. In addition, James M. Landis, *Report on Regulatory Agencies to the President-Elect* (December 1960), stressed the need for a drastic administrative overhaul to improve the effectiveness of the ICC.

heavier reliance on the forces of competition. Since the failure of Congress to pass the bills requested in the Kennedy transportation message, pressures for a change in present policies have been uneven. The Johnson administration concentrated its efforts on establishing a Department of Transportation and failed to recommend more sweeping changes.[2] Whatever the transport policies of the Nixon administration, it is likely that the problems of Vietnam and the cities will take precedence over the problems of the transport sector.

Thus this seems to be an opportune time to review the basic issues: to trace the development of existing regulatory policies, to indicate why and in what ways they are not working well, and to analyze the probable effects of alternative policies. This study is therefore concerned with the costs and benefits of alternative transportation policies in both a qualitative and a quantitative way.

Briefly, the problem is this. When regulation of railroads was first introduced in 1887, it was widely supported. Small, isolated shippers wanted it to protect them from the monopoly power of the railroads. Western communities wanted it to limit the railroads' heavy-handed exercise of economic power over rates, routes, and the placement of depots. The general public wanted it to control the frequent rate wars, the watered stock, the irresponsible land speculation, and the many bankruptcies and reorganizations. The federal government wanted it to ensure relatively low freight rates on goods coming from the West to encourage the continued settlement and development of this region. The railroads supported it (or at least acquiesced to it) to formalize the existing rate structure and to end the instability created by frequent rate wars.[3] Thus, the Interstate Commerce Act of 1887 and the regulatory structure it established enjoyed wide support. Regulation controlled the monopolistic excesses of the railroads while permitting them to maintain a rate structure that benefited not only the railroads but society.

2. See "Special Message to the Congress on Transportation," March 2, 1966, in *Public Papers of the Presidents of the United States: Lyndon B. Johnson*, Book 1 (1967), pp. 250–63. The bill to create a Department of Transportation was passed in October 1966. In its present form the department has relatively few powers to enforce an overall and unified transportation policy.

3. For an elaboration of these views see Solon Justus Buck, *The Granger Movement, 1870–1880* (Harvard University Press, 1913); Gabriel Kolko, *Railroads and Regulation, 1877–1916* (Princeton University Press, 1965); Lee Benson, *Merchants, Farmers, and Railroads: Railroad Regulation and New York Politics, 1850–1887* (Harvard University Press, 1955); Ida Tarbell, *The History of the Standard Oil Company* (Macmillan, 1904), 2 vols.

The first four sections of the Interstate Commerce Act of 1887 effectively prohibited the monopoly exploitation of the small shippers by requiring that rates be just and reasonable (Section 1) and by explicitly prohibiting personal discrimination (Section 2), undue preference between persons, localities, and types of traffic (Section 3), and the practice of charging more for a short haul than a long haul over a common line (Section 4). Section 5 was specifically aimed at the railroads' practice of pooling their earnings on a joint profit-maximizing basis, which was the main means of cartelizing the industry. Thus the body of the act was designed to curtail the unacceptable monopoly practices of the railroads. Nevertheless, the act made no mention of the most prevalent form of price discrimination used by the railroads—the practice of value-of-service pricing, under which low-value agricultural products and raw materials were shipped at rates considerably lower than those applied to high-value manufactured goods.

Commodity price discrimination that permitted low-value bulk and agricultural commodities to travel at low rates while high rates were charged for manufactured commodities satisfied important social goals. Low rates on agricultural products and raw materials produced in the West enabled them to compete with alternative sources of supply closer to the large eastern markets and thus assisted its development. Similarly, low rates supported farm incomes at a level which encouraged people to undertake the risks and hardships of settling the western and southwestern lands. If the supply of agricultural goods had been fixed in the short run, rate increases would have been pushed back to producers, reducing their income; this in turn would have had the long-run effect of slowing the development of these areas. Furthermore, the high rates on manufactured goods encouraged the industrial development of the West by effectively protecting its infant manufacturing industries from the more efficient eastern producers. Although this rate structure tended to turn the terms of trade against the western and southwestern farmers and raw material producers by encouraging low prices for their raw material exports and high prices for their manufactured imports, its net effect was to encourage the development of the West.

The railroad rate structure that met these social goals was also in the long-run, profit-maximizing interest of the railroads. Because of rapid expansion of capacity, the railroads had developed a cost structure characterized by large fixed costs relative to variable costs. This meant that where competitive pressures prevailed, rail rates tended to be pushed down to variable costs. Where few competitive pressures existed, rail rates tended to rise considerably above average total costs.

Bulk commodities were subject to considerable competitive pressures because of water competition, alternative sources of supply, and the high proportion of freight costs in the final-goods price, which ensured that a rate increase would be reflected in it. Thus these commodities had a highly elastic demand for rail services; any rate change would have led to a more than proportional change in traffic. On the other hand, no other means of transport was as well suited as railroads for carrying high-value manufactured goods, and the small proportion of freight costs in their final prices ensured that rate increases would have an insignificant effect on them. Hence these commodities had an inelastic demand for rail services; any rate change would have led to a less than proportional change in traffic.

In view of their cost structure and the nature of the demand for their services on the part of low-value bulk commodities and high-value manufactured commodities, the railroads would have evolved a value-of-service rate structure in any event. Thus the form of commodity price discrimination that encouraged the development of the West also maximized the railroads' profits. Regulation simply institutionalized these pricing policies while restraining the monopoly power of the railroads in other areas.

Regulation of the railroads and manipulation of the rate structure for policy purposes made sense in the late nineteenth century. At that time, the structure of government was uncomplicated, and the tools available to it were few and limited in scope. Since their interests were similar, relatively little conflict arose between government and the railroads over regulatory policies. Because there were virtually no other means of transport for many commodities, few distortions resulted from rate regulation. When it was initially instituted, regulation led to substantial social benefits and created few social costs.

As long as the policy tools available to the government remained limited, and as long as the elasticities of demand of manufactured goods for rail services remained low, employing the railroad rate structure as one such tool could be defended. However, the technology and related market circumstances that made the entire system desirable in the early twentieth century have changed, if not vanished, in the wake of subsequent development of other modes of transport—pipelines, highway transportation, and barges. Transport demands have become increasingly sensitive to cost differentials. Railroads have steadily lost high-value traffic to trucks, which, faster and more flexible, can deprive the railroads of traffic even while charging identical rates. Similarly, as their costs fall, barges and pipelines are making inroads into the bulk traffic market. The result has been considerable excess capacity throughout the transportation system.

Thus the main issue facing freight transportation today is the extent to which the present system of value-of-service pricing can and should be maintained. If continued use of transport rates for redistributive purposes is deemed desirable, it is probably necessary both to intensify and to broaden the regulatory process. If, however, the costs of continuing the present rate structure are considered too great, relaxed regulation and increased competition may be in order.

New policies are probably required. Changes in technology, in demographic and social structures, and in demand may mean that present policies are no longer either desirable or viable. The movement of population to large urban centers and changes in consumption patterns may well bring the initial goal of income maintenance for producers of raw materials and agricultural commodities into question. Moreover, even if this goal is still accepted, there is considerable doubt about whether the transport rate structure is the appropriate or the sole tool by which to achieve it. Stockpiling procedures and the farm program have, for example, been effective in maintaining incomes in this sector. As alternative means of both regulated and unregulated transport have developed, existing rate policies have imposed considerable social costs through misallocation of traffic. Although policies such as increasing the degree and extent of regulation could probably make the existing system work, it is important to ask whether their costs are too large relative to the benefits derived from them, or whether there are alternative means to achieve the same goals at lower cost.

Once it is decided that the present system cannot be maintained, the emphasis must be on alternatives. Then the heart of the matter lies in solving the difficulties of transition from the existing joint public-private management system, which was tailored to the circumstances of the early 1900s, to modern and considerably different circumstances. The central problem of freight transportation becomes one of devising a scheme that will ease the transition from inefficiency in traffic allocation and in location of many producers and shippers to greater rationality in the structure of transport itself and in the geographical distribution of an important group of its users. Since, however, such a rationalization would undoubtedly accelerate the economic decline of certain misplaced industries or transportation properties, there are clear-cut costs involved in this course of action.

Obviously, this study cannot make definitive quantitative estimates of the arguments for and against present and alternative policies. It can, however, lay out the costs and benefits of alternatives and systematically analyze their consequences. In this way, it seeks to provide the basis for more rational decisions concerning the policy that will lead to the greatest social gain.

Chapter 2 reviews the historical basis of present policies to indicate the premises underlying them. The nature of the costs of transport services and the demand for them are analyzed in Chapter 3. Chapter 4 estimates the costs of maintaining present policies. Even if these costs do not seem excessive, it is likely that certain technological and structural changes are taking place in transport that undermine the present structure in the absence of increased and extended regulation. Thus Chapter 5 attempts to outline the forces that are eroding the present regulatory structure, and discusses the growth of private and exempt carriage and the potential impact of piggybacking and other innovations. Chapter 6 is concerned with alternatives to present regulatory policy (cost-based rates and increased regulation, competition and deregulation, the formation of integrated transportation companies, and other proposals) to determine the nature and probable extent of the gains and losses associated with them. Chapter 7 attempts to assess the possible alternatives in the context of the fate of the Kennedy bills, to determine the most likely and desirable policy. Finally, Chapter 8 summarizes the findings of a conference of experts which was organized by the Brookings Institution to discuss and evaluate alternative policies to improve transportation policy in the United States.

CHAPTER TWO

The Rationale of Regulation

REGULATION IS THE EXCEPTION rather than the rule in the United States. Competition is considered "workable" in that it leads to a reasonably efficient allocation of resources and prevents a socially undesirable exercise of economic power. Government regulation is usually justified as an effort to promote economic efficiency or to further some goal concerning income distribution. It generally has the following purposes: (1) to prevent unreasonable prices and earnings in situations where technological and demand conditions create natural monopolies; (2) to prevent discrimination among groups with unequal bargaining power; (3) to maintain certain types of services considered to be in the broad public interest; and (4) to ensure sufficient profits for the development and expansion of an industry in situations where competition and large divergences between average total and average variable or marginal costs make it profitable to cut rates to the floor of variable costs and thus foster rate wars and instability.[1]

Of these purposes, only the last is concerned solely with economic efficiency. Regulation appears, therefore, to be aimed primarily at prohibiting the antisocial exercise of monopoly power or at promoting uneconomic but socially desirable services. Economic efficiency and the allocation of resources seem to be matters of less concern.

While the Interstate Commerce Commission (ICC) has always recognized the need for a stable transportation industry, the concept of economic efficiency has generally been ignored. Whether given traffic volumes could move at a lower cost if rates or regulatory policy were

1. John R. Meyer and others, *The Economics of Competition in the Transportation Industries* (Harvard University Press, 1959), p. 11.

7

altered, whether technological change is stimulated or retarded, whether capacity is used as fully as possible are questions that the Commission has not asked or analyzed.

In contrast, questions concerning income groups have always been given considerable attention. The extent to which a given rate discriminates unduly against a given shipper or a given rate or policy change would adversely affect groups of producers, shippers, or competing modes is a question that has dominated the Commission's proceedings. The specific impact of rates or regulatory policy on various income groups has almost always been given more weight than their general impact on the abstract consideration of resource allocation.

This emphasis on distributional goals can be seen throughout the history of the ICC, from the pressures that caused the adoption of the Interstate Commerce Act of 1887 to the present controversy over minimum rate regulation and the desirable extent of regulation.

Pressures behind the Adoption of the Interstate Commerce Act of 1887

Part of the Commission's concern with social considerations can be traced to the social pressures behind the adoption of the Interstate Commerce Act of 1887. Through a policy of land grants, loans, and tax concessions, the federal, state, and local governments encouraged the rapid expansion of rail facilities into previously inaccessible areas. In all, the federal government gave the railroads west of the Mississippi land grants equal to 9.5 percent of the area of the twenty-six states receiving land grants and 6.8 percent of the total land area in the nation.[2] Moreover, the transcontinental railroads received almost half of their construction costs from the government under easy terms. In all, the federal financial aid to the railroads probably amounted to $175 million, while the combined aid of the state and local governments matched this sum.[3]

Indicative of the feelings of the time was the statement of Senator Wilson of Massachusetts who said, "What are seventy-five or a hundred millions of dollars in opening a railroad across the central regions of this

2. John F. Stover, *American Railroads* (University of Chicago Press, 1961), p. 88.

3. See Carter Goodrich, *Government Promotion of American Canals and Railroads, 1800–1890* (Columbia University Press, 1960), pp. 269–71.

continent which will connect the people of the Atlantic and Pacific and bind them together?"[4] When the railroads began to exploit the economic power that had been invested in them through the various public aids, however, their behavior was found to be socially intolerable.

At the end of the Civil War, there were 35,085 miles of track in the United States. Within the next decade this figure had more than doubled to 74,096 miles, and by 1887 there were 149,214 miles of road in operation. Thus, within a period of 22 years, the railroad right-of-way had increased by 325 percent.[5] Having expanded so rapidly, the railroads found themselves with a large amount of capacity relative to demand and large divergences between average total and average variable or marginal costs.

In this situation, any firm will attempt to utilize as much capacity as possible by practicing price discrimination and charging different markups over costs to different buyers. Suppose, for example, that a railroad knows that it has two different kinds of shippers: one with a highly elastic demand that is very sensitive to rates and one with a highly inelastic demand that is not very sensitive to rates. If the railroad can separate these two groups of shippers, it will maximize its profits with respect to each group and charge low rates relative to costs to the former group and high rates relative to costs to the latter group. If it is forced to charge a common rate relative to costs, its profits will be reduced. Any increase in rates on the traffic with an elastic demand will lead to a more than proportional reduction in traffic and thus reduce the revenues on those shipments. Similarly, any reduction of rates on the traffic with an inelastic demand will lead to a less than proportional increase in traffic and thus reduce the revenues on those shipments. Since more traffic is lost than is gained, total output is reduced and total costs increased. Consequently, charging a common rate will lead to reduced revenues and increased costs. Profits and capacity utilization will be greater under price discrimination than under a common rate.

In the 1870s and 1880s, the railroads were subject to competitive pressures from water transport, from other railroads, and from the locational advantage of their shippers relative to the major consuming and producing centers. Since these pressures affected the demand for rail ser-

4. Quoted in P. Harvey Middleton, *Railways and Public Opinion: Eleven Decades* (Railway Business Association, 1941), p. 49.
5. U.S. Bureau of the Census, *Historical Statistics of the United States, Colonial Times to 1957* (1960), p. 427.

vices in different ways, the railroads reacted by evolving an extensive system of price discrimination with respect to commodities, localities, and shippers.

Water competition and market pressures formed the basis of the rate differentials between high-value and low-value goods. Since many bulk commodities could use water transport, since the majority of the major consuming centers were served by several sources of supply, and since transport costs formed a significant percentage of their final goods price, the elasticity of demand for rail transport on the part of most agricultural commodities and raw materials was quite high; changes in rail rates would have led to more than proportional changes in traffic.

Similarly, since high-valued manufactured goods had few other means of transport, and since transport costs formed a relatively small percentage of the final-goods price, the elasticity of demand for rail transport on the part of these commodities was quite low. Changes in rail rates would have led to less than proportional changes in traffic. In view of these different elasticities, the practice of charging higher rates relative to costs to high-value commodities than to low-value commodities represented rational, profit-maximizing behavior on the part of the railroads. Because the railroads based their rate differentials on the value of the commodity, which was inversely related to the elasticity of demand for rail services, this form of commodity price discrimination became known as value-of-service pricing.

Differences in the degree of monopoly power that a given railroad enjoyed with respect to different communities caused the railroads to practice extensive locational price discrimination. If a railroad enjoyed a complete transportation monopoly with respect to a given community, the limits to the rates it could charge would be set by market forces such as the location of that community relative to the major consuming and producing centers, the importance of rail costs in the final prices of the commodities shipped, and the elasticity of demand for the commodities shipped. If a railroad faced water competition in a given community, the limits to the rates it could charge would be set by the water rates, which would generally be low. Similarly, if a railroad faced rail competition in a given community, the limits to the rates it could charge would be set by the rates charged by the other railroads. Since the railroads rarely colluded effectively to maximize their joint profits, rail competition generally served to increase the elasticity of demand facing any given railroad. Consequently, communities served by several railroads or by water carriers typically enjoyed rates considerably below those charged to communities in which a railroad had a transport monopoly. It was not uncommon for the railroads to charge a higher rate for a haul between an isolated community and a major consuming center than for a haul between two major consuming centers, even though the isolated community lay on the common rail line between those centers. Because this form of long-haul, short-haul discrimination was widespread and noticeable, it aroused considerable hostility among shippers in the relatively isolated communities.

Competition among the railroads also engendered pricing behavior that aroused considerable hostility on the part of the public. During the 1870s and 1880s the market structure of the railroads was particularly unsettled because of their rapid expansion of capacity and entry of new rail lines into certain geographical areas. Although the railroads serving a given market area were aware of the interdependence of their actions and tried to cartelize the industry to prevent competitive pricing, they were not very successful.[6] The large amounts of excess capacity facing each railroad made it tempting to shade prices to utilize more capacity and reduce unit costs. Since overt price cutting would be met by retaliation on the part of the other railroads, covert price cutting in the form of rebates was particularly attractive. In this way, large shippers such as the Standard Oil Company were able to achieve considerable rate reductions that were not open to their smaller competitors.

Rate cutting was not limited to rebates, however, since the discipline among the railroads was not sufficiently great to maintain rates at their monopoly levels. Whenever a railroad tried to enter a new market or expand its market share, it cut rates in an attempt to take traffic away from the other railroads. This engendered retaliatory pricing and eventually led to a rate war. Consequently, the 1870s and 1880s were marked by widely fluctuating rates arising from the periods of attempted cartelization and rate wars.

Thus prior to the passage of the Interstate Commerce Act of 1887, the railroad rate structure was characterized by pervasive price discrimination among shippers, localities, and commodities. Small-lot shippers with no countervailing power, isolated communities with no alternative means of transport, and high-value commodities were charged rates far

6. For a good discussion of the efforts to cartelize the railroad industry, see Paul W. MacAvoy, *The Economic Effects of Regulation: The Trunk-line Railroad Cartels and the Interstate Commerce Commission Before 1900* (M.I.T. Press, 1965).

in excess of those charged for comparable services where railroads faced competitive pressures. Large-volume shippers, communities served by several means of transport or alternative sources of supply, and low-value commodities generally enjoyed low rates. Moreover, the competitive behavior among the railroads only served to widen these differentials because the railroads would usually concentrate their rate-cutting on those shipments with an elastic demand. Thus in addition to creating great instability in rates, competition among the railroads served to increase the extent of price discrimination in the rate structure.

Social Goals of Regulation before the First World War

The Interstate Commerce Act of 1887 was primarily a reaction against specific forms of price discrimination with respect to persons, companies, and localities and the chronic instability of the rail industry rather than a reaction against monopoly power and price discrimination per se. Hence the act required that rates be just and reasonable and prohibited personal price discrimination; undue preference between persons, companies, or localities; the practice of charging higher rates for short hauls than long hauls along a common line; and the practice of pooling, which was the main means of cartelizing the industry. However, in failing to mention the most prevalent form of price discrimination, namely value-of-service pricing, the Interstate Commerce Act preserved the major profit-maximizing element in the railroad rate structure.

The importance of commodity price discrimination was recognized by the ICC and explicitly defended in its first annual report which said:

The public interest is best served when the rates are so apportioned as to encourage the largest practicable exchange of products between different sections of our country and with foreign countries; and this can only be done by making value an important consideration, and by placing upon the higher classes of freight some share of the burden that on a relatively equal apportionment, if service alone were considered, would fall upon those of less value. With this method of arranging tariffs little fault is found, and perhaps none at all by persons who consider the subject from the standpoint of public interest.[7]

A similar statement was contained in the second annual report: ". . .

7. *First Annual Report of the Interstate Commerce Commission, 1887*, p. 36.

This exchange [of commodities] . . . would be restricted to comparatively small sections if articles which are at once bulky and cheap and articles which in small compass comprise very great value were alike charged rates for transportation which disregarded the value as an element of estimation. . . ."[8]

Thus, in addition to its implicit approval by the Interstate Commerce Act, value-of-service pricing received explicit approbation by the Interstate Commerce Commission. Although the ICC was doubtless concerned with the financial health of the railroads, it is unlikely that the railroad rate structure would have been singled out for praise on these grounds alone. In addition to satisfying the interests of the railroads, it seems clear that value-of-service pricing met very important social goals.

A desire to maintain frontier incomes sufficiently high to encourage the development of the western regions has played an important role in American life. At the time when regulation was instituted, farm incomes were low and the cry of the National Grange for the adoption of "such laws as will alleviate the oppression imposed upon us by the transportation monopolies, [for] . . . the surplus of our farms is wrenched from us to enrich the giant monopolies" was doubtless not left unheeded.[9] Evidence in support of this view is given by the directive that the Senate made to the Commission in 1890 to investigate the relations of freight rates and the depressed condition of agriculture in the Middle West. As a result of this investigation, the Commission prescribed reduced rates on corn, wheat, and flour.[10]

Freight rates determine the difference between the market price of a given commodity and the farmer's received price. Hence, a general increase in freight rates has much the same effect as the imposition of a tax on a specific commodity, reducing the farmer's received price by the amount of the rate increase. In the short run when the supply of agricultural commodities is fixed, the farmer has no choice but to absorb any rate increases. Farm incomes fall and railroad revenues rise by the amount of the rate increase.

The impact of rate increases on farm incomes can be seen in Figure 2.1 which shows the supply and demand curves of a commodity such as

8. *Second Annual Report of the Interstate Commerce Commission, 1888*, p. 35.
9. Quoted in Gabriel Kolko, *Railroads and Regulation* (Princeton University Press, 1965), p. 23.
10. 4 ICC 48 (1890). See discussion in Interstate Commerce Commission, Bureau of Transport Economics and Statistics, *Value of Service in Rate-Making*, Statement 5912 (1959), p. 10.

FIGURE 2.1. Rail Freight Rate Increase Effect on Producer Incomes

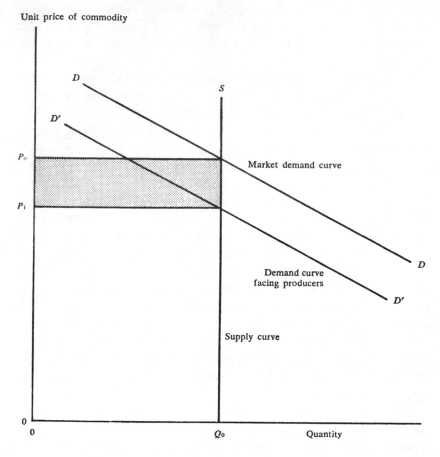

wheat. The supply curve drawn is perfectly inelastic; the demand curves are drawn to be quite elastic. At the initial equilibrium, Q_0 bushels of wheat are produced and sold at a price P_0 per bushel. Suppose that railroads increase the rates on wheat. The market demand curve DD does not change, but so long as railroads are the only source of transport, the effective demand curve $D'D'$ facing the producers falls by the amount of the rate increase. The received price falls to P_1, and the farmer's revenue or income falls by the shaded area, which also represents the increase in the railroads' revenues. For the large portions of the West and Southwest that lacked alternative means of transport, this could be the expected outcome of a general rate increase.

Once producers have a chance to react to changes in received income, the impact of rate increases becomes less predictable. In general, the more elastic the demand curve relative to the supply curve, the more will rate increases tend to be pushed back to producers. Moreover, the more elastic are both the demand and the supply curves, the more will output be reduced in response to rate increases. Thus in a situation characterized by an elastic demand curve, an inelastic short-run supply curve, and an elastic long-run supply curve, rate increases would initially be pushed back to producers who would then curtail production in response to the reductions in their incomes derived from the commodities subject to the rate increases.

It is likely that these demand and supply curves characterized western agricultural and raw materials markets at the turn of the century. Since western agricultural products and raw materials were competing with alternative sources of supply, the demand curves for these western commodities were probably quite elastic. Similarly, the short-run supply curves of these commodities were doubtless quite inelastic since production decisions are difficult to change in the short run. However, the long-run supply curves were probably quite elastic since high incomes were needed to compensate people for the risks and hardships encountered in developing the West. Consequently, rate increases on agricultural commodities and raw materials would probably have curtailed the development of the West by reducing producers' received incomes. Although the need for low freight rates to maintain western agricultural and raw materials producers' incomes sufficiently high to encourage the development of the West was never explicitly stated, the Commission's emphasis on the need to maintain a free flow of traffic indicates that this was a real, if implicit, consideration in the maintenance of low freight rates on agricultural products and raw materials.

The statement that value should play an important part in determining rates also implies that rates should be high on high-value commodities. Since the demand for high-value manufactured goods was typically inelastic, these high rates tended to be pushed forward to the consumers. Thus the rate structure led to transfers between different income groups as well as between different commodity groups. If not subsidized in the sense that they failed to cover the incremental costs associated with their transport, the low-value goods tended to make smaller contributions to overhead than high-value goods.[11] Moreover, through the rate differen-

11. Strictly speaking, these differential contributions must be stated in per unit terms. If the volume is sufficiently large, the total contribution to overhead

tials, the western producers of agricultural commodities and raw materials tended to receive income transfers from the consumers of manufactured goods. Of course, to some extent these were one and the same, since the producers who could ship their goods out cheaply were also the consumers who had to pay high rates on their purchases of manufactured goods. However, it seems unlikely that the balance was complete. Not every consumer in the West was also a producer. Moreover, most of the consumption and production of manufactured goods took place in the northern and eastern sections of the country. Hence, to a large extent, the cross subsidization was between regions and between income groups. The railroad rate structure was effectively used as a tax and subsidy to redistribute income to stimulate the development of the West.

Thus during the initial period of regulation the interests of the railroads and of the ICC coincided. The rate structure that maximized the railroad profits was also the rate structure that encouraged the development of the West. At that time, regulation unquestionably served important social goals and created few, if any, losses in terms of economic efficiency.

Regulation in the Interwar Period

After the First World War, however, the long-run profit maximizing interests of the railroads and those of the government as expressed by the ICC began to diverge. Similarly, the rate and investment policies that helped maintain western farm and raw materials producers' incomes began to diverge from the rate and investment policies that would have used the transportation resources most efficiently.[12]

Divergences between the Interests of the Railroads and the ICC

During the period of government control, the railroads had been forced to curtail their new and replacement investment. Since the war

---

can be quite large even though the contribution per unit is quite small. This is true in the case of bituminous coal today. Data are lacking, however, to determine whether this was the case during the early period of regulation.

12. The following argument draws on the paper by Robert A. Nelson and William R. Greiner, "The Relevance of the Common Carrier under Modern Economic Conditions," in *Transportation Economics* (Columbia University Press for the National Bureau of Economic Research, 1965), pp. 351–74.

had also increased the flow of interregional traffic and induced firms to move to areas distant from market centers, the demand for rail transport had increased substantially relative to the existing plant. Consequently, after the First World War nondiscriminatory policies might have been pursued without leading to excessive losses. Moreover, the reduction in capacity meant that the railroads had the possibility of making new investments that would gear revenues to less discriminatory policies. Hence, the restoration of the railroads to private management in 1920 presented an excellent opportunity to reappraise the existing regulatory practices and policies.

At that time, however, neither the government nor the railroads seemed to be particularly interested in such a reappraisal. Agriculture was in a depressed state, and the government was quite sensitive to discontent in the farm states. Since a policy aimed at rationalization of the rate and investment structure would have meant less investment, curtailment of service, and higher rates in the sparsely settled regions that generated low traffic volumes, it would have affected the farmers in the western and plains states adversely.

Moreover, it seems unlikely that the railroads would have voluntarily given up value-of-service pricing at that time. Although the automobile was gaining wide acceptance as the highway network spread, the truck was hardly viewed as a menace in 1920. The railroads still viewed the demand for high-value manufactured goods as relatively inelastic. This in itself would have been sufficient to maintain the traditional rate structure unless considerable pressure had been brought to bear to change it on the part of the government.

Nevertheless, conflicts between the ICC and the railroads concerning the level of agricultural rates began to arise shortly after the passage of the Transportation Act of 1920, which established "fair return on fair value" as the rule of rate making to be followed by the ICC. The railroads interpreted this as meaning that they were free to increase rates wherever they saw fit; that is, that they were free to pursue pricing policies that would maximize their profits, subject only to the restraints against personal price discrimination. Western roads in particular found it advantageous to raise rates on the eastern bulk shipments, because of changes in their cost structure. Population location had become such that there was a basic imbalance between East-West and North-South freight movements, with the West and the South sending bulk commodities to the East and North and receiving manufactured commodities in return.

The increasingly self-sufficient regions of the West and South demanded relatively few shipments of manufactured goods, and the result was a car shortage in the eastern movements and a surplus in the western movements. The proper response of the railroads to these changed cost conditions should have been to increase rates on the eastbound movements and to reduce them on the westbound movements to utilize the excess supply of cars.

The ICC viewed any efforts to change the traditional rate structure with considerable suspicion, however. On one occasion in 1921, it requested the railroads to reduce their rates on livestock, and later that year it required reduced rates on grain, citing the depressed state of agriculture in both cases.[13]

It was not until 1925, however, when Congress passed the Hoch-Smith Resolution, that the need to maintain the traditional rate structure to help agricultural producers became a formal policy. The resolution gave explicit directions to the ICC to regulate the rates so that ". . . the conditions which at any given time prevail in our several industries should be considered in so far as it is legally possible to do so, to the end that commodities may freely move." It authorized and directed the Commission to make a thorough investigation of the rate structure to determine to what extent

. . . existing rates and charges may be unjust, unreasonable, unjustly discriminatory, or unduly preferential, thereby imposing undue burdens, or giving undue advantage as between the various localities and parts of the country, the various classes of traffic, and the various classes and kinds of commodities, and to make, in accordance with law, such changes, adjustments, and redistribution of rates and charges as may be found necessary to correct any defects so found to exist. In making any such change, adjustment, or redistribution the commission shall give due regard, among other factors, to the general and comparative levels in market value of the various classes and kinds of commodities as indicated over a reasonable period of years, to a natural and proper development of the country as a whole, and to the maintenance of an adequate system of transportation.

The resolution singled out agriculture, saying:

In view of the existing depression in agriculture, the Commission is hereby directed to effect with the least practicable delay such lawful changes in the rate structure of the country as will promote the freedom of movement by

13. *National Livestock S.L.* v. *Atchison, Topeka, and Santa Fe Ry. Co.,* 63 ICC 107, 117 (1921) and *Rates on Grain, Grain Products, and Hay,* 64 ICC 85, 93, 100 (1921). See Interstate Commerce Commission, Bureau of Transport Economics and Statistics, *Value of Service in Rate-Making,* p. 105.

common carriers of the products of agriculture affected by that depression, including livestock, at the lowest possible lawful rates compatible with the maintenance of adequate transportation service. . . .[14]

Thus the Hoch-Smith Resolution gave a clear legislative sanction to the maintenance of the traditional rate structure and the continuation of value-of-service pricing. Reacting to this directive, the ICC began to limit the range of rate increases and to widen the spectrum of commodities subject to reduced rates.[15] Fearing a reduction in revenues, the railroads appealed to the courts. In a case that eventually went to the Supreme Court, the Court held that the resolutions had not negated the principle of fair return on fair value, but had merely made explicit the legality of value of service as a rate-making principle.[16] Since fair return on fair value was still a basic tenet of the law, the Court nullified some rate reductions that the ICC had required. Nevertheless, insofar as the resolution asserted the right of Congress to establish principles of rate making, it diminished the role of the Commission by making it clear that value-of-service rate making should be pursued as long as it did not conflict with other aspects of the law.[17] It seems clear that the Commission was influenced by the Hoch-Smith Resolution in its later decisions.[18]

14. 43 Stat. 801 (1925).

15. For example, the Commission required reduced rates on fertilizers in the Southern Territory, dairy products in New England, and peaches and hay. Moreover, the Commission justified rate increases on iron and steel in terms of the resolution. The cases cited respectively are *Fertilizer Between Southern Points*, 113 ICC 389, 392, 421 (1926); *Milk and Cream Between New England Points*, 126 ICC 38, 68 (1927); *Georgia Peach Growers Exc.* v. *Alabama G.S. R. Co.*, 139 ICC 143, 147, 161 (1928); *Hay, Straw, and Excelsior*, 146 ICC 664, 670, 676 (1928); *Iron and Steel Articles*, 155 ICC 517 (1929). For full discussion, see Interstate Commerce Commission, Bureau of Transport Economics and Statistics, *Value of Service in Rate-Making*, pp. 106–07.

16. *Ann Arbor Railway Co.* v. *U.S.*, 281 U.S. 658 (1930).

17. Nelson and Greiner, "Relevance of the Common Carrier," pp. 361–62.

18. For example, in 1930 the Commission refused to grant desired rate increases, citing the depressed state of agriculture (*Grain and Grain Products*, 164 ICC 619 [July 1930]). Similarly, in 1931, when the railroads requested a general rate increase of 15 percent, the Commission called attention to the "general industrial collapse," and pointed out that agriculture was in a "much worse plight than the railroads" (*Fifteen Percent Case, 1931*, 178 ICC 539, 566, 578, 587–90 [1931]). During the industrial decline of 1937, the ICC again refused to grant the desired rate increases on agricultural goods (*Fifteen Percent Case, 1937–1938*, 226 ICC 41, 85–99, 138–39 [1938]). After the Second World War, the railroads contended that rates on agriculture were too low since they had been held down during the depression of the 1930s. While permitting a general rate increase of 20 percent, the ICC limited the railroads to an increase of 15

Although the railroads attempted to raise agricultural rates throughout this period, it is unlikely that they wanted any basic change in the system of value-of-service pricing. For the most part, their view toward the growth of trucking was very shortsighted, and they were unwilling to cut rates to retain the 10 percent of the traffic they were losing to the truckers for fear of the losses on the other 90 percent. In an effort to maintain their short-run profits, the railroads made no effort to change the rate structure and consequently permitted trucks to capture a good deal of the most profitable rail traffic. This loss of traffic does much to explain the railroads' desire to increase rates on agricultural commodities and raw materials during this period.

Problems of the Railroads in the Depression of the 1930s

The depression of the 1930s followed a period of considerable expansion of rail capacity and indebtedness. Consequently, the railroads were hard hit by the reduction in demand and suffered from considerable excess capacity and revenue losses. The traditional response of the railroads to this situation would have been to raise rates on high-value manufactured goods because of their traditional low elasticity of demand for rail services. This course of action was no longer open to the railroads because of the rapid growth of trucking, which provided an alternative means of transport for these commodities. Manufactured commodities were sufficiently sensitive to rail rates that any increase in rates would surely have been met by a more than proportional loss in traffic and reduced revenues. Because of the large amounts of excess capacity in the trucking industry, any reductions in rail rates would probably have been met by reduced trucking rates. The only other means of increased revenue came from the bulk and agricultural commodities, whose elasticity of

---

percent on agricultural products. (*Increased Railway Rates, Fares, and Charges, 1946,* 264 ICC 695 [June 1946].) Finally, as late as 1956, the railroads were not permitted to raise agricultural rates as much as those on other commodities. (*Increased Freight Rates, 1956,* 298 ICC 279, 307–27 [1956].) Moreover, in a similar case involving requests by eastern and western carriers later that year, the Commission justified its refusal by saying that "The Hoch-Smith Resolution is still in effect." (*Increased Freight Rates, E.W. & S. Territories, 1956,* 299 ICC 429, 441, and 451–59 [December 1956].) Thus, in spite of the Supreme Court ruling, the resolution seems to play an important role in the Commission's decisions. For a full discussion see Interstate Commerce Commission, Bureau of Transport Economics and Statistics, *Value of Service in Rate-Making,* pp. 105–20.

supply was such that rate increases could have been pushed back to the producers with relatively little reduction in traffic. At a time when gross farm incomes from grain had fallen by 75 percent, however, from $1.3 billion in 1929 to $0.3 billion in 1932, the Commission felt that this was an unacceptable course of action.[19]

Congress affirmed this view in the Transportation Act of 1933, which directed the Commission to regulate rates so that the traffic would move freely at the "lowest charges consistent with the cost of providing service."[20] Thus fair return on fair value was abandoned as the major principle in rate making. The revenues of the railroads were to be considered only to ensure the maintenance of adequate transportation service.[21]

The Transportation Act of 1933 proved inadequate to ensure sufficient rail revenues. Bankruptcy threatened many railroads, and the accompanying disruption of existing transport facilities was feared. Further legislation was required to ensure adequate rail revenues. This was provided in the Transportation Act of 1935, which brought motor carriers under regulation.

Regulation of Motor Carriers

The motives of Congress in passing this law are difficult to assess. This was a period of the deepest depression experienced by the United States. Faced with large amounts of excess capacity throughout the economy and the resulting losses and cut-throat competition, Congress reacted by passing laws that were essentially aimed at the cartelization of previously competitive industries. The Robinson-Patman Act, the Agricultural Adjustment Act, the National Industrial Recovery Act, and the Motor Carrier Act were all based on a common desire to limit entry, to control price reductions, and to maintain discipline in an industry so that the remaining firms could enjoy adequate profits.

The support of the Motor Carrier Act from the large truckers, who desired some modification in the extent of the price competition, and the shippers, who favored rate stabilization, was based on a desire to limit the excesses of competition. It also seems clear that Congress wanted to maintain the traditional rate structure and to keep rates on agricultural products low. To this end, it exempted agricultural commodities from

19. *Ibid.*, pp. 109–10.
20. 41 Stat. 488 (1933); as subsequently amended, 49 U.S.C. 15(a)(2).
21. Nelson and Greiner, "Relevance of the Common Carrier," p. 363.

trucking regulation. Moreover, it seems clear that Congress wanted to help the railroads maintain adequate profit levels, not for the railroads themselves, but because

Help for the railroads meant preservation of the rail pricing system and retention of depressed rates on some commodities. Truck competition clearly threatened the viability of that price structure and, if allowed to persist, would have necessitated the increase of some rail rates. Control of truck competition through regulation may have held out the prospect of helping the railroads . . . but, nevertheless, chief among the confluence of interests which brought about passage of the act was pressure from certain shippers and representatives of certain regions to retain the benefits of value-of-service rates.[22]

This desire to maintain the traditional rate structure was not lost on the ICC, which based trucking rates on the existing level of rail rates. Thus the value-of-service structure became even further ingrained, and the ICC used its minimum rate powers to increase truck rates whenever they threatened the railroads.

Regulation of Water Carriers

Since the railroads continued to be harassed by barge and other water competition, the Transportation Act of 1940 brought water carriers under regulation for the first time. This regulation was limited and exempted bulk movements as long as there were no more than three commodities to a tow. Perhaps the most significant aspect of the 1940 act was what it did not contain. The act began as a bill to bring all water carriers under regulation. This was effectively blocked by the water-minded congressmen who wanted to keep water rates low. Implicit in the acceptance of their argument by the rest of Congress was a desire to keep agricultural rates as low as possible by maintaining effective water competition. This interpretation receives some confirmation from the fate of the Miller-Wadsworth Amendment, which was introduced to prevent selective rate cutting by the railroads which might undermine the barges' competitive position. As passed by the Senate the amendment read:

In order that the public at large may enjoy the benefit and economy afforded by each type of transportation, the Commission shall permit each type of carrier or carriers to reduce rates so long as rates maintain a compensatory return to the carrier or carriers after taking into consideration overhead and all the elements entering into the cost to the carrier or carriers for the service rendered.[23]

22. *Ibid.*, p. 364.
23. *Congressional Record*, Vol. 84, 76 Cong. 1 sess. (1939), p. 6074.

The logical result of this amendment would have been a shift to a system of rates based on costs and the abandonment of the value-of-service structure. Thus it is highly significant that when Congress realized the implications of the amendment, it refused to pass it.[24] This can only be construed as another congressional insistence on the value-of-service rate structure. Although the preamble to the 1940 act stressed the need to "foster sound economic conditions in transportation and among the several carriers,"[25] the fate of the Miller-Wadsworth Amendment implies that this must be done subject to the constraints of maintaining low rates on agricultural products and raw materials.

Question of Minimum Rate Regulation

The history of regulation since the 1940 act is primarily characterized by the effort of the ICC to implement the conflicting tenets of the National Transportation Policy, which was the preamble to the 1940 act. Briefly, the preamble directed the Commission to do the following: (1) "to provide for fair and impartial regulation of all modes of transportation"; (2) "to recognize and preserve the inherent advantages of each"; (3) "to promote safe, adequate, economical, and efficient service and foster sound economic conditions in transportation and among the several carriers"; (4) "to encourage the establishment and maintenance of reasonable charges for transportation services, without unjust discriminations, undue preferences or advantages, or unfair or destructive competitive practices"; (5) "to cooperate with the several States and the duly authorized officials thereof"; (6) "to encourage fair wages and equitable working conditions;—all to the end of developing, coordinating, and preserving a national transportation system by water, highway, and rail, as well as other means, adequate to meet the needs of the commerce of the United States, of the Postal Service, and of the national defense."

Probably the most important issue facing the ICC in the postwar period has been the question of minimum rate regulation. The railroads have consistently pushed for reduced rates to compete more effectively with the water and motor carriers. The ICC has been apparently inconsistent in granting these. On the one hand, it has recognized that lower rates on bulk commodities are desirable and has thus permitted the railroads

24. For a full explanation of the fate of the amendment see Nelson and Greiner, "Relevance of the Common Carrier," pp. 364–67.
25. 54 Stat. 899 (1940), Preamble.

to cut rates down to out-of-pocket costs to meet barge competition. On the other hand, it has generally been unwilling to grant rate reductions on high-value goods. Because of this, it has often been accused of preventing railroads from exploiting their true competitive position. If truck and railroad rates are kept at comparable levels, the traffic will usually go to the trucks, which offer better service at the same cost. Thus in its unwillingness to permit rate reductions, the ICC has prevented the railroads from exercising their only means of competition.

The ICC has received substantial criticism for its failure to permit competitive forces to determine the structure of rates. Since considerable evidence indicates that the existing rate policies lead to substantial inefficiencies in the allocation of traffic between modes,[26] one can only conclude that the Commission has given more weight to distributional considerations than to the social costs associated with a misallocation of economic resources. In this light, the continued emphasis on the maintenance of the traditional rate structure and the importance of preventing "destructive competition" makes sense.

If the Commission takes as a basic constraint that rates on agricultural commodities and raw materials should be kept low, its pattern of behavior seems to be reasonably consistent. Bulk commodities are subject to water competition and therefore form the majority of the cases having to do with minimum rates. In view of the desire to keep rates low on bulk commodities, one would expect the Commission to permit the railroads to reduce rates whenever they desired. In fact, the Commission seems to have established the general principle that rates of the high-cost carrier (rail) cannot go below its own out-of-pocket cost or fully distributed cost or that of the low-cost carrier (water), whichever is higher. Although considerable freight moves at less than out-of-pocket cost,[27] it

26. See, for example, Meyer and others, *Competition in the Transportation Industries,* Chap. 6; Merton J. Peck, "Competitive Policy for Transportation?" in Almarin Phillips, ed., *Perspectives on Antitrust Policy* (Princeton University Press, 1965).

27. In 1961, it was estimated that 22 percent of all freight failed to cover out-of-pocket cost. The bulk of this was due to intraterritory shipments of sand and gravel, crushed stone, pulpwood and phosphate rock. Thus the rail losses on bulk commodities are primarily due to raw materials rather than agricultural commodities. (See *Transportation Acts Amendments, 1962,* Hearings before the House Committee on Interstate and Foreign Commerce, 87 Cong. 2 sess. [1962], p. 386.)

The ICC estimates of the costs of transporting bulk commodities may be subject to considerable error. For example, if the cost estimates are correct, one

seems clear that the Commission is reluctant to permit free rate competition on water-competitive traffic. Apparently, the Commission feels that if rail revenues fell sufficiently low on this traffic, the railroads would have to cover their losses from increased revenues from other traffic. Because competitive pressures preclude rate increases on motor competitive traffic and because the Commission prevents rate reductions on this traffic, the only other possible sources of revenue would be on noncompetitive bulk traffic. However, rate increases on agricultural products and raw materials from the West would be a reversal of the traditional rate structure. Consequently, the Commission wants to ensure that the railroads maintain a reasonable return on their water-competitive traffic.

The Commission's stand in favor of limiting the exemption on agricultural commodities and on bulk commodities carried by barges can also be explained in these terms, in spite of the apparent inconsistency with the desire to maintain low agricultural and bulk rates. The ICC apparently believes that the existence of these exemptions undermines the financial viability of the railroads. If the position of the railroads becomes seriously undermined, the maintenance of the traditional rate structure is no longer feasible. Therefore, the argument for ending the exemptions is almost identical to the argument made for regulating the motor carriers in the 1930s and the water carriers in 1940; namely, that financially strong railroads are necessary for the maintenance of the traditional rate structure and that these are not possible if there are large segments of the transportation industry undermining their competitive position. Thus if the traditional rate structure is to be maintained, regulation must be extended to all modes.

Similarly, the Commission's reluctance to grant rate reductions on high-value manufactured goods seems to arise from a fear that any marked reduction in the average return over out-of-pocket costs on manufactured goods would mean a reduction in rail revenues and thus in the ability of the railroads to maintain relatively low rates on agricultural products and raw materials. Although the ICC has granted rate reduc-

---

would expect the Norfolk and Western and Chesapeake and Ohio Railroads to lose money, since their traffic is heavily concentrated in bituminous coal which only covers 86 percent of its fully distributed costs. However, they are two of the most profitable in the nation. See Systems Analysis Research Corporation, *Cost-Based Freight Rates—Desirability and Feasibility,* prepared for the Under Secretary for Transportation, U.S. Department of Commerce (August 1966), p. 60. See also Chap. 3 below for a discussion of the biases in the ICC cost estimates.

tions for technological changes,[28] it has been unwilling to permit the railroads to cut rates to "regain or to retain a fair share" of the traffic, even though the new rate is "remunerative."[29] On occasion, the ICC has made it clear that it sees the maintenance of the traditional rate differentials as inviolate and has refused rate reductions because they would "place an undue transportation burden on the [carrier's] other traffic. . . ."[30]

Of course, whether such a burden would in fact occur depends on the elasticity of the demand for rail services. If the demand were sufficiently elastic, the railroads could cut rates and expect increases in revenues. Moreover, if the railroads attempt to maximize profits, it seems unlikely that they would attempt to cut rates unless they thought the demand was sufficiently elastic.[31] Thus, in preventing the railroads from cutting high-value rates, the Commission either must believe that the railroads are not rational profit maximizers or must be attempting to protect trucking interests. From the discussion in the various proceedings, it appears that the Commission has taken both stands at various times.[32]

Thus the Commission's rate and regulatory policies are understandable if one accepts the following basic premises: (1) rates on agricultural and bulk commodities must be kept down; and (2) competitive rate making would undermine the financial strength of the railroads and cause them to increase rates on their noncompetitive bulk traffic. From these premises follow most of the Commission's rulings with regard to rates and regulation. Consequently, the Commission's policies have been fairly consistent when viewed in this light. Whether they have been misguided is the subject of the remainder of this study.

The first question to consider is whether the income redistribution implied by the maintenance of the traditional rate structure is desirable. Traditionally, American public policy has favored such a redistribution. The farm subsidy, the stockpiling procedures for raw materials, the high

28. See, for example, *New Automobiles in Interstate Commerce*, 259 ICC 475 (1945).
29. For a full discussion see Henry J. Friendly, *The Federal Administrative Agencies* (Harvard University Press, 1962), p. 130. Ernest W. Williams, Jr., *The Regulation of Rail-Motor Rate Competition* (Harper & Bros., 1958), has a full discussion of ICC rulings and policies with regard to truck and rail competition.
30. Quoted in Friendly, *Federal Administrative Agencies*, p. 130.
31. For a full discussion of this point, see Chap. 6 below.
32. See Friendly, *Federal Administrative Agencies*, and Williams, *Regulation of Rail-Motor Competition*.

tariffs, the railroad rate structure, and the provision for transportation in the sparsely settled areas are all indications of this past policy. Whether this policy will be accepted indefinitely is problematical. The rapid urbanization of the country, the increasing emphasis on urban problems, the formation of the Department of Housing and Urban Development, and the reapportionment rulings may indicate that the pendulum is swinging away from agricultural and rural interests. While it is still too early to say, it is quite likely that the next twenty-five years will see a shift of power from the rural to the urban forces in the legislatures and from the southern and western agricultural and mining interests in Congress to those of the industrialized areas. If so, the general consensus supporting the past patterns of redistribution will dissolve. If this happens, the support for the traditional rate structure will also disappear.

The antagonism to the Kennedy message and bills indicates that this change in sentiment is not imminent. Thus, it must be assumed for the present that such an income redistribution is generally considered to be desirable. In that case, the question becomes whether freight-rate policy is the best means of achieving this redistribution. Here, I think, the answer must be no; the existing policies are neither efficient nor viable. If this view is accepted, then the question becomes one of easing the transition of moving from a system of joint public-private management adapted to a set of technological, institutional, and market circumstances that existed around 1900 to a modern and considerably different set of circumstances. The fundamental difficulty or objection to many proposals for reforming or rationalizing transportation is that such a rationalization would imply the end of redistribution and accelerate the decline of certain misplaced industrial or transportation properties. However, it is probable that the costs of the present policies are underestimated since they are diffused, while the cost of moving to alternative policies are overestimated, since they are concentrated on certain groups. Thus the remainder of this study will attempt to analyze the costs and benefits of the present and alternative policies to determine which will lead to the greatest social welfare.

CHAPTER THREE

Supply and Demand in Transportation Services

IT IS DIFFICULT to make definitive statements about the merits of the present policies or their alternatives without understanding the nature of the supply of and demand for different transportation services. Thus this chapter seeks to quantify the supply and demand relationships, insofar as it is possible, as background to subsequent analysis. Since data on these relationships are scarce and not very reliable, however, the analysis will be somewhat qualitative and suggestive. Nevertheless, a fairly clear idea should emerge of the comparative advantage of the different modes and the nature of the demand for transport services.

The Supply of Transport Services

Determining costs in the transportation industries is hazardous, in part because of the conceptual problems of defining relevant costs; in part because of statistical difficulties in estimating these costs; and in part because of differences between costs facing shippers and carriers and true social costs associated with a given movement. Cost estimates are sensitive to the way in which each of these factors is treated. The problems are therefore discussed in detail before actual cost estimates are considered.

Problems of Cost Concepts

In considering costs, it is important to distinguish between fixed, variable, and total costs and between marginal and average costs. Total costs are the sum of variable and fixed costs. Variable costs are those that vary with output for a given plant and equipment, and include labor, materials, energy, and so on. In contrast, fixed costs do not vary with output. They must be incurred once the decision to produce has been made, and they encompass rental and interest costs associated with the plant and fixed levels of equipment, management costs, and similar expenses. Fixed costs can only be eliminated by going out of business. For any type of costs, average costs are the cost per unit. Thus it is possible to refer to average total costs, average fixed costs, and average variable costs. Finally, marginal costs are the additional costs incurred by producing an additional unit of output. If average costs are falling, marginal cost must lie below average cost. If average costs are rising, marginal cost must lie above average cost. Only if average cost is constant, will the two coincide. Figure 3.1 illustrates these cost concepts for a given plant and equipment on a short-run basis.

The fixity and variability of costs depend on the time horizon under consideration. As the time horizon extends, machinery can be scrapped or replaced, plant locations changed, mortgages or loans renegotiated. Thus the longer the time horizon, the greater the variability of the costs; indeed, in the longest run all costs become variable. The relationship between the long-run total cost (LRTC) and several short-run total cost curves (S_1, S_2, and S_3) can be seen in Figure 3.2. For any expected scale of output, the firm chooses the plant size that minimizes its total costs of producing that scale of output. Once the plant size is given, the short-run cost curve is determined. The long-run cost curve is a composite of all the short-run curves and is defined by the envelope of these curves. Thus the long-run cost curve represents the minimum possible cost of producing each level of output.

It should be pointed out that cost curves have a clear meaning only for a single-product firm, whose output can be defined unambiguously. However, because transportation firms typically provide a wide range of services, the appropriate definition of output is not clear. For example, in the railroad industry, car-miles may be a more appropriate unit of measurement than ton-miles,[1] which is commonly used as the standard unit of output. Moreover, the costs of shipping various commodities may differ. The costs per car-mile (or per ton-mile) associated with transporting

1. For a discussion of this point see George W. Wilson, *Essays on Some Unsettled Questions in the Economics of Transportation* (Indiana University Library, 1962), pp. 14–24.

FIGURE 3.1. Short-Run Cost Curves for a Given Plant and Equipment

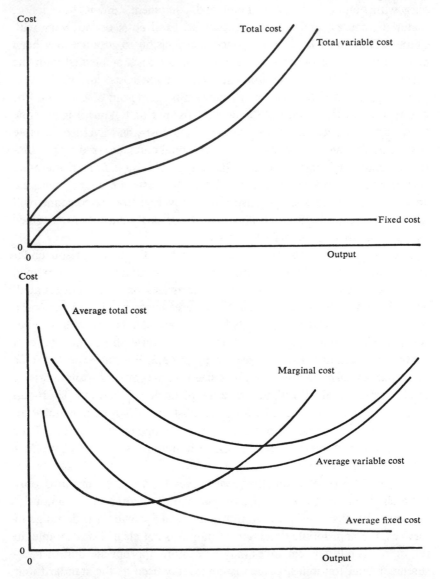

highly perishable vegetables will be very different from those associated
with transporting coal. Consequently, although standard cost curves will
be employed throughout this book, it is important to remember that they
are generalizations and refer to a similar range of commodities; they
have no meaning for specific commodity shipments or specific carriers.

FIGURE 3.2. Relation between Short-Run Total Cost Curves and the
Long-Run Total Cost Curve

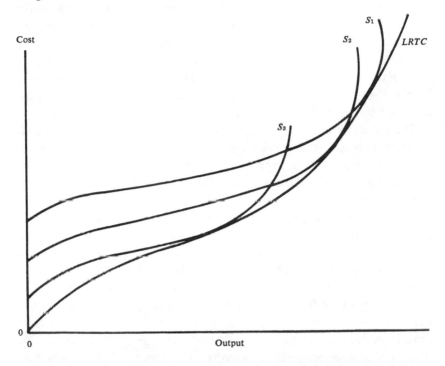

In assessing the relative costs of the various modes, it seems to be generally agreed that long-run marginal costs are the relevant carrier costs.
Since these costs reflect society's valuation of the additional resources required to produce an additional unit of output when the carrier under
consideration is producing that level of output as efficiently as possible,
long-run marginal costs reflect the inherent advantages of the various
carriers in making a given shipment. Consequently, the supply of transport services will be discussed in the context of long-run marginal costs
or, in the parlance of the transportation industry, out-of-pocket costs.

Statistical Problems

The estimation of out-of-pocket costs is extremely difficult. Because
transportation firms typically produce many kinds of services and have
many common and joint costs, specific cost estimates must necessarily be
somewhat arbitrary. This is particularly true for the railroads, which

have large fixed and common cost elements and a wide range of diverse operations; but it is also true for all other modes to a lesser extent. The Interstate Commerce Commission (ICC) provides extensive and readily available estimates of out-of-pocket costs; hence its cost data form the basis of the relative costs that will be given later in this chapter. The ICC cost data, however, seem to be subject to considerable error and bias, particularly with respect to the railroads. Thus, to view the cost estimates in this chapter in perspective, the nature of the biases associated with the ICC costing techniques will be outlined here and in Appendix A.

The criticisms of the ICC cost estimates are primarily aimed at the allocation of costs between passenger and freight services and the use of out-of-pocket costs as an approximation of long-run marginal costs. The ICC allocates overhead costs between freight and passenger services on the basis of the revenues derived from each source. This is quite arbitrary since the general roadbed, yard facilities, management, and so on are true common costs that must be incurred regardless of the level or division of traffic. Moreover, the allocation of costs between variable and fixed portions is equally arbitrary and introduces a bias into the ICC cost estimates that bring their usefulness into considerable question.

According to the ICC, out-of-pocket rail costs "reflect the costs which over the long-run period and at the average postwar density of traffic, have been found to be variable with traffic changes."[2] They include 80 percent of the operating expenses, rents, and taxes (excluding federal income taxes) plus a return of 4 percent after federal income taxes on 100 percent of the equipment used in freight service and on 50 percent of road property. Thus the ICC estimates of out-of-pocket costs are based on the following assumptions: 80 percent of the operating expenses are variable with output; 100 percent of the equipment is variable with output; 50 percent of the road property is variable with output; and the average rate of return after taxes is 4 percent.

Since the ICC determines out-of-pocket costs by applying a figure of 80 percent variable to the total costs derived by conventional cost accounting techniques, the estimation of the percent variable is of crucial importance. The validity of the ICC estimates of out-of-pocket costs largely depends on the validity of its estimates of the percent variable; and it is here that the main problems and ambiguities connected with the

2. Interstate Commerce Commission, Bureau of Accounts, *Rail Carload Cost Scales by Territories for the Year 1962*, Statement 2–64 (March 1, 1964), p. 3.

ICC cost estimates lie. The percent variable is defined to be that percentage of total expenses that is variable with output. If a linear cost function is estimated, so that $C = a + bX$, the percent variable is given by bX/C. Since b is also the marginal cost of the output, the percent variable is also equal to marginal cost divided by average cost.[3] This is precisely the elasticity of costs, which indicates the percentage increase in costs associated with a percentage increase in output. A figure of 80 percent implies that a 10 percent increase in output will be accompanied by an 8 percent increase in costs. Thus by applying a figure of 80 percent variable to all railroads, the ICC is in effect assuming that all railroads are producing under identical increasing returns to scale.

However, railroads differ dramatically in terms of their relation of output to capacity. At any given point in time, it is highly unlikely that any given railroad will have costs that are 80 percent variable. Since the ICC insists on applying the same percentage variable to all railroads, its estimates of out-of-pocket costs are often meaningless for specific point to point movements.

Since operating expenses comprise the bulk of out-of-pocket costs,[4] the ICC practice of rigidly applying a figure of 80 percent variable to total operating expenses creates the primary bias in its estimates of out-of-pocket costs. However, it is worth pointing out the somewhat cavalier method used by the ICC in determining the percentages of the capital expenses that can be called variable.

The treatment of the investment in equipment as 100 percent variable was based on the *assumption* that the carrier's ownership of motive power and freight train cars would be adjusted (over an extended period with some lag) to the needs of the traffic. The use of a figure of 50 percent for road property and 100 percent for equipment is approximately equivalent to the use of an

3. The percent variable equals variable cost divided by total cost. If the cost function can be described by $C = a + bX$, total cost is given by C, total variable cost is given by bX, marginal cost is given by b, and average total cost is given by C/X. Hence percent variable equals $bX/C = (b)(X/C) = $ marginal cost/average cost.

4. For example, operating expenses comprised 89.5 percent of all out-of-pocket costs in 1962, when average operating expenses per railroad were $116.4 million; the average value of equipment was $103.9 million; the average value of road property was $311.9 million. Hence the variable capital expenses totaled $10.4 million (4 percent of 100 percent of the value of the equipment and 4 percent of 50 percent of the value of the road property), while the variable operating expenses totaled $93.12 million (80 percent of total operating expenses); out-of-pocket costs totaled $104.02 million.

overall figure for road and equipment of 60 percent. The latter figure is in accord with the conclusion reached [in regression estimates] that the percent variable for the plant investment was 50 percent or more.[5]

In addition, the use of the low rate of return of 4 percent to determine capital expenses adds an additional bias to the estimates of out-of-pocket costs. Most studies estimate that the social rate of return to capital in the United States is on the order of 15 to 20 percent.[6] This would imply an after tax return of approximately 8 to 10 percent, or more than double the return attributed to the railroads by the ICC. If the rate of return to rail capital were as low as 4 percent, it is unlikely that the railroads could either attract or keep capital. While the railroads appear to have some difficulty in obtaining access to capital markets, the difficulties are not nearly as great as those implied by a 4 percent rate of return.[7] Consequently, it seems likely that the true after-tax rate of return on rail capital is greater than 4 percent and that the ICC cost estimates are biased downward. For example, if an after-tax rate of return of 8 percent or 6 percent were used, the ICC estimates of out-of-pocket costs would increase by approximately 12 percent or 6 percent.

Enough should have been said to make the reader wary of accepting any ICC estimates of out-of-pocket costs. Because of their biases, they have little relevance for specific railroads or specific commodity shipments. At most, ICC cost data can be used to describe general cost behavior of the railroads. Thus, it is important to remember that the cost data used in this study only reflect the general behavior of the various modes, but in no way should be used to assess the relative costs of a specific point-to-point commodity movement.

Problems of Social Costs

The social costs of transportation differ from those considered by shippers or carriers. The costs incurred by the shipper include the rate he is charged, pickup, delivery, and terminal costs he must specifically incur,

5. Interstate Commerce Commission, Bureau of Accounts, *Explanation of Rail Cost Findings, Procedures and Principles Relating to the Use of Costs,* Statement 7-63 (1963), pp. 86–87. Italics added.
6. See, for example, Robert M. Solow, *Capital Theory and the Rate of Return* (Amsterdam: North Holland Publishing Company, 1963), Chap. 3.
7. See the summary of the conference of experts, Chap. 8, for a discussion of this point.

and inventory costs assigned to goods in transit. The costs incurred by the carrier include the expenses associated with making the shipment plus a sufficient return on overhead to remain in business, which can be allocated differently among different shippers.

Neither shipper nor carrier costs adequately reflect the true social costs, which include certain aspects of each of these costs. Social costs include the resource costs required to get the shipment from its point of origin to its point of destination such as handling, pickup and delivery, and line-haul transportation, and the inventory costs associated with the goods in transit. The carrier costs will tend to underestimate the resource costs for several reasons. First, the shipper or consignee typically provides some of the pickup or delivery or handling services. Second, insofar as the right-of-way is subsidized or differentially taxed, the costs facing the carrier will diverge from the resource costs. Third, the carrier usually does not have to carry the inventory costs of the goods in transit. If the rates charged the shipper adequately reflected the true resource costs, shipper costs would reflect social costs. Since there is often little relation between rates and costs, however, the costs facing the shipper will as a rule diverge from social costs.

For expositional purposes, the social costs of transportation can be broken down into three components: terminal, line-haul, and inventory costs. Terminal costs include all of the handling costs associated with making the shipment ready for the line-haul journey, the expenses incurred in carrying the shipment to and from the line-haul vehicle, and billing and collecting costs. Line-haul costs arise in carrying the shipment from its general area of departure to its general area of destination. They include the costs required to run the vehicle between the points of origin and destination and to keep the vehicle in operable condition, the costs associated with constructing and maintaining the right-of-way, and other allocation of overhead. Inventory costs arise because goods in transit are a form of working capital and, as such, generate additional inventory costs due to time in transit, shipment size, and so on.

The nature of these costs varies by mode and type of shipment. Since costs are particularly sensitive to such things as density of the commodity, volume shipped over a given time period, fragility and perishability, both the line-haul and terminal costs of bulk and high-value shipments will vary within each mode. Therefore, the costs associated with transporting each of these commodity types will be considered separately.

Cost of Transporting High-Value Commodities

Railroad terminal operations are considerably more complex than those of trucking and consequently tend to be more expensive for all but the largest shipments. The basic trucking terminal operations of pickup and delivery, handling, and billing and collecting are similar to those of rail operations. However, while a loaded truck can go directly to its point of destination, a loaded boxcar must be weighed, classified, and switched onto the proper train at its point of origin and go through a similar process at its point of destination. Siding operations involve additional costs to maintain the spur lines. Therefore, although high-car utilization can reduce rail terminal costs below those of trucking, trucking terminal costs are less than those of rail for shipment sizes less than 30 tons.

While rail terminal costs are expensive relative to those of trucking, rail line-haul costs are relatively cheap. The friction of a flanged wheel on a steel track is minimal, and a diesel engine is particularly well-adapted to handling large loads. Consequently, rail costs are quite low for relatively large shipments and long hauls and can reach 6 to 7 mills a ton-mile. In contrast, most trucks have a maximum capacity of 20 to 30 tons and do not have the basic economies associated with large loads and long hauls. Hence, line-haul trucking costs are greater than those of rail for all shipment sizes. For example, assuming a maximum truck capacity of 20 tons, the minimum trucking line-haul costs are 11 mills a ton-mile.

Trucks have a decided inventory advantage over rails. Therefore, rail costs must be adjusted upward to take this into account. Since inventories are a form of working capital, anything that increases inventory holdings will increase inventory costs. Because rail operations force the shipper to hold larger inventories than trucking operations, rail costs must be adjusted upward to incorporate these additional inventory costs. There are two basic sources of inventory costs: those due to shipment size and those due to transit time. Since the optimal boxcar capacity is approximately twice that of a truck, rail operations force a shipper to hold larger inventories between orders. Moreover, since rail operations are considerably slower than trucking operations, a shipper must hold larger inventories after the date of order. Consequently, the increased level of inventories associated with rail transportation substantially increases the rail costs incurred by a shipper. For a high-value commodity, the inventory costs could double the nominal rail terminal costs and increase the rail line-haul costs by almost 50 percent. For a low-value commodity, these inventory costs would be negligible. Nevertheless, for many high-value goods, inventory costs can increase nominal rail costs by at least 50 percent, thereby forcing rail rates to be proportionately lower to ensure shipper indifference between truck and rail service.

There is considerable controversy whether rail or trucking costs need to be further adjusted to take social costs into account. The issue revolves around two points: First, should railroad right-of-way be subject to local property taxes? Second, do trucks pay their full share of the construction costs of highways? The answer to the first question is probably affirmative, while the answer to the second is negative.

With regard to the first question, the railroads have consistently held that property taxes on their right-of-way are unjust. Nevertheless, in a sense, these tax costs are true social costs associated with railroad operations. The railroad right-of-way is provided solely for railroad use and is reserved exclusively for use by passenger or freight trains. Since passenger traffic is such a small percentage of most railroad traffic, if freight traffic were removed, there would be no alternative demand for the right-of-way, which could be no longer maintained. Since railroad right-of-way is privately provided and is primarily used by freight operations, any costs associated with providing the railroad right-of-way are properly included as true social costs. In this respect, the property tax on railroad right-of-way is as much a cost of railroading as the maintenance costs on that right-of-way.

In contrast, it is generally agreed that the publicly provided rights-of-way of highways and waterways should not be subject to property taxes. In deciding to have the government provide the highways or waterways, society presumably felt that these facilities would provide important social benefits that could not be captured through private development. Therefore, as public facilities, they belong to society as a whole and should not be made subject to local taxes. That individual trucking operators derive an advantage from using a public facility cannot be denied. However, these benefits should not be thought of as an unfair advantage, but rather as a basic difference in the structure of providing rail and trucking services.[8]

Nevertheless, it is important to ensure that trucks pay their full share of the costs of constructing and maintaining the highway. Because a highway is a joint facility that is provided for trucks and private automobiles, any cost allocation must be arbitrary. However, the following

8. For a full discussion of these points see Chap. 5 below, pp. 105–11.

allocation seems reasonable. Since automobiles require much lower highway design standards than trucks, automobiles should only be held responsible for their share of the costs of constructing a highway to meet their needs. Trucks should then be made responsible for bearing the full incremental or additional costs needed to build a highway to meet their requirements. Since trucks contribute to the wear and tear of the basic roadway, they should also contribute to its cost in proportion to their use. Thus costs should be allocated among different types of vehicles on an average-marginal basis in which all vehicles proportionately share in each of the cost increments for which they can be held responsible. Recent studies made by the U.S. Bureau of Public Roads indicate that heavy diesel trucks fail to pay their full share of the costs of highway construction on the basis of this cost allocation. If these vehicles were charged their full share, their federal highway tax payments would increase from approximately 1.4 cents to 1.8 cents per vehicle mile,[9] and the estimated trucking costs should be inflated by this differential.

Table 3.1 summarizes the relevant terminal and line-haul costs of railroads and trucks. From this table and the previous discussion two main facts should stand out: trucking terminal costs are relatively low and rail line-haul costs are relatively low. This implies that if rail and truck operations could be combined in some fashion to take advantage of these economies, considerable savings could result. Piggybacking is precisely such an operation and provides a coordinated rail-truck movement from the point of origin to the point of destination.

One of the major advantages of piggybacking arises from the fact that the unit of transport is the truck trailer instead of the boxcar. Thus the optimum size of shipment is between 15 and 20 tons instead of between 30 and 40 tons. This permits several economies. For truckload piggyback shipments only one loading and unloading is required at the origin and destination. In contrast, similar boxcar loads must be shed-handled and thus they involve four more handlings (two each at the origin and destination in transferring the freight from the cartage vehicle to the shed and then from the shed to the railroad car). Although many truck shipments are more economically handled through a shed, the dividing line is 10 tons instead of 20 tons or more. Thus a considerable portion of less than carload lot train shipments would be full truckload shipments. This leads to considerable economies in handling costs through piggybacking.

9. *Supplementary Report of the Highway Cost Allocation Study,* Letter from the Secretary of Commerce, H. Doc. 124, 89 Cong. 1 sess. (1965), Table 2, p. 4.

TABLE 3.1. Terminal and Line-Haul Costs for Rail and Truck, by Size and Value of Shipment, Eastern-Central United States, 1964

Type of cost	Shipment size (tons)							
	1	5	10	15	20	30	40	50
Rail terminal costs (dollars per ton)								
Basic	66.28	13.34	6.73	4.54	3.42	2.29	1.76	1.43
Inventory due to shipment size[a]								
High value	—	—	—	0.08	0.17	0.41	0.60	0.88
Low value	—	—	—	-0.02	-0.01	0.01	0.03	0.06
Inventory due to transit time[a]								
High value	1.06	1.06	1.06	1.06	1.06	1.06	1.06	1.06
Low value	0.03	0.03	0.03	0.03	0.03	0.03	0.03	0.03
Total rail								
High value	67.34	14.40	7.79	5.68	4.66	3.76	3.42	3.37
Low value	66.31	13.37	6.76	4.56	3.44	2.33	1.83	1.53
Truck terminal costs (dollars per ton)	21.28	9.24	4.98	3.62	3.12	3.74	3.12	3.49
Rail line-haul costs (cents per ton-mile)								
Basic	18.71	3.91	2.06	1.45	1.13	0.82	0.67	0.58
Inventory due to transit time[a]								
High value	0.22	0.22	0.22	0.22	0.22	0.22	0.22	0.22
Low value	0.01	0.01	0.01	0.01	0.01	0.01	0.01	0.01
Total rail								
High value	18.93	4.13	2.28	1.67	1.35	1.04	0.89	0.80
Low value	18.71	3.91	2.06	1.45	1.14	0.82	0.68	0.58
Truck line-haul costs (cents per ton-mile)								
Basic	40.92	10.37	5.55	5.28	4.64	5.28	4.64	4.02
Incremental highway share	0.51	0.10	0.05	0.03	0.03	0.02	0.01	0.01
Total truck	41.43	10.47	5.60	5.31	4.67	5.30	4.65	4.03

Source: See App. B for derivation of cost data. Figures are rounded and will not necessarily add to totals.
a. High-value goods are assumed to have a value of $1,943 per ton, while low-value goods are assumed to have a value of $60 per ton.

39

Moreover, the smaller shipment size removes the service differential of trucking operations due to shipment size.

Another simplification in piggybacking operations comes from bypassing the railroad yard classification at the point of origin and destination. Piggyback operations need only an initial classification yard consisting of nothing more than a trailer ramp site and a parking lot. Classification of cars by destination usually can be accomplished in the process of loading the trailer onto the flatcar at origin. Moreover, classification yards en route can often be bypassed. Finally, switching en route in most circumstances can be done by a diesel road switcher locomotive simply by dropping cars at trailer ramps located outside major cities.[10]

Thus piggybacking permits railroad operations to achieve the usual trucking economies of smaller shipment size, faster service, and increased flexibility in service. Since the unit of piggybacking is the truck trailer, trucks gain no inventory differential due to smaller shipment size.[11] Loading and unloading the trailers onto flatcars may be performed away from the major railroad yards, with pickup and delivery service performed by the truck. Complete trains of trailers may be made up and classified by destinations at such sites, which reduces the possibility of freight being held up in railroad yards and terminals. By comparison, private siding operations often require more time in switching than piggybacking requires in total delivery time, and unless the plant at the siding has a very large transport demand, additional waiting time is necessary to make up a carload to minimize switching expenses. For the increasing number of industrial plants and warehouses located off a siding, piggybacking makes railroad service available on a door to door basis, and thus offers the same degree of flexibility as the highway truck.

10. More specifically, the ICC has estimated that the switching minutes per car in piggyback operations are about 40 percent less than those associated with ordinary car movements. The ratio of loaded to empties is twice those of ordinary boxcars and almost three times that of more specialized cars. The costs are about 60 percent lower for general switching and about 20 percent lower for interchange switching costs. See Interstate Commerce Commission, Bureau of Accounts, *Rail Carload Unit Costs by Territories for the Year 1963*, Statement 5–65 (March 1965), Tables 9, 10, 13, 15.

11. The New York Central system instituted a piggyback express service between New York and Chicago that took just under 24 hours. This is as fast, if not faster, than most trucking operations. Therefore, one day delivery is possible. The Santa Fe Railway Company offers three-day service between New York and Los Angeles, and two-day service between Chicago and Los Angeles. See R. E. Clancy, "Growth, Economics and Future of Piggybacking" (Master's thesis, Massachusetts Institute of Technology, 1963).

TABLE 3.2. Terminal and Line-Haul Piggybacking Costs, by Size and Value of Shipment, Eastern-Central United States, 1964

Type of cost	Shipment size (tons)							
	1	5	10	15	20	30	40	50
Terminal costs (dollars per ton)								
Basic	52.35	10.48	5.24	3.50	2.63	1.75	1.32	1.05
Inventory due to transit time								
Low value	0.02	0.02	0.02	0.02	0.02	0.02	0.02	0.02
High value	0.53	0.53	0.53	0.53	0.53	0.53	0.53	0.53
Total terminal costs								
Low value	52.37	10.50	5.25	3.52	2.65	1.77	1.34	1.07
High value	52.88	11.01	5.77	4.03	3.16	2.28	1.85	1.58
Line-haul costs (cents per ton-mile)								
Basic	21.10	4.38	2.30	1.60	1.24	0.90	0.73	0.62
Trailer	1.65	0.33	0.17	0.11	0.08	0.06	0.04	0.03
Inventory due to transit time								
Low value[a]	—	—	—	—	—	—	—	—
High value	0.11	0.11	0.11	0.11	0.11	0.11	0.11	0.11
Total line-haul costs								
Low value	22.75	4.72	2.46	1.72	1.33	0.96	0.77	0.66
High value	22.85	4.82	2.57	1.82	1.43	1.06	0.83	0.76

Source: See App. B for derivation of piggyback costs. Figures are rounded and will not necessarily add to totals.
a. Less than 0.01.

Table 3.2 summarizes the elements of piggybacking costs and shows that piggybacking operations can reduce rail terminal costs substantially, while incurring line-haul costs that are only slightly higher than those of ordinary boxcar operations.

Having estimated the costs associated with railroad, trucking, and piggybacking operations, it should be possible to determine the proper allocation of traffic among these three modes. Because of the differences in the value of the commodities, inventory costs may have a significant effect on this allocation. Hence, transport costs of each mode should be compared for a high-value good and a low-value good. The results of these comparisons are given in Table 3.3 for various shipment weights.[12]

TABLE 3.3. Efficient Allocation of Truck, Piggyback, and Rail Traffic, by Size and Value of Shipment

| Size of shipment (tons) | Most efficient distances (miles) | | | | | |
| | High-value commodities | | | Low-value commodities | | |
	Truck	Piggyback	Rail	Truck	Piggyback	Rail
1	226[a]	226–369	369[b]	220[a]	220–340	340[b]
5	132[a]	132–497	497[b]	123[a]	123–363	363[b]
10	121[a]	121–709	709[b]	105[a]	105–380	380[b]
15	107[a]	107–1148	1148[b]	89[a]	89–412	412[b]
20	91[a]	91–1882	1882[b]	73[a]	73–407	407[b]
30	43[a]	43[b]	—	30[a]	30–420	420[b]
40[c]	43[a]	43[b]	—	29[a]	29–537	537[b]

Source: Based on data in Tables 3.1 and 3.2. Piggybacking and rail terminal costs were adjusted upward to take pickup and delivery costs into account.
a. Maximum.
b. Minimum.
c. Piggyback containers are assumed to have a maximum capacity of 20 tons, with a maximum flatcar capacity of two containers. Since boxcar capacity can reach 70 tons or more, the assumed discontinuity in piggybacking capacity ensures that rails will have the cost advantage for shipments greater than 40 tons.

In studying this table, it is well to keep in mind the rather shaky foundations on which the cost estimates were built. Thus the traffic allocation implied should not be taken as definitive, but rather as descriptive. Clearly a 30-ton high-value shipment traveling 100 miles should not go by piggyback if the piggybacking terminal is far from the point of origin

12. Trucking costs were estimated on the assumption that optimal trucking operations were for shipment sizes of 20 tons. This probably underestimates trucking costs for large shipments. Piggybacking and rail costs were adjusted upward to take pickup and delivery costs into account.

and delivery and if piggyback service is infrequent. Nevertheless, the thrust of the argument is probably correct. Piggybacking has a decided cost advantage over either rail or truck for most high-value commodities in medium shipment sizes traveling medium distances. The advantage of piggybacking in transporting low-value commodities is less pronounced because of the small inventory costs associated with these commodities. Nevertheless, even for these commodities piggybacking seems to have a cost advantage for shipments traveling between 200 and 400 miles.

From this analysis, the potential importance of piggybacking operations to the railroads should be evident. Extensive development and use of piggybacking could capture much of the existing truck traffic for the railroads without diverting much of the existing rail traffic from conventional rail operations. Hence, the railroads should concentrate their efforts on the introduction and utilization of piggybacking operations.[13]

Costs of Transporting Bulk Commodities

Bulk commodities generally have a low value and must be moved in large volume. Therefore the most important attribute of the means of transport suited to carry bulk commodities is the ability to handle very large shipment sizes at low unit costs. This can be provided by water, rail, and pipelines.

WATER TRANSPORT. It is difficult to make generalizations about the costs of shipments by water, since there are various types of water transport. The cost characteristics of inland waterway transport, Great Lakes transport, and intercoastal package freighter are all different. For purposes of this study, it is sufficient to consider only the costs of inland water transport since this is the most important in terms of rail competition and is the mode that is usually involved in rail-water litigations. Hence, although Great Lakes steamers and package freighters play an important part in the transportation spectrum, they will be ignored here.

As was true in the case of high-value commodities, it is necessary to consider the social costs of shipping a commodity from a given specific

13. This view apparently is shared by the railroad management, since piggybacking headed the list of innovations important to the next decade (see Edwin Mansfield, "Innovation and Technical Change in the Railroad Industry," in *Transportation Economics* [Columbia University Press for the National Bureau of Economic Research, 1965], p. 192). However, if piggybacking is to be effective, the restrictions associated with its use must be removed. For a full discussion of this point see Chap. 5.

point of origin to a given specific point of destination. Thus, the terminal costs, the social line-haul costs, and the inventory costs of barge transportation must be analyzed. Since adequate data are lacking to analyze the costs in this detail, the discussion must be somewhat cursory and suggestive.[14]

Terminal costs vary with the commodity shipped and the location of the waterway with respect to the original point of departure. If the initial shipping point is inland, the commodity must be moved to a waterway terminal where it will incur handling and storage charges. These pickup and delivery operations will usually be necessary unless the mine, refinery, or factory is on the waterway. Since the volumes associated with water transport are very large, rail operations would usually be used for pickup and delivery operations between the waterway and the point of origin or destination.

The actual terminal costs depend on the commodity shipped. Most terminals are specialized and designed to handle one good. Some terminals are equipped to handle only oil or grain (which can usually be pumped), coal or ores (which can be shoveled or moved on conveyor belts), lumber or logs (which must usually be handled by a crane), and package freight (which also requires a crane). Costs thus vary with the volume handled, the extent of mechanization, and so on. In general, however, the greater the mechanization, the lower the terminal costs. This minimizes the labor or stevedoring costs and the demurrage and operating costs of the vessel while in the harbor. Hence water carriers operate the most effectively in handling bulk commodities (sand, grain, petroleum, ores) for which there is special equipment for rapid loading and unloading, and low- to medium-value goods over long hauls for which their low line-haul costs can offset high terminal costs. Since specific estimates of terminal costs are not available, it is impossible to make a more detailed analysis of these costs.

Somewhat more information is available on line-haul costs, which vary with the speed, the characteristics of the flotilla (length, breadth, and draft), the characteristics of the waterway (width and depth), the amount of push needed to be generated, the amount of lockage involved, and so on.

Most estimates place barge costs at about 3 mills per ton-mile. These

14. This lack of data should be rectified in the near future when a major study by a group at Northwestern University is completed. The results of their study are not yet available, however.

are fully distributed costs, and presumably include terminal costs as well as a return to overhead.[15] It is difficult to separate the line-haul component of this fully distributed cost of 3 mills a ton-mile, but it has been estimated that the line-haul component is as low as 0.7 mill per ton-mile.[16]

Because waterways are provided by the government, but made available to waterway operators free of charge, the nominal costs differ from the social costs. By 1961, approximately $7 billion had been spent on waterway development by the federal government.[17] It is estimated that, at the present time, the federal government is spending $200 million on new construction and $50 million on operating and maintenance expenditures.[18]

Nothing can be done about past construction expenditures. These are sunk costs and to charge the present operators for past investments over which they had no control would be both inequitable and inefficient. However, there is no reason barges should not be charged the current construction and operating and maintenance costs. The estimated current costs of $250 million should, therefore, be allocated to the current users.[19]

Any allocation of these costs among the users must be somewhat arbitrary and depends on the relative use of the waterway between barge and other means of transport and their relative needs in terms of waterway design. Since barges comprise the bulk of waterway users, for the purposes of approximating social line-haul costs it is reasonable to assume that barges must pay for all of the current construction costs of $200 million. The actual costs charged to barge operations will then depend on the rate of interest and the period of amortization charges applied to the current construction costs. Thus, if a 10 percent capital recovery

15. John R. Meyer, "A Comparison of the Advantages and Disadvantages of the Various Modes of Transport," in Robert S. Nelson and Edward M. Johnson, eds., *Technological Change and the Future of the Railways* (Northwestern University, Transportation Center, 1961), p. 7.

16. Lester Lave, unpublished manuscript for Corps of Engineers, 1966.

17. Doyle Report, p. 172.

18. U.S. Bureau of the Budget, "Transportation User Charges" (memorandum, 1965).

19. The problem is more complicated than stated here because waterway investments are usually part of large multiple purpose developments. Consequently, the allocation of the costs between waterway developments and other aspects of the project is rather arbitrary, and the figure of $250 million may be subject to considerable error.

factor is used[20] on the $200 million annual construction costs, $70 million must be allocated among the users.[21] The annual freight carried by barges is approximately 100 billion ton-miles. An allocation of the current costs among the existing traffic would increase the ton-mile costs by 0.7 mill.[22] This would increase the costs of barge transport to almost 4 mills per ton-mile. If a 5 percent capital recovery factor is used, ton-mile costs would increase by 0.6 mill.

The significance of inventory costs is probably not very great for bulk commodities. Table 3.4 shows that the bulk of barge shipments is in extremely low-value commodities. Nevertheless, generalizations about inventory costs are difficult to make since data are lacking on relative speeds, the optimal size of shipments, and so on. An example can indicate the relative importance of these costs. The cost of delaying a ton of steel one hour is approximately 0.06 cent. A typical rail shipment between New Orleans and Chicago takes approximately 60 hours; a similar barge movement can often take 500 hours.[23] At a cost of 0.06 cent a ton for each hour delayed, this would amount to a cost of about 26 cents a ton for the journey. Since the distance between New Orleans and Chicago is 1,000 miles, the inventory costs for this shipment would be 0.26 mill a ton-mile. Since steel is a relatively high-value commodity shipped by barge and since specialized tows can reduce transit time considerably, this figure represents a maximum inventory cost. A specialized petroleum tow might make the Chicago-New Orleans trip in seven to ten days. Because the cost of delaying a ton of petroleum one hour is roughly 0.03 cent, inventory differentials would increase the cost per ton by approximately 5.4 cents for the journey. This would only increase inventory costs by 0.054 mill per ton-mile—a relatively insignificant amount.

20. This should be compared with a rate of 6 percent used by Meyer, Kain, and Wohl in their analysis of urban transport investments. See John R. Meyer, John F. Kain, and Martin Wohl, *The Urban Transportation Problem* (Harvard University Press, 1965), p. 177.

21. In many cases the line between maintenance and investment expenditures is not very clear. Nevertheless, although the distinction is somewhat arbitrary, it will be made for the purpose of exposition.

22. This figure should be reduced somewhat to reflect the share of the current costs paid by other waterway users. Nevertheless, this estimate probably represents a minimum since the imposition of user charges would doubtless reduce the traffic on the waterways. Thus a higher rate would be needed to produce the desired revenue.

23. John R. Meyer and others, *The Economics of Competition in the Transportation Industries* (Harvard University Press, 1959), p. 121.

TABLE 3.4. Waterborne Traffic in United States, by Value of Commodity, 1959, and Tonnage Distribution, 1961

Commodity	Percentage of waterborne tonnage	Value of commodity (dollars per ton)
Petroleum and products	41.8	24.64
Coal and coke	15.4	8.93
Iron ore and iron and steel products	10.8	85.26
Sand, gravel, stone	8.3	2.77
Grains	4.2	58.06
Logs and lumber	3.1	88.60
Chemicals	2.8	436.91
Seashells	1.9	n.a.
	88.3	
Other	11.7	
Total	100.0	

Sources: Waterborne tonnage, W. A. C. Connelly, "Statistics on Waterborne Commerce Compiled by the Corps of Engineers, U.S. Army," *Freight Transportation*, Highway Research Record 82 (Highway Research Board, 1965), p. 35; value of commodities, Interstate Commerce Commission, Bureau of Transport Economics and Statistics, *Freight Revenue and Wholesale Value at Destination of Commodities Transported by Class I Line-Haul Railroads*, 1959, Statement 6112 (October 1961), App. A.
n.a. Not available.

Thus, when all of the costs associated with barge transport are considered, the social costs may reach a maximum of 4 mills a ton-mile—3 mills for the basic carrier cost plus 0.7 mill for the current capital costs and 0.3 mill for inventory costs. However, it is important to remember that many barge shipments can go for considerably less than this. For example, oil is shipped up the Ohio River in direct competition with pipelines that charge 1 mill a ton-mile. Since the barge company involved has been replacing equipment and expanding its operation, one must conclude that their fully distributed costs must also be on the order of 1 mill a ton-mile.

RAIL TRANSPORT. The rail costs associated with the transportation of bulk commodities differ radically depending on the type of equipment used and load carried. The line-haul costs of a 40-ton boxcar can reach 7 mills a ton-mile; those of a 70-ton load can fall as low as 4 mills a ton-mile.[24] To these must be added the terminal costs of $1.06 a ton for a 40-ton shipment and 60 cents a ton for a 70-ton load. For a journey of

24. See Interstate Commerce Commission, *Rail Carload Cost Scales by Territories for the Year 1962*, Pocahontas Region, Table 2, p. 68.

1,000 miles, a 40-ton boxcar shipment could cost as low as 6 mills a ton-mile; a 70-ton shipment could cost as low as 4.5 mills a ton-mile. However, most trips are considerably shorter. For an average journey of 300 miles, a 40-ton shipment would cost 8 mills a ton-mile; a 70-ton shipment would cost 6 mills. This should be compared with Meyer's estimate of 7 mills a ton-mile for ordinary bulk commodity operations,[25] which seems to be a reasonable approximation of the costs associated with bulk shipments.

These costs can be significantly reduced if the shipments can be made in larger sizes. To capitalize on the economies of large-scale shipments, the railroads have recently instituted special service and rates for large-volume shipments. Of these, the two most important are the Big John cars and the unit trains. Faced with a steady erosion of its grain traffic by trucks and water carriers, the Southern Railway developed specially designed hopper (Big John) cars with 100-ton capacity, which led to substantial cost reductions through higher utilization, cheaper maintenance, and the terminal economies associated with large shipment size. On multiple car shipments of 450 tons (five cars, each carrying 90 tons) the Southern reduced its rates by some 60 percent to levels of 5 mills per ton-mile.[26] Although considerable litigation resulted from this and similar reductions, the courts ruled in the Southern's favor and the rates have been accepted as compensatory, that is, covering out-of-pocket costs. Thus on the Big John cars, costs approach levels that are competitive with water transport.

Unit trains are another recent innovation and have been developed to enable coal to meet the competition of other energy sources.[27] These represent large multiple-car shipments, usually from the mine to the utility, and are quoted for annual volumes. A typical unit train is composed of 100 cars, each carrying 100 tons. Thus the total shipment load is 10,000 tons, approximately one-fourth the size of a single barge tow. The economies arising from unit-train operations come from reduced switching expenses, since the trains are only made up and broken at the points of origin and destination, faster turnabout times, reduced clerical expenses,

25. Meyer, "A Comparison of the Advantages and Disadvantages of the Various Modes of Transport," p. 17.

26. For example, the rate between Birmingham and St. Louis was reduced from $8.70 to $3.12 a ton or from 12.83 mills to 5.02 mills per ton-mile.

27. The technology associated with unit trains has been in existence for many years, but the railroads have been blocked from using it by the ICC regulatory policies until recently. For a full discussion of this problem see Chap. 4.

and higher levels of utilization. Estimates of unit-train costs indicate that they are in the neighborhood of 5 mills a ton-mile.[28] However, published rates have fallen as low as 4.5 mills.[29] Since these rates have not been challenged, they presumably cover out-of-pocket costs. Thus costs of 4 mills a ton-mile may be feasible for unit trains. This implies that under the proper conditions rail operations are competitive with barge operations. For this to happen, however, large shipment sizes are needed. Consequently, for all but the largest volumes of rail shipments, water transport probably retains a competitive edge over rail transport.

TRANSPORT BY PIPELINE. Pipelines are presently used to carry most crude oil, natural gas, and refined petroleum products moving overland and have been used successfully in the transportation of coal and some ores. Since the volume of throughput increases more than proportionately with the size of the pipe, pipeline costs drop dramatically as volume of throughput rises. For example, the minimum costs of shipment through a 10-inch pipeline are considerably more than three times the minimum cost of shipment through a 30-inch pipeline.

At their most efficient level of operation, pipelines are very cheap. A large pipeline built to carry 400,000 barrels a day can achieve costs as low as 0.6 mill a ton-mile.[30] However, a more representative figure is probably 1.2 mills a ton-mile, which is still very cheap.[31] Moreover, even at their least efficient operation, pipelines can carry crude oil for a cost as low as 3.7 mills a ton-mile.[32] Thus when pipelines can be utilized they are cheaper than any other mode.

If pipelines are used for commodities other than gas and oil, additional costs must be incurred to enable the commodity to be carried through the pipe. For example, slurry pipelines carrying coal must incur additional costs to liquify and deliquify the coal. The one experiment with slurry coal pipelines, the pipeline between Cadiz and Cleveland,

28. See Paul W. MacAvoy and James Sloss, *Regulation of Transport Innovation: The ICC and Unit Coal Trains to the East Coast* (Random House, 1967), pp. 37–61.

29. See M. A. Adelman, "American Coal in Western Europe," *Journal of Industrial Economics,* Vol. 14 (July 1966), p. 206.

30. Meyer and others, *Competition in the Transportation Industries,* p. 131. Their estimates were inflated to 1963 prices by the GNP deflator.

31. Meyer, "A Comparison of the Advantages and Disadvantages of the Various Modes of Transport," p. 7.

32. Meyer and others, *Competition in the Transportation Industries,* p. 129, inflated by GNP deflator to 1963 prices.

Ohio, yielded costs of 13.6 mills a ton-mile.[33] Although initially competitive with rail rates, the pipeline proved to be noncompetitive when the railroads reduced their rates in 1963. Since then, no slurry coal pipeline has been in commercial operation.

Because the pipeline used in the Cadiz-Cleveland operation was of less than optimal size in terms of length and diameter, its costs do not represent the possible costs associated with slurry pipeline operations. Some idea of possible costs can be obtained from a study made by Robert R. Nathan Associates, which analyzed the feasibility of using pipelines to carry coal in the West from the mine to the utility. Their estimates ranged from 10 to 4 mills a ton-mile, depending on the length of the haul and the volume to be carried. From their study, it appears that slurry pipelines, unit trains, and barges could all compete effectively for the coal traffic.[34]

Because costs vary with commodity, length of haul, and size of shipment it is difficult to give a single dimensional figure for transport costs of each mode. Nevertheless, Table 3.5 attempts to provide such a figure for each mode discussed here. At their most efficient, rail operations can probably compete with some water operations. Moreover, at their most efficient, piggyback operations lead to considerable economies over ordinary rail or truck service. However, it is important to stress the approximate nature of the costs—particularly with regard to high-value commodities whose costs vary radically with length of haul and shipment size. Thus these figures should be taken as indicative of the general cost characteristics and not as representative of the costs associated with carrying a specific commodity a specific distance.

The Demand for Transport Services

While considerable empirical work has been done on transport costs, relatively little has been done on demand. The few existing studies are

33. *Ibid.*, p. 133, inflated by GNP deflator to 1963 prices.
34. *The Potential Markets for Far Western Coal and Lignite,* Report to the U.S. Department of the Interior, Office of Coal Research, Dec. 27, 1965. Whether pipelines could be used for other commodities is problematical. The fact that they have not been used for many other minerals suggests that the costs of liquifying and deliquifying may be too high to make pipelines profitable. Moreover, when a pipeline was used to transport grain in Washington, it was found to be unsatisfactory because the friction burned the grain.

TABLE 3.5. Long-Run Marginal Costs for Optimal Freight Transport
Operations, by Mode of Transport, 1963[a]

Mode of transport	Marginal costs (mills per ton-mile)
Pipeline	1.0
Water	
Manufactured commodities	4.0–5.0
Bulk commodities	1.0–2.0
Rail	
Bulk multiple car	4.0–5.0
Bulk boxcar	7.0
Piggyback	11.4
High-value commodities	15.6
Truck	21.7

Source: Estimated by author.
a. Assumes shipments of 500 miles, capacity operations.

highly aggregative and not entirely satisfactory.[35] Thus the ensuing discussion will be primarily qualitative, but will introduce quantitative data
whenever possible.

It is important to realize that freight transportation is not wanted in its
own right, but only for the service it provides in the process of production. Thus demand for it is a derived demand and can be treated the
same way as the demand for any other factor of production. In general,
the demand for a factor of production will be less elastic: (1) the less
elastic the demand for the commodity using the factor; (2) the less important the price of the factor in the cost of producing the commodity;
(3) the less factor substitution is possible in the process of production;
and (4) the less willing other factors are to match reductions in the cost
of a given factor.

By applying these premises to transportation services, much can be
determined about the nature of the demand for these services. The de-

35. H. Benishay and G. E. Whitaker, Jr., "Demand and Supply in Freight
Transportation," *Journal of Industrial Economics,* Vol. 14 (July 1966), pp. 243–
62; Eugene D. Perle, *The Demand for Transportation: Regional and Commodity
Studies in the United States* (University of Chicago, Department of Geography,
1964); E. Silberg, "The Demand for Inland Waterway Transportation" (Ph.D.
thesis, Purdue University, 1964); Arthur P. Hurter, Jr., "Some Aspects of the Demand for Inland Waterway Transportation" (processed, Northwestern University,
Transportation Center, September 1965).

mand for general transportation will be considered first to determine its probable elasticity. Then the demand for specific types of transportation will be considered to determine their probable elasticities.

General Transport

Probably the two main elements determining the elasticity of demand for an input or factor are the extent of substitution among the factors or inputs and the extent that the cost of the factor or input appears in the final-goods price.[36] In the short run, there is probably relatively little substitution between transport and other inputs. Once a locational decision has been made, the transport needs of a firm are more or less set. In the longer run, however, as locations become flexible, transport could be substituted for other services. Thus the elasticity of demand for transport services should be greater in the long run than in the short run.

The input-output table of 1958 gives some indication of the importance of total transportation services in the final-goods price of each commodity, since the estimate of the direct transport inputs per dollar of output are a direct measure of the importance of transport in the final-goods price. Although transport is used ubiquitously, it does not constitute a significant proportion of the total inputs of any commodity. Transportation is most important in ferrous mining (9.1 percent of the final-goods price), chemical and fertilizer mineral mining (6.4 percent of the final-goods price), lumber and wood products (5.1 percent of the final-goods price), stone and clay products (6.0 percent of the final-goods price), and primary iron and steel products (5.3 percent of the final-goods price). However, for most commodities, transportation accounts for no more than 2 percent of the final-goods price.[37] Since the elasticity of transport demand is given by the product of the elasticity of the final-goods demand and the proportion of transport costs in the final-goods

36. The elasticity of demand for transport will vary between localities, commodities, and so forth. Moreover, since elasticity is a point concept, its numerical value should change with output and prices. Hence, to say that demand is relatively inelastic implies that it is inelastic within the existing area of production and consumption. At different levels of output, the elasticity would be different.

37. Warehousing is included in the transport sector in "The Transactions Table of the 1958 Input-Output Study and Revised Direct and Total Requirements," in *Survey of Current Business* (September 1965). Thus the figure tends to overestimate the importance of transport. Since transport is large relative to warehousing, the error introduced should not be too great. See Table 2, pp. 40–42.

price,[38] the demand for transport services must necessarily be quite inelastic unless the demand for the commodity is highly elastic.[39]

In the short run, therefore, it seems likely that the demand for transport services is quite inelastic. Because few substitutes are available in the short run and because transport costs do not significantly affect the final-goods price of most commodities, it seems likely that within the relevant range of the elasticity of the demand for the commodity, the demand for transport should be quite insensitive to changes in the price of transport services.

Even though the demand for transport as a homogeneous factor may be inelastic, this is not likely to be true for the demand for a given mode. Thus transportation is probably characterized by an overall low elasticity and high cross elasticities between modes.

Alternative Modes of Transport

A given transport mode has several characteristics for a given shipment and offers a certain price, a certain speed or time of delivery, a certain reliability or probability that the shipment will arrive undamaged and within the time period specified, and a certain minimum shipment size that it can handle the most economically. These are usually known to the shipper and can be treated as data when he is making his decision concerning the proper mode to employ. Thus for any given shipper, the demand for any given mode will depend on the rate and service characteristic (speed, reliability, minimum optimal size of shipment) offered by that and all competing modes.

The nature of the demand depends in part on the nature of the commodity to be shipped. All commodities have different characteristics that

38. Formally, the elasticity of demand for transport is given by the expression $E_t = q/r$, where q is the percentage change in freight volume and r is the percentage change in rates. If f is the percentage of transport costs in the final-goods price, a rate increase of r percent will increase the final-goods price by rf percent. This will in turn reduce the quantity purchased of that commodity by $(E_c)(rf)$ percent, where E_c is the elasticity of demand for that commodity. If the reduction of output is reflected proportionally in transport demand, then $q = (E_c)(rf)$. Hence $E_t = (E_c)(f)$.

39. Considering the direct and indirect requirements does not change the conclusions. Thus, the maximum direct and indirect transport requirements occur in the ferrous mining industry where 11.64 cents' worth of transport services are needed for every $1.00 output of the ferrous mining industry. For most industries the requirements are considerably less. *Ibid.*, Table 3, pp. 45–49.

make them sensitive to different aspects of transport costs. Of these, probably the most important are value, density, volume, and fragility or perishability. Since some of these affect the cost and some affect the demand, generalizations are difficult. Density should primarily affect the shipment costs per ton. Since the unit of supply is the truck or boxcar instead of the ton, the greater the density, the greater the possible load per vehicle mile; hence the lower the cost per vehicle mile. This implies that dense commodities should have a relatively lower percentage of transport costs embodied in their final-goods price. Thus, the elasticity of demand with respect to rates should be rather low for dense commodities. This is not true with respect to the other determinants of demand, however. Since a given transport vehicle (barge, boxcar, or truck) can transport a larger tonnage of a dense commodity, the value of the shipment will be greater than that for a less dense commodity. This will increase the inventory costs associated with a shipment. Hence for dense commodities, the elasticity of demand with respect to speed, minimum shipment volume, and reliability should be rather high.

Value affects transport demand in a fashion similar to density. Since high-value commodities usually have a low percentage of transport costs in their final-goods price, their elasticity with respect to rates should be fairly low. Similarly, because any given shipment will incur higher inventory costs as the value of the commodity rises, high-value goods should have a relatively high elasticity with respect to speed, minimum shipment volume, and reliability.

Volume refers to quantity shipped per unit of time. Therefore, the larger the volume to be shipped the more sensitive should shippers be to rate differentials and the greater should be the elasticity of demand with respect to rates. Large-volume shippers would probably not be very sensitive to the other elements of transport demand. Since a large volume implies a relatively constant throughput, speed or reliability should not affect the transport demand of high-volume shippers very much.

Fragility should make a commodity sensitive to such factors as speed and reliability. Moreover, since the minimum shipment size will determine the amount of the loss in case of accident, fragile commodities should also be sensitive to minimum shipment size. It is likely that fragile commodities will be more sensitive to these service characteristics than to rate differentials.

To recapitulate, low-value, average-density commodities with a large annual shipment volume should be sensitive to rates and not particularly sensitive to the inventory costs associated with speed, minimum shipment size, and reliability. High-value, dense, or fragile commodities should be relatively insensitive to rates, but sensitive to the factors affecting inventory costs. From this analysis, it should be possible to predict the pricing policies followed by the different modes and the probable modal splits.

The ICC has five broad categories of commodities: products of agriculture; animals and products; products of mines; products of forests; and manufactures and miscellaneous. Table 3.6 gives the general characteristics of these commodity groups.

The products of mines as shown have a low value. Although data are available only for the railroads, they are suggestive of other aspects of these commodities. For those commodities that go by rail, freight charges form an important component of the final-goods price. This suggests that the elasticity of transport demand for these products should be rather high and that price would have to be fairly responsive to costs. This is corroborated by the relatively low ratio of rail revenues to out-of-pocket costs for these commodities.[40] Although there are no available data on the modal split of these commodities, because of their bulky nature, low value, and high ratio of freight costs to final price, they are likely to go by either rail or water. Where barge transportation is available to compete with rail transport, competition should force prices down toward marginal costs. Unless rails could carry the commodities in large volumes,

---

40. If the railroads were profit maximizing, the elasticities of rail demand could be estimated directly from the ICC data on the ratio of rail revenues to cost. A profit-maximizing firm will set its price so that $E = P/(P - mc)$ where E = elasticity of demand with respect to price, P = price, and mc = marginal cost. The ICC data on the ratio of rail revenues to out-of-pocket costs is roughly equivalent to the price-marginal cost ratio. By designating this ratio as a and substituting into the above elasticity equation, a direct estimate of elasticity can be derived: $E = a/(a - 1)$ where a = the ratio of rail revenues to out-of-pocket costs. Since the railroads are not free to set profit maximizing rates, marginal revenue (mr) does not equal marginal cost (mc); hence $mr = \gamma mc$, and the actual elasticity under which the railroads are operating is $E^* = a/(a - \gamma)$. If the railroads are prevented from raising rates, γ is less than unity and E^* is less than E; the inferred elasticity overstates the true elasticity. On the other hand, if the railroads are prevented from reducing rates, γ is greater than one and E^* is greater than E; the inferred elasticity understates the true elasticity. Thus, to the extent that railroads are forced to hold down rates on bulk commodities and maintain rates on manufactured commodities, the elasticities inferred from the ICC data on the ratio of rail revenues to out-of-pocket costs would overestimate the true elasticity of demand under which the railroads are operating for bulk commodities and underestimate that for manufactured commodities. Consequently, the ICC data on the ratio of rail revenues to out-of-pocket costs do not provide a useful means of estimating elasticities.

TABLE 3.6. Characteristics of Rail Freight, by Commodity Group, United States, 1952–61

Variable and year	Products of agriculture	Animals and products	Products of mines	Products of forests	Manufactures and miscellaneous	All commodities
Value per ton (dollars), 1959	101.31	601.44	11.16	57.97	280.60	120.85
Rail volume (millions of tons), 1961	1.46	0.09	6.12	0.71	3.16	11.57
Rail freight cost as percentage of value, 1959	8.20	3.96	28.13	14.21	5.06	5.77
Rail revenue as percentage of out-of-pocket costs:						
1952	137	121	125	132	185	152
1953	128	115	121	128	185	149
1954	128	112	112	127	174	141
1955	130	118	122	131	177	146
1956	126	112	121	127	173	142
1957	124	111	117	125	169	139
1958	128	110	114	124	163	137
1959	122	109	113	122	159	135
1960	119	107	109	118	152	129
1961	118	111	106	117	148	127

Sources: Value and rail freight cost, Interstate Commerce Commission, Bureau of Transport Economics and Statistics, *Freight Revenue and Wholesale Value at Destination of Commodities Transported by Class I Line-Haul Railroads, 1959,* App. A, pp. 16–21; percentage costs and volume, Interstate Commerce Commission, Bureau of Accounts, *Distribution of the Rail Revenue Contribution by Commodity Groups, 1961,* Statement 6-64 (June 1964), p. 12 and Table 7.

the advantage would probably go to barges. For petroleum products, pipelines would have a clear advantage.

Animal products have a very high value, and freight plays a small role
in the final-goods price. Moreover, the demand for these commodities is
relatively inelastic. This implies that their overall transport demand
should be relatively inelastic. However, the rail markup on these commodities is low, indicating that the elasticity of demand for rail services
must be fairly high, probably due to the competitive nature of the products' transport markets. Since animals and many animal products fall
under the agricultural exemption, these commodities are subject to ubiquitous, unregulated truck competition. Because most of the products
have a high value, relative inventory costs play an important part in
determining the modal split. Here the advantage goes to the trucks, which
because they are unregulated tend to cut their rates down to costs.
If the railroads want to maintain any traffic, they must keep rates low
because of truck competition. Thus effective competition can do much
to keep rates close to marginal costs.

The rail markups on agricultural and forest materials are similar. Both
commodities have relatively low values, and rail-freight costs play a significant role in their final-goods price. Thus the rail transport demand for
these commodities should be fairly elastic. Although this might be offset
somewhat by the low elasticity of demand for these commodities, it is
unlikely that their transport demand would be significantly affected.
Hence one would expect them to travel at rates that are close to costs,
particularly in view of the historical bias of the ICC in favor of keeping
these rates low.

It is somewhat surprising, therefore, that the rail markups over cost
are as high as they are. This can only be explained by the lack of effective intermodal competition. Since rails are often the only effective
means of transporting these commodities, they can set their rates on the
basis of the general transport elasticity instead of on the modal cross
elasticity. Where water competition exists, rail rates are significantly
lower. These considerations are seen in Table 3.7 which shows the regional rate differentials for agricultural and forest products. Water
competition is generally available in the southern and official territories,
which contain the Mississippi, Missouri, and Ohio River systems, but not
in the western territory. Thus one would expect rail rates to be lower in
the first two territories than in the last. Although there is some evidence
of this differential, the traditional bias in favor of low freight rates from
the West often masks it.

TABLE 3.7. Rail Revenue as Percentage of Out-of-Pocket Costs for Selected Agricultural and Forest Products, by Direction of Shipment, United States, 1961

Direction of shipment by region[a]

Agricultural or forest product	Official to official	Southern to southern	Western to western	Official to southern	Southern to official	Official to western	Western to official	Southern to western	Western to southern	United States to United States
Wheat	140	172	193	122	227	103	200	147	167	185
Flour	72	84	84	94	—	129	119	—	128	94
Corn	118	167	159	96	128	240	206	237	119	140
Pulpwood	62	79	77	—	77	76	107	92	47	76
Shingles	126	158	144	180	163	156	118	174	132	134

Source: Interstate Commerce Commission, Bureau of Accounts, *Distribution of Rail Revenue Contribution by Commodity Groups, 1961*, Table 7.

a. Official territory: Maine, Vermont, New Hampshire, Massachusetts, Connecticut, Rhode Island, New York, Pennsylvania, New Jersey, Ohio, Indiana, Michigan, West Virginia, Maryland, Virginia, District of Columbia, Illinois (eastern half).
Southern territory: North Carolina, South Carolina, Georgia, Florida, Alabama, Mississippi, Tennessee, Kentucky.
Western territory: Rest of the country (everything west of the Mississippi plus Wisconsin and western half of Illinois).

Nevertheless, where competition exists, it seems to be an effective means of keeping freight rates low. Moreover, a lack of effective competition and the resulting low elasticity of demand for rail transport seems to permit relatively high rates, even though the ICC has tried to keep key rates down on raw materials and agricultural products coming from the West. Thus, market forces seem to be a more effective regulator of rates than policy.

The rail markup over out-of-pocket costs on manufactured goods is striking. The ability of the railroads to maintain that differential is due to several factors. First is the nature of their transport demand. Because these goods have a high value and relatively low freight costs embodied in their final-goods price, their general transport demand should be relatively inelastic. In the early days of transport development, when the railroads were the sole means of transport, the ICC and the railroads recognized this inelasticity and capitalized on it. This formed the basis of the historical rate differentials between low-value and high-value goods.

With the development of the trucking industry, however, the cross elasticity of rail demand should have risen; rates should have fallen in response to truck competition. Their failure to do so can only be explained by regulation and the application of the railroad rate structure to the trucking industry. Thus competition has taken place in the service area. Here, the high value of the commodities has made them particularly sensitive to the elements of speed, reliability, and minimum shipment size associated with inventory costs. Consequently, the allocation of traffic between rail and truck should primarily be determined by service rather than rate differentials.

The *Census of Transportation 1963* made data available to pursue these hypotheses.[41] If railroads and trucks were free to compete on the basis of rates, the share of trucking should be positively correlated with the ratio of rail revenues to out-of-pocket cost. Since they are not, the competition should be on the basis of service and relative inventory costs. Because rail inventory costs rise with the value of the commodity, the share of trucking should be more highly correlated with the value of the commodity than the ratio of rail revenues to out-of-pocket cost. The rank correlations of tons and ton-miles shipped by truck to value per ton were 0.706 and 0.709, respectively (both significant at the 1 percent level). The rank correlations of tons and ton-miles shipped by truck to

41. U.S. Bureau of the Census, *Census of Transportation, 1963:* Vol. III, *Commodity Transportation Survey,* Pt. 3, "Shipper Groups," Table 1, pp. 18 ff.

the ratio of rail revenue to out-of-pocket costs were 0.140 and 0.226, respectively. In the first case, the correlations are high and highly significant; in the second case, they are low and statistically insignificant. Thus, because of inflexibilities in the rate structure, the transport demand of manufactured goods appears to be much more sensitive to relative inventory costs than to rates.

From this discussion, it should be clear that price discrimination is ubiquitous in transportation, and particularly in rail transportation. The extent of this discrimination can be seen from the rail-freight tariff schedules. The rate classification lists 31 classes, each of which has a separate rate per ton-mile ranging from 400 percent to 13 percent of the first-class rate. However, this classification covers only 15 percent of rail freight; the other 85 percent goes by commodity rates, which are quoted for specific point to point movements of a specific commodity of a specific shipment size. Thus the number of rates probably goes into the trillions. Rates not only differ for shipments with similar costs, but are equal for shipments with widely varying costs.

The Interstate Commerce Act permits railroads to practice commodity price discrimination in the form of value-of-service pricing, while limiting locational price discrimination and prohibiting personal price discrimination. However, all forms of price discrimination are ubiquitous in the transport industry. Although the existence of truck competition should increase the sensitivity of high-value goods to truck-rail rate differentials, the regulatory policies have effectively limited rate competition. Hence the railroads have been able to maintain effective commodity price discrimination and charge relatively higher rates for high-value commodities than for low-value commodities.

A recent study of the relative degrees of price discrimination within various freight commodities concluded that there was more price discrimination within low-value commodities than within high-value commodities. Although this conclusion may seem surprising, a little reflection will indicate that it is to be expected. High-value freight is carried almost exclusively by rails or motor carriers, which are highly regulated and have very little rate competition. Low-value freight is carried by rails or barge carriers. Since rails are regulated and most water carriers are not, the ICC permits railroads to pursue rate competition with respect to the water carriers. Consequently, rates will tend to fall in competitive situations, but remain high in situations where the railroads have monopoly power. The result of these competitive and regulatory pressures should be a more homogeneous rate structure for high-value than for bulk commodities. This was precisely the finding of Oi and Hurter.[42] Thus value-of-service pricing has remained an integral aspect of the transport rate structure.

In addition to commodity price discrimination, the railroads practice extensive locational price discrimination. Since many small intermediate towns have more limited transport facilities than large consuming and producing centers, market pressures tend to make rates on shipments to these towns higher than rates on larger shipments between two major consuming centers. Although Section 4A of the Interstate Commerce Act is specifically supposed to limit this form of price discrimination, the ICC has generally permitted relatively higher rates between the major center and the intermediate points than between the major centers if the carrier can show the existence of competitive pressures. This is particularly true if the railroad faces water competition.

Locational price discrimination is particularly evident on shipments of bulk commodities. Since the general elasticity of demand for transport on the part of bulk commodities is relatively high and the cross elasticity between modes is higher, the existence of water competition should push rates down toward marginal cost. Where competition does not exist, however, the railroads can exercise their monopoly power, subject only to the forces of market competition. Table 3.8 indicates that where water competition exists, rates are approximately two-thirds to one-half of those where competition does not exist. Thus the degree of locational price discrimination seems to be considerable.

Market competition can also give rise to substantial locational price discrimination. When a consuming center has several alternative sources of supply, the elasticity of demand facing any given carrier should be considerably higher than that facing a carrier in a consuming center with limited sources of supply. Thus the markups over carrier cost will generally be lower for the former center than the latter.

The market for coal on the East Coast gives a good example of the significance of market competition. The large coastal utilities can obtain coal from the Appalachian mines or oil from abroad or via pipeline, while the small inland utilities can generally use only coal. Consequently, the elasticity of demand for rail transport is much higher on the part of

42. See Walter Y. Oi and Arthur P. Hurter, Jr., *Economics of Private Truck Transportation* (William C. Brown Company for the Transportation Center, Northwestern University, 1965), Chap. 7.

TABLE 3.8. Extent of Railroad Price Discrimination Due to Water Competition, Selected United States Routes, 1963

Origin and destination	Distance (miles)	Water competition	Rail rate (dollars per ton)	Rail rate (cents per ton-mile)	Ton-mile rate, long route as percentage of ton-mile rate, short route	Commodity
New Orleans, La. to Little Rock, Ark.	436	No	12.10	2.78	45	Sugar
New Orleans, La. to Cincinnati, Ohio	834	Yes	10.50	1.26	62	Structural steel
St. Louis, Mo. to Detroit, Mich.	473	No	12.70	2.68		
St. Louis, Mo. to Pittsburgh, Pa.	604	Yes	10.00	1.66	44	Limestone
Baton Rouge, La. to Bauxite, Ark.	346	No	4.39	1.27		
Baton Rouge, La. to Prairie du Rocher, Ill.	735	Yes	2.40	0.33	63	Newsprint
Calhoun, Tenn. to Oklahoma City, Okla.	828	No	17.20	2.08		
Calhoun, Tenn. to Houston, Tex.	854	Yes	11.02	1.31	65	Iron and steel plates
St. Louis, Mo. to Jackson, Miss.	505	No	10.01	1.98		
St. Louis, Mo. to New Orleans, La.	685	Yes	8.89	1.30	60	Coal
West Va. to Concord, N.H.	722	No	6.04	0.84		
West Kentucky to Tampa, Fla.	770	Yes	3.87	0.50	55	Phosphate rock
Bartow, Fla. to Greensboro, N.C.	667	No	7.44	1.12		
Bartow, Fla. to Norfolk, Va.	802	Yes	4.95	0.62	40	Aluminum billets
Riverdale, Ia. to Jones Mills, Ark.	614	No	13.80	2.25		
Riverdale, Ia. to Gregory, Tex.	1,189	Yes	10.69	0.90	47	Hydrofluoric acid
Houston, Tex. to Danville, Ill.	928	No	23.00	2.48		
Houston, Tex. to Chicago, Ill.	1,039	Yes	1.21	1.16	65	Wheat for export
New Orleans, La. to Oklahoma City	673	No	8.00	1.19		
New Orleans, La. to St. Louis, Mo.	685	Yes	5.30	0.77	58	Wheat for export
Amarillo, Tex. to Houston, Tex.	596	No	8.00	1.34		
St. Louis, Mo. to New Orleans, La.	685	Yes	5.30	0.77	54	Coal
West Frankfort, Ill. to Menominee, Mich.	556	No	5.62	1.01		
West Frankfort, Ill. to Minneapolis, Minn.	619	Yes	3.37	0.54	67	Phosphate rock
Bartow, Fla. to Montgomery, Ala.	464	No	6.33	1.36		
Bartow, Fla. to Pensacola, Fla.	462	Yes	4.25	0.92	46	Phosphate rock
Bartow, Fla. to Greensboro, N.C.	667	No	7.44	1.12		
Bartow, Fla. to Des Plaines, Ill.	1,205	Yes	6.25	0.52	50	Phosphate rock
Bartow, Fla. to Spartanburg, S.C.	559	No	6.91	1.24		
Bartow, Fla. to Norfolk, Va.	802	Yes	4.95	0.62		

the large coastal stations than on the part of the inland stations. Mac-Avoy and Sloss have estimated that the elasticity of demand for rail services with respect to rates is only -0.397 for small, non-oil-using inland generating stations while the comparable elasticity of large oil-using coastal generating stations is -4.612.[43] Rates vary accordingly. For example, the price-marginal cost ratio on carload shipments from the coal producing regions to the coastal centers of Boston, New York, Philadelphia, and Baltimore are some 10 to 20 percent lower than the price-marginal cost ratio on carload shipments to closer, but inland centers.[44]

Personal price discrimination exists whenever two shippers are charged different prices for identical services. This was explicitly prohibited by the Interstate Commerce Act of 1887 and is still considered illegal. The basic tenet seems to be that shippers be treated equally for equal services. The difficulty is to determine what equal services are. Differences in location and in commodities shipped seem to be interpreted as differences in services. Except for carload and less-than-carload traffic, differences in volume do not.[45] This has led to situations where small, inefficient mine operators have been able to compete with large, efficient operators. Since the freight of the very large-volume shippers can be carried for substantially less than the freight of small-volume shippers, this insistence on equality has effectively acted as a form of personal price discrimination. However, the rapid development of the unit train is changing this situation. Moreover, although evidence on this point is lacking, the extremely low rates on many commodities that do not seem to be subject to competitive or ICC pressures indicate that the shippers must be exercising some monopsony power.[46]

Price discrimination is probably a necessary aspect of the transportation industry. Different shippers have different elasticities of demand and are faced with different marginal costs for their shipments. Railroads have large fixed costs relative to their variable and marginal costs. As long as substantial excess capacity prevails, the optimal use of capacity requires price discrimination.[47] The marginal shipper with a high elasticity of demand can be accommodated at close to marginal cost, while the

43. MacAvoy and Sloss, *Regulation of Transport Innovation*, pp. 77–85.
44. *Ibid.*, pp. 67–68. It should be pointed out that the introduction of unit-train service in 1964 changed these rate relationships somewhat.
45. The ICC has granted volume rate reductions in certain situations. *Ibid.*
46. See the summary of the conference of experts, Chap. 8, for an elaboration of this point.
47. See Chap. 6, below, for a full discussion of this point.

captive shipper with a low elasticity of demand can be used to cover the overhead and charged rates considerably above costs. Without price discrimination all shippers would be charged the same rate and less traffic would move. Thus price discrimination enables the railroads (or other modes) to capture the consumers' surplus of the low-elasticity shipper to enable them to carry the goods of the high-elasticity shipper. So long as the railroads are operating in the falling or constant portions of their cost curves, this leads to the maximum use of resources and thus is socially desirable (assuming, of course, that the income redistribution implied by this is also deemed socially desirable).

CHAPTER FOUR

Consequences of the Present Regulatory Policies

PRESENT REGULATORY POLICIES impose substantial costs on the United States economy by encouraging continued resource misallocation in shipping and production relationships. The nature and extent of these costs are the subject of this chapter.

Static Costs

Under present regulatory policies, many shipments fail to go by the low-cost carrier. Although the static losses to society resulting from this resource misallocation may reach $500 million a year, the resulting adjustments in transportation using industries impose additional costs that are probably even greater than this figure. The reasons for these static costs are discussed below.

Economic Efficiency and the Present Traffic Allocation

Much has been written about the probable misallocation of traffic caused by a discriminatory rate structure based on the value of the commodity.[1] This practice, termed value-of-service rate making, worked initially because the railroads were the only means of transportation; it

1. See, for example, John R. Meyer and others, *The Economics of Competition in the Transportation Industries* (Harvard University Press, 1959), Chaps. 6 and 7; Merton J. Peck, "Competitive Policy for Transportation," in Almarin Phillips, ed., *Perspectives on Antitrust Policy* (Princeton University Press, 1965).

has continued to work up to the present time because the railroad rate structure has been applied to other regulated modes. Since shippers of high-value commodities are sensitive to inventory cost differentials, competition has centered on service. Here the trucks have a clear advantage. In the absence of effective rate competition, they have been able to attract considerable traffic that could go more cheaply by rail even when the inventory cost differentials are taken into account. Thus there is a presumption that traffic would shift from truck to rail if rates more accurately reflected costs.

In their path-breaking work, Meyer and his associates estimated that: "Trucks have a clear cost advantage for traffic of less than 100 miles, the rails a narrow cost advantage at 100 miles, and a clear and increasing cost advantage for traffic moving over 200 miles. . . ." Since 91 percent of all trucking shipments are sent for distances of over 200 miles, the implication is clear: much traffic goes by truck that could go more cheaply by rail; the present insistence of the Interstate Commerce Commission (ICC) on the maintenance of value-of-service rate making leads to substantial misallocation of traffic.[2]

Data recently became available to test this hypothesis more fully. The *1963 Census of Transportation* made possible the generation of statistics that give the modal split by shipment size and length of haul for a large number of commodity groups in the manufacturing sector.[3] By calculating the inventory costs associated with each commodity[4] and adding them to the relevant railroad costs given by the ICC, the costs of rail operations for each commodity can be estimated. The estimates can then be compared with the relevant trucking costs to determine the distance at which it is cheaper to ship each commodity by rail. Table 4.1 gives these distances for each commodity group and representative shipment sizes and the allocation of shipments between truck and rail.

The evidence in Table 4.1 should not be taken as definitive, but it suggests that substantial misallocation of traffic exists. Although railroads have a clear cost advantage for all 10- and 20-ton commodity shipments

2. Meyer and others, *Competition in the Transportation Industries*, pp. 194, 195.

3. I am indebted to Donald Church of the U.S. Bureau of the Census for making these unpublished data from the 1963 census of transportation available to me.

4. This was done according to the formulas outlined in App. B, below. The value of each commodity was obtained by taking a weighted average of all the commodities in the ICC classification included in the relevant Census of Transportation commodity group.

TABLE 4.1. Distance Beyond Which Shipments Should Go by Rail and Actual Method of Shipment, by Commodity and Shipment Size, United States, 1963

Commodity	Value (dollars per ton)	Distance (miles) beyond which shipments should go by rail, by shipment size (tons)				Percentage of traffic shipped less than 200 miles by truck, by shipment size (tons)				Percentage of traffic shipped more than 200 miles by truck, by shipment size (tons)			
		1	10	20	40	1	10	20	40	1	10	20	40
Cutlery, hand tools, and hardware	1,942.78	249	159	135	87	94.8	89.4	28.4	100.0	84.9	71.9	47.3	—
Tires and tubes	1,508.65	248	152	124	76	99.4	97.2	12.4	—	97.8	79.1	29.9	19.7
Motor vehicles and equipment	1,283.46	247	148	117	70	96.8	74.1	58.3	7.6	65.6	39.7	21.9	1.8
Plastics and related materials, etc.	1,181.62	247	147	117	67	97.2	96.0	94.2	36.0	93.7	96.0	74.5	11.4
Paints, varnishes, etc.	593.00	244	137	103	54	97.0	95.3	95.5	77.3	95.2	92.0	79.0	58.2
Beverages and flavoring extracts	339.75	243	134	98	48	99.6	99.3	93.9	6.1	80.9	85.6	77.9	14.0
Paper and paper products	297.49	243	133	96	46	98.4	94.4	58.8	33.2	66.9	58.6	47.1	10.4
Industrial chemicals	202.68	243	131	95	44	98.8	96.7	93.8	20.0	95.4	76.9	57.3	3.2
Iron and steel castings	190.01	243	131	94	44	97.8	93.0	92.1	25.2	95.3	89.7	80.2	13.7
Steel and rolling mill products	176.72	243	131	94	44	98.6	98.0	97.5	29.6	93.6	92.0	85.0	8.2
Products of petroleum refining	59.50	242	129	92	43	80.3	78.8	92.2	34.3	83.7	59.7	49.1	2.2

Source: Distance figures are based on cost data in App. B. Percentages are calculated from unpublished data from U.S. Bureau of the Census, *Census of Transportation, 1963.*

traveling more than 150 miles, the bulk of these shipments traveling more than 200 miles goes by truck. Moreover, the large amount of one-ton shipments traveling over 200 miles by truck indicates that substantial misallocation exists in this traffic. Nevertheless, since trucks carry virtually all one-ton shipments traveling less than 200 miles, the allocation of the small-size, short-haul traffic seems to be quite efficient. Moreover, since the bulk of all 40-ton shipments traveling more than 200 miles goes by rail, the allocation of the large-size, long-haul traffic seems to be reasonably efficient.

Thus the main source of traffic misallocation seems to exist in the small-to-medium-size shipments and the medium-to-long hauls. Since this traffic forms a large proportion of existing truck traffic, a reallocation of traffic to reflect relative costs should lead to substantial diversion of trucking traffic to the rails. Moreover, since piggyback operations increase the advantage of rails in this area, their extensive introduction would probably lead to even greater traffic diversion. Consequently, present regulatory policies that prevent the railroads from practicing effective rate competition have enabled the trucks to maintain an uneconomic share of the traffic in high-value manufactured goods.

In addition, present regulatory policies force the railroads to provide a great deal of retail or distribution service for which trucks are better suited. The present blanket-rate structure requires railroads to charge identical rates to shippers in wide geographical areas, regardless of the density of the traffic or the costs of performing the service. Moreover, Section 4 of the Interstate Commerce Act prohibits rates between two major consuming centers from being lower than the rates between either center and an intermediate point, regardless of its traffic characteristics.

Railroads are best suited to carrying high-density traffic with a minimum number of distribution points. The costs of service to relatively small, isolated communities with low traffic densities and inefficient means of distribution are substantially higher than the costs of service to communities with high traffic densities and efficient means of distribution. However, rates cannot generally reflect these cost differences.

The problem is compounded by the Commission's use of average costs in intermodal rate cases. Although efficient railroad operations may have a substantial cost advantage over trucks, the average cost data used by the Commission may not reflect it if the railroads perform a large amount of low-density service. Similarly, although trucking operations may have a substantial cost advantage over low-density rail service, the average cost data used by the Commission may not reflect it if the railroad performs a substantial amount of high-density, efficient service. By considering only average costs, the Commission effectively prevents each mode from adopting rates that would reflect their true cost advantage.

An efficient traffic allocation would permit the railroads to perform a wholesaling service and specialize in handling high-density traffic between major centers. It would permit trucks to perform a retail or distribution service and specialize in handling relatively low-density traffic. Such specialization would lead to a diversion of large-volume trucking traffic to rails, a diversion of low-volume rail traffic to trucks, and lower transport costs. By refusing to let rates reflect relative costs, the Commission ensures a continued traffic misallocation and excessively high transport costs.

The Losses of Misallocation

Although such estimations are always subject to error and qualification, it is interesting to estimate the social costs of this misallocation of traffic. This can be done by calculating the deadweight loss associated with noncompetitive pricing.[5]

In a perfectly competitive market, the supply curve will represent marginal cost, and price must necessarily be equal to marginal cost. If firms offer only the commodity at marginal cost plus some markup, the equilibrium price will rise, and the equilibrium output will fall. Consequently, consumers will be worse off while producers will be better off. Since the producers' gains will fail to offset the consumers' losses, society as a whole will be worse off as a result of the noncompetitive pricing policies, which are said to create a deadweight loss.

These considerations can be seen in Figure 4.1, which shows a com-

5. This method was initially outlined by Hotelling and has been employed by Harberger rather extensively in recent years. See Harold Hotelling, "The General Welfare in Relation to Problems of Taxation and of Railway and Utility Rates," *Econometrica*, Vol. 6 (1938), reprinted in Richard A. Musgrave and Carl S. Shoup, eds., *Readings in the Economics of Taxation* (Richard D. Irwin for American Economic Association, 1959), pp. 139–67; and Arnold C. Harberger, "Taxation, Resource Allocation, and Welfare," in *The Role of Direct and Indirect Taxes in the Federal Revenue System*, A Conference Report of the National Bureau of Economic Research and the Brookings Institution (Princeton University Press, 1964), pp. 25–70. See also Arnold C. Harberger, "The Measurement of Waste," American Economic Association, *Papers and Proceedings of the Seventy-sixth Annual Meeting, 1963, American Economic Review*, Vol. 54 (May 1964), pp. 58–76.

FIGURE 4.1. Deadweight Loss Caused by Noncompetitive Pricing

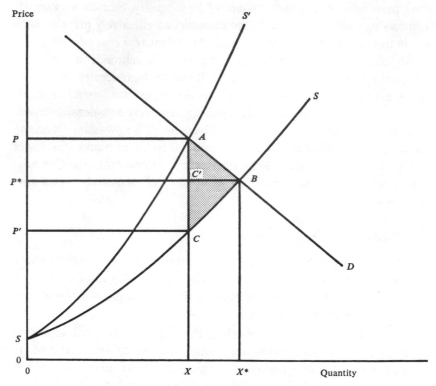

petitive equilibrium, where price equals P^* and output equals X^*. So long as the industry is perfectly competitive, the supply curve, SS, represents the summation of each firm's marginal-cost curve. Hence, price equals marginal cost. Suppose that for some reason producers do not move along their marginal-cost curve but insist on receiving their marginal cost plus a constant percentage markup. The supply curve is effectively raised to SS'; the equilibrium consumers' price rises to P; the equilibrium quantity falls to X. The loss in consumers' surplus is given by the area PP^*BA; the gain in producers' surplus is given by the rectangle $PP^*C'A$. The gain does not offset the loss, however. The triangle ABC represents the deadweight loss to society for which there is no compensation. This triangle is composed of the net loss in consumers' surplus ABC' and the net loss in producers' surplus $C'BC$. So long as the demand and supply curves are reasonably linear over the relevant range, the deadweight loss

associated with the noncompetitive pricing of a single commodity can be
given by

$$L = \tfrac{1}{2} \Delta P \Delta X$$

where $\Delta P =$ the divergence between the actual price P and the marginal
cost P' at that output, and $\Delta X =$ the divergence between the competitive
output X^* and the actual output X. This is the area of the triangle ABC.
By summing over all commodities for which price diverges from marginal
cost, the deadweight loss to society can be given by

$$L = \tfrac{1}{2} \sum_i \Delta P_i \Delta X_i$$

where $\Delta P_i =$ the divergence between price and marginal cost for the ith
commodity, and $\Delta X_i =$ the divergence between actual and competitive
output for the ith commodity.

With a little manipulation this expression can be rewritten as

$$L/\sum_i P_i X_i = \tfrac{1}{2} \sum_i Z_i \delta_i^2 E_i$$

where $\sum_i P_i X_i$ equals the total output, Z_i equals the share of total output
produced by commodity type i, δ_i represents the ratio of the divergence
between price and marginal cost to price for commodity type i, and E_i
represents the elasticity of demand for the ith commodity.[6] Thus this
expression gives the loss as a proportion of total output.

It is important to realize that there are many assumptions involved in
this procedure. One of the most important is that all people have the
same weight given to an increment or deduction of income. Otherwise,
the transfer of income from the consumers to the producers could not be

6. This expression is derived by multiplying $\tfrac{1}{2} \Delta P_i \Delta X_i$ by the fraction $(\Delta P_i P_i^2 X_i)/$
$(\Delta P_i P_i^2 X_i)$ which is equal to unity. Hence

$$L = \frac{1}{2} \sum_i \left[\Delta P_i \Delta X_i \left(\frac{P_i^2 X_i \Delta P_i}{P_i^2 X_i \Delta P_i} \right) \right] = \frac{1}{2} \sum_i \left[P_i X_i \left(\frac{\Delta P_i}{P_i} \right)^2 \left(\frac{\Delta X_i}{\Delta P_i} \cdot \frac{P_i}{X_i} \right) \right].$$

Let $Z_i = (P_i X_i)/(\sum_i P_i X_i)$; $\delta_i = \Delta P_i/P_i$; and

$$E_i = \frac{\Delta X_i}{\Delta P_i} \cdot \frac{P_i}{X_i}.$$

Z_i is the share of the total output accruing to commodity type i, δ_i is the ratio of the divergence between price and marginal cost to price for commodity type i and E_i is the
elasticity of demand for commodity type i. See Walter Y. Oi and Arthur P. Hurter, Jr.,
Economics of Private Truck Transportation (William C. Brown Co. for the Transportation
Center at Northwestern University, 1965), pp. 333–57, and Harberger, "Taxation,
Resource Allocation, and Welfare," and "The Measurement of Waste," for a full discussion.

canceled out. Another important assumption is that price equal to marginal cost is the proper norm.[7] It should also be pointed out that this approach to estimating the losses is extremely partial and does not take all of the interactions within the economy into account. Thus the ensuing analysis should be taken as illustrative, but not as definitive.

THE LOSSES FROM RAILROAD PRICING. The above formula can be used to estimate the losses associated with railroad pricing policies. If the share of the total traffic (Z's), the elasticities (E's), and the divergences from marginal costs (δ's) are known for each commodity type, it is a straightforward matter to estimate the losses.

The ICC provides sufficient data to estimate the Z's and the δ's for a wide range of commodities. For each commodity, it gives the total revenues derived from its transportation and the ratio of revenues to out-of-pocket cost. The Z's can easily be computed by taking the ratio of the revenues derived from transporting a given commodity to the total rail revenues. The δ's can be estimated from the ICC data on the ratios of rail revenues to out-of-pocket costs. Data on elasticities are scarce and not very reliable.[8] However, Perle's estimates are suggestive and thus can be used to give an order of magnitude of the losses.[9]

The calculations needed to estimate the losses are given in Table 4.2

7. The implication of this assumption will be discussed below, pp. 75–77.

8. The elasticities inferred from the ICC data on the ratio of rail revenues to out-of-pocket cost are no help in estimating the deadweight loss. The ICC data reflect the average markup of price over marginal cost for all railroads and as such reflect the average monopoly power exercised by each railroad. Consequently, the elasticities inferred from these data reflect the average elasticity of demand facing each railroad (subject to the biases outlined above, p. 55, note 40).

However, in estimating the deadweight loss, it is the market demand that is relevant rather than the firm demand. The elasticity of the market demand will always be less than the elasticity of the firm demand (unless the firm is a monopolist), and there is no reason it cannot be less than one while the elasticity of the firm demand is greater than unity. (In a perfectly competitive industry, the elasticity of each firm's demand will be infinite, while the elasticity of the market demand could be less than unity.) Since the ratios of rail revenues to out-of-pocket costs are based on average figures, there is no way of going from the inferred average elasticity of demand facing the firm to the market demand.

9. Eugene D. Perle, *The Demand for Transportation: Regional and Commodity Studies in the United States* (University of Chicago, Department of Geography, 1964). Perle's study gives numerous estimates of the elasticity of demand that vary with the specific arguments used in his demand functions. Consequently, the elasticities of demand given in Table 4.2 do not reflect specific estimates given by Perle, but rather my assessment of the most probable value of the elasticities based on his numerous regressions.

TABLE 4.2. Losses Associated with United States Railroad Pricing Policies as a Proportion of Rail Revenue, 1961

Commodity group	Pricing policy: Optimal price equals out-of-pocket costs				Pricing policy: Optimal price equals fully distributed cost			
	Proportion of total revenue Z_i	Ratio of deviation from optimal price to actual price δ_i	Absolute value of elasticity of demand E_i	Loss as proportion of revenue $(0.05)(Z_i\delta_i^2 E_i)$	Proportion of total revenue Z_i	Ratio of deviation from optimal price to actual price δ_i	Absolute value of elasticity of demand E_i	Loss as proportion of revenue $(0.05)(Z_i\delta_i^2 E_i)$
Products of agriculture	0.15	0.15	0.5	0.0008	0.15	−0.07	0.5	0.0002
Animals and products	0.03	0.10	0.6	0.0001	0.03	−0.02	0.6	[a]
Products of mines	0.25	0.06	1.2	0.0005	0.25	−0.28	1.2	0.0118
Products of forests	0.07	0.15	0.9	0.0007	0.07	−0.11	0.9	0.0004
Manufactures and miscellaneous	0.50	0.32	0.7	0.0179	0.50	0.17	0.7	0.0050
All commodities				0.0201				0.0174

Sources: The first, second, fifth, and sixth columns from Interstate Commerce Commission, Bureau of Accounts, Distribution of the Rail Revenue Contribution by Commodity Groups, 1961, Statement 6–64 (June 1964); the third and seventh columns from Eugene D. Perle, The Demand for Transportation: Regional and Commodity Studies in the United States (University of Chicago, Department of Geography, 1964).
a. The figure for animals and products is less than 0.00004.

and indicate that the loss attributed to railroad pricing is on the order of 2 percent of all rail-freight revenues. In 1964, these revenues were $8.5 billion; hence the welfare loss roughly equals $170 million. Even if all these elasticities were doubled, the loss would come only to $340 million.[10] Since the elasticities needed to make the estimated losses equal $340 million are rather high, it seems more reasonable to estimate that the welfare losses might come to $200 to $300 million annually.

THE LOSSES FROM TRUCK PRICING. Because the trucking rate structure follows rather closely that of the railroads, there should also be some losses associated with truck pricing. Unfortunately, data are lacking to estimate these losses in a disaggregated fashion. Estimates of the relationships between revenue and costs of truck commodity shipments do not exist. There are no adequate estimates of the elasticity of trucking demand by different commodity groups with respect to price.[11] Thus gross estimates will have to be made. Benishay and Whitaker have estimated the gross demand for trucking services with respect to price.[12] Since their estimated elasticity of 1.151 more or less agrees with Perle's estimates, for the purposes of estimating the losses associated with trucking operations, an elasticity of unity can be taken as a reasonable approximation of the true elasticity. The ICC keeps no record of the ratio of revenue to out-of-pocket costs for trucking operations.

The best indication of the divergence between costs and rates lies in the behavior of rates when certain agricultural commodities were deregulated.[13] The deregulation of frozen poultry led to reductions in rates of some 30 percent; similar reductions were found to occur in the case of frozen fruits and vegetables. Thus, as approximation, the divergence between rates and costs can be taken to be 20 percent. This leads to a welfare loss of 1.4 percent of the trucking revenues of regulated carriers.[14] In 1964, the revenues were $6.1 billion, yielding a welfare loss on trucking operations of approximately $85 million. Hence the total

10. The *Economic Report of the President, January 1966,* estimated cost savings of $400 million accruing to shippers if railroad rates were based on costs, p. 127.

11. Although Perle does have some estimates of these elasticities, they are not very satisfactory and seem to suffer from considerable biases.

12. See H. Benishay and G. E. Whitaker, Jr., "Demand and Supply in Freight Transportation," *Journal of Industrial Economics,* Vol. 14 (July 1966).

13. See C. Peter Schumaier, "Characteristics of Agriculturally Exempt Motor Carriers," in *Private and Unregulated Carriage* (Northwestern University, Transportation Center, 1963), pp. 77–95.

14. $Z = 1.0$; $\delta = 0.167$; $\delta^2 = 0.028$; $E = 1.0$; $L = (\frac{1}{2})Z\delta^2 E = 0.014$.

welfare loss arising from value-of-service pricing can be estimated at approximately $300 to $400 million annually or approximately 2 to 3 percent of the revenues of regulated motor and rail carriers.

THE PROBLEM OF "SECOND BEST." It should be stressed that these estimates are the grossest possible sort and overestimate the welfare losses in some respects and underestimate them in others. The estimation of the losses has been based on the assumption that out-of-pocket or marginal cost has a normative significance and is the proper price to charge from the point of view of social welfare. So long as price is equal to marginal cost throughout the economy, this assumption is proper. If prices are generally greater than marginal cost, price should not be required to equal marginal cost in any given sector. This would lead to an overutilization of resources in that sector. Thus if price is generally greater than marginal cost throughout the economy, the normative price should also be greater than marginal cost. Hence the estimates of the losses made on the basis of the divergences between revenues and out-of-pocket or marginal costs should overestimate the losses.

However, once it is admitted that price is not equal to marginal cost throughout the economy, the proper price to charge in any one sector becomes virtually impossible to determine. Estimation of the optimal divergence between price and marginal cost in each sector requires the quantitative knowledge of the actual divergence between price and marginal cost in all sectors and the way in which marginal rates of substitution and of transformation between goods react to changes in the consumption and production of other goods.[15] Since the required information is not available, there is no way to quantify the proper relationship between price and marginal cost in any one sector.

In the United States economy, average-cost pricing is generally followed instead of marginal-cost pricing. This throws it into the world of second best where normative prescriptions are virtually impossible to make. Nevertheless, it is interesting to pursue the problem a little and make some rough adjustments in the previous estimates of the losses. For the manufacturing sector as a whole, the markup of prices to average total cost is approximately 5 percent.[16] Since this figure is based on

15. For a full discussion of this point see R. G. Lipsey and Kelvin Lancaster, "The General Theory of Second Best," *Review of Economic Studies,* Vol. 24 (December 1956), pp. 11–32.

16. The rate of return to sales is approximately 5 percent. See U.S. Federal Trade Commission–Securities and Exchange Commission, *Quarterly Financial Report for Manu-*

accounting costs, it does not include a return for normal profit. This normal return is approximately 3 percent on sales.[17] Therefore, the excess profit on sales is approximately 2 percent; the average divergence between prices and costs is on the order of 2 percent.

Since the average divergence between price and average total costs is on the order of 2 percent throughout the economy, relatively little misallocation should exist if the transportation industry maintained this same relationship between prices and average total costs.[18] Moreover, as long as the railroads are subject to considerable excess capacity, average-cost pricing is necessary to enable them to obtain sufficient revenues to remain in business in the absence of subsidies.[19] Therefore it is relevant to

---

facturing Corporations, various issues. By some simple algebraic manipulation, it can be shown that this is the same as the markup of price to costs.

$$\text{Rate of return to sales} = \frac{TR - TC}{TR} = \frac{(P)(Q) - (AC)(Q)}{(P)(Q)} = \frac{P - AC}{P}$$

where TR = total revenue; TC = total cost; P = price; Q = output; and AC = average cost.

17. This figure was derived in the following way. The rate of return on equity can be related to the rate of return to sales by the formula

$$\left(\frac{TR - TC}{V}\right)\left(\frac{V}{TR}\right) = \frac{TR - TC}{TR}$$

where TR = total revenues, TC = total costs, V = the value of equity. The average return to equity in the United States has been about 10 percent. Since the average return to sales is approximately 5 percent, the ratio of equity to revenues should be approximately one-half. Since the "normal" return to equity is considered to be approximately 5 percent, this implies that the "normal" return to sales should be approximately $2\frac{1}{2}$ percent. For a full discussion of the relationships involved, see Joe Bain, *Industrial Organization* (2d ed., John Wiley and Sons, 1964), pp. 387–412.

18. Strictly speaking, this statement will be correct only under stringent conditions. If the ratio of average total cost to marginal cost is the same for all industries, and if the ratio of average total cost to price is the same for all industries, the ratio of price to marginal cost will be the same for all industries. If factors are in fixed supply, equal price-marginal cost ratios will lead to an optimal use of resources. For a discussion of the "proportionality rule," see Abba P. Lerner, *The Economics of Control: Principles of Welfare Economics* (Macmillan, 1944); Lionel W. McKenzie, "Ideal Output and the Interdependence of Firms," *Economic Journal,* Vol. 61 (1951), pp. 785–803; J. deV. Graaf, *Theoretical Welfare Economics* (Cambridge: Cambridge University Press, 1957).

19. Although price discrimination could enable the railroads to obtain sufficient revenues to stay in business, it implies wide variation in the price-marginal-cost ratios. Thus in terms of pure static efficiency, it would probably lead to greater losses than those associated with average-cost pricing. Nevertheless, as an operational pricing policy, price discrimination may be preferable to average-cost pricing. Because of the multiproduct nature of a railroad and the interdependencies

reestimate the losses from rail pricing taking the general price-average-cost ratio that exists in the United States economy as a norm. Calculations to determine the losses in this case are also given in Table 4.2. The losses from rail pricing then fall to 1.74 percent of revenues and are consequently reduced by approximately 13 percent.

FURTHER DISTORTIONS. The losses estimated for the transport sector represent only the first round, however. Since transport is used as an intermediate good, the distortions and misallocations existing in the transport sector will be magnified in the other sectors. In particular, the depressed rates for mining and forestry materials indicate that freight rates do not adequately reflect the costs of transporting these commodities. Since producers base their production decisions on rates rather than costs, the costs that they consider will be less than the true social costs. This will tend to lead to the overutilization of mining and forestry raw materials, which, in turn, may lead to the development of submarginal mines or timber lands.

Moreover, poor locational decisions may take place. Because of relatively high rates on manufactured commodities and low rates on raw materials, manufacturing firms may locate too close to consuming centers and too far from raw-material centers. The rate structure encourages the substitution of raw-material shipments for manufactured-goods shipments. This may lead to increasing industrial concentration in the large urban centers. If freight rates reflected costs more closely, the pattern of industrial location might be considerably more diversified. It may not be entirely coincidental that within the highly industrialized northeast the ratio of revenues to out-of-pocket costs for manufactured goods are the highest in the country.

In addition to the distortions in production and location decisions, the freight-rate structure should also lead to distortions in consumption decisions. Goods that heavily use forestry and mining raw materials may in fact be underpriced because of the low freight rates. Similarly, manufactured goods may be overpriced because of their high freight rates. This means that the general price level may be distorted; the relative prices facing the final consumers may have little bearing on the relative costs of producing them. The extent of these distortions is almost impossible to pin down. Products of mines are used as raw materials for manufactur-

between costs, output, and demand, it is virtually impossible to define railroad costs operationally and hence to set prices that are equal to average total costs. For a full discussion of this point see Chap. 6, pp. 131–35, below.

ing industries and not as finished goods. When they are transformed into manufactured goods, they are subject to excessively high rates. Thus the relationship between the delivered prices of the manufactured goods and the prices that would prevail if rates reflected costs might be rather close.

That the freight-rate structure has led to some misallocation of resources is clear. What is far from clear, however, is the quantitative impact of this misallocation. Clearly, goods are not transported as efficiently as possible, and a restructuring of freight rates would lead to considerable social savings. The impact of the rate structure on other economic relationships is more difficult to assess. Possibly its impact has been greater on locational decisions than on the basic production and consumption decisions. Thus the economies of agglomeration that the urban geographers discuss may not be true economies, but reflections of distorted transport costs. Unfortunately, however, without more information, the true impact of the rate structure on the economy can only be a source of conjecture. The direct costs of the rate structure in the transport industries are probably on the order of $500 million per year. Although the indirect costs exist, their magnitude must remain a question mark until data become available to make an analysis.

Dynamic Costs

The present regulatory policies lead to the dynamic costs of poor utilization of capacity and poor investment decisions. If the capital invested in the transport industries could be rationalized and used more efficiently, the United States economy could achieve a higher level of investment and growth. Although these losses are virtually impossible to quantify, they may be more important than those arising from the misallocation of shipments between modes. The nature of these dynamic costs will be discussed below.

Excess Capacity and the Regulatory Process

It is possible to argue that the large amount of excess capacity existing in the transport industries is due to regulation. The concept of the common carrier has doubtless encouraged capacity expansion in the transport industry. Common carriers have a responsibility to the public to provide adequate transportation services; they must be available to carry goods to and from isolated locations; they must have sufficient capacity to meet the peak demands. These requirements would not necessarily lead to excessive capacity expansion if the carriers were permitted to charge rates that reflected the higher costs associated with irregular route or peak demand service. However, rate differentials of this type have traditionally been forbidden by the Commission. Since rationing the facilities through the price mechanism has been precluded, the carriers have found it profitable to maintain sufficient capacity to handle all irregular demands without prohibitive increases in costs.

The grain shipments pose an interesting problem in this respect since they are the primary source of the seasonality in rail demand. Faced with the regulatory constraint of maintaining constant rates over the course of the year, the railroads have maintained sufficient capacity to handle the demands of this peak period without an excessive increase in costs. This has led to considerable excess capacity in other periods. Although a flexible rate policy would enable the railroads to utilize their equipment more evenly over the year and thus to carry the same volume of traffic at a lower level of plant and equipment, seasonal pricing would tend to increase the rates on agricultural commodities coming from the West. In view of its stand in favor of the traditional rate structure, it is not surprising that the Commission has been unwilling to permit seasonal rate differentials. In maintaining this position, however, the Commission has encouraged the railroads to expand capacity.[20]

In addition, the regulatory emphasis on "fair return on fair value" has done much to encourage expansion in capacity. Under current regulatory policies, a railroad that achieves "excessive" profits may be under pressure to lower rates to reduce its level of profitability. Few railroads will willingly reduce rates in this situation because of uncertainty concerning future traffic levels. Once rates have been reduced to ensure "normal" rates of return at the existing traffic levels, any reduction in traffic will lead to subnormal profits. Since upward rate adjustments are often met with litigation and delays, this period of low profitability could last for some time. Consequently, the railroads may tend to hide excessive profitability by increasing investment in equipment and the modernization of facilities. These actions will reduce the observed rate of return and permit the railroads to maintain a constant rate of profit by curtailing replace-

20. For a rigorous discussion of the relation of inflexible rates to excess capacity see George H. Borts, "Increasing Returns in the Railway Industry," *Journal of Political Economy*, Vol. 62 (1954), pp. 316–33.

ment investment in periods of recession without experiencing a concomitant increase in costs. Thus instead of leading to rate reductions, the emphasis on fair return on fair value has tended to encourage the railroads to increase capacity to mask any returns over permissible levels.[21]

Finally, the maintenance of value-of-service pricing has doubtless contributed to the maintenance of excess capacity by the railroads. Value-of-service pricing was initially instituted to permit the railroads to receive sufficient return on their capital, which was built far ahead of demand. Since price discrimination can be justified only when there is excess capacity, continued value-of-service pricing has required continued capacity expansion to justify its use. In view of their traditional stance in favor of rate differentials between high-value and low-value commodities, it is not surprising that both the Commission and the Congress have encouraged capacity expansion on the part of the railroads. In view of the regulatory constraints placed on them, capacity expansion has been a rational pattern of behavior for the railroads to follow.

THE NATURE OF EXCESS CAPACITY IN THE RAIL INDUSTRY. Because of the difficulties associated with measuring capacity utilization, data on excess capacity are quite scarce and not very reliable. Nevertheless, all the available evidence indicates that substantial excess capacity exists in the transportation industries.

Before considering the extent of excess capacity in the rail industry, it is interesting to consider its nature. This can be done by utilizing the existing studies of rail costs. Cost functions usually express costs as a function of output; that is, $C = a + bX$, where C represents total cost and X represents output. Once the parameters (the a and the b) are estimated, it is a straightforward procedure to estimate the percent variable or the elasticity of costs for the railroad industry. Any percent variable less than 100 necessarily reflects increasing returns and a less than optimal use of capacity. Moreover, if the percent variable of the short-run curve is less than the percent variable of the long-run curve, this is a clear indication that the existing plant has excess capacity.

This can be seen from Figure 4.2, which shows a long-run total cost curve ($LRTC$), three short-run total cost curves (S_1, S_2, and S_3), and the

21. For a somewhat different view of the effect of regulation on investment see Harvey Averch and Leland L. Johnson, "Behavior of the Firm under Regulatory Constraint," *American Economic Review*, Vol. 52 (1962), pp. 1052–77. Their analysis was based on a guaranteed return on investment which the railroads do not have.

FIGURE 4.2. Relation between Long-Run and Short-Run Total Cost and Average Total Cost Curves for the Railroad Industry

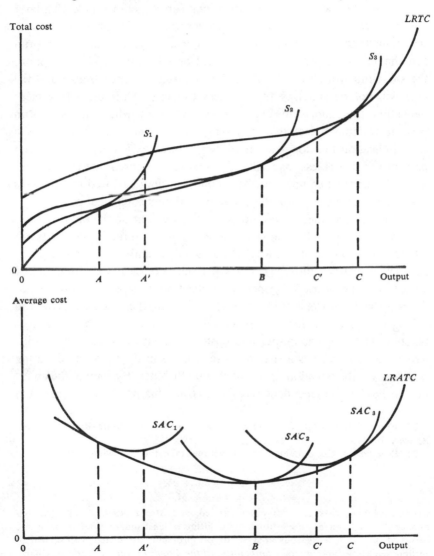

associated average total cost curves ($LRATC$, SAC_1, SAC_2, and SAC_3). At any output beyond B, the percent variable on the long-run curve will be greater than 100. Moreover, for any output between C' and C, both the long-run and the short-run percent variables will be more than 100.

However, within this range, the output could be produced with a smaller-scale plant than that implied by S_3, and the observed short-run percent variable will be less than the observed long-run percent variable. Similarly outputs between A and A' could be produced more cheaply with a larger-size plant than that implied by S_1. Thus, even though both the long-run and the short-run percent variables will be less than 100 at this point, the short-run will be greater than the long-run percent variable and the firm will not be suffering from excess capacity. Thus there is a clear indication that short-run excess capacity exists when the short-run percent variable is less than the long-run percent variable; there is a clear indication that long-run increasing returns exist when the long-run percent variable is less than 100. The first can be cured by the abandon·ment of plant and equipment; the second can only be cured by increases in demand sufficient to use the capacity of the most efficient plants.[22]

The existing studies on rail costs shed some light on the nature of excess capacity. Typically, rail costs are estimated in three forms: costs are a function of output alone; a function of output and some capacity measure (usually track mileage); costs per mile of track are a function of output per mile of track.[23] Since the utilization of capacity figures introduces a short-run element into the cost function, the first form is akin to a long-run cost function, the second form is akin to a short-run cost function. Deflating the output and costs by mileage has a somewhat different effect. Insofar as a size measure remains in the equation, deflating by size gives the equation some short-run attributes. By forcing the equation to have no independent threshold costs, this procedure merges the

22. For a full analysis of these points see Borts, "Increasing Returns in the Railway Industry."

23. Specifically, the estimated cost functions take the following forms:

$$C = a + bX$$
$$C = a + bX + cM$$
$$C/M = a + bX/M$$

where C = total costs, X = ton-miles carried, and M = miles of track. The parameters (a, b, and c) are estimated by fitting a least-squares line through the observed data. For a rigorous analysis of the problems associated with statistical costing, see Meyer and others, *Competition in the Transportation Industries*, Chaps. 2 and 3; and John R. Meyer and Gerald Kraft, "The Evaluation of Statistical Costing Techniques as Applied in the Transportation Industry," American Economic Association, *Papers and Proceedings of the Seventy-third Annual Meeting, 1960*, American Economic Review, Vol. 51 (May 1961), pp. 313–34.

size-related and fixed or common costs.[24] Thus in this form, the equation is something of a hybrid between a short-run and a long-run cost function. Moreover, by giving the same weight to small and large railroads, deflating by size gives disproportionate weight to the large numbers of small railroads. Thus, estimating the equation in this form for all railroads will bias the estimates toward the smaller railroads. When, however, the sample is divided between large and small railroads, the equation for each size class can only be interpreted as a hybrid between short-run and long-run cost functions.

Studies of increasing returns in the railroad industry are scarce and the available evidence is sketchy. For determining the causes of increasing returns to scale in railroads, a recent study by Griliches is probably the most appropriate.[25] Table 4.3 summarizes his results. Although he did not estimate the cost function in its short-run form, the normalized form can be taken to represent the short-run cost function since it is essentially a hybrid between a short-run and a long-run cost function.[26] From this table several interesting facts emerge. First, the percent variable for small firms is well under 100, but seems to be independent of the form of the equation. Second, the percent variable for large firms is approximately 100 when estimated by the long-run form but is considerably below 100 when estimated by the short-run form.

Although the evidence is hardly definitive, it suggests the following conclusions. (1) The marked increasing returns found in small firms come from an inefficiently sized plant rather than from excess capacity.

24. As estimated, the equation reads $C/M = a + bX/M$. This is equivalent to estimating the equation in the form of $C = aM + bX$. The lack of an independent term either implies that common and size-related costs have been merged or that no common costs exist. Since this latter assumption is unrealistic, the former interpretation seems more correct.

25. Zvi Griliches, *Rules to Govern the Assembling and Presenting of Cost Evidence,* Interstate Commerce Commission Docket 34013, Vol. 2 (April 1965). George Borts has made several more sophisticated studies of increasing returns in the rail industry. However, they are not as appropriate as the Griliches study for purposes of this study since they do not distinguish between the short-run and long-run forms of the equations. See George H. Borts, "Production Relations in the Railway Industry," *Econometrica,* Vol. 20 (January 1952), pp. 71–9 and "The Estimation of Rail Cost Functions," *Econometrica,* Vol. 28 (January 1960), pp. 108–31.

26. However, when estimated in this form the equation tends to yield less reliable results. See Meyer and others, *Competition in the Transportation Industries,* for a full discussion.

TABLE 4.3. Estimated Percent Variables for Railroad Industry, by Size of Firm and Cost Function, United States, 1957–61 Average[a]

Size of Firm	Total cost: $C = a + bX$	Cost per mile of track: $C/M = a + bX/M$
All railroads	97	75
	(5)	(11)
Small railroads	70	67
	(15)	(12)
Large railroads	99	77
	(6)	(11)

Source: Zvi Griliches, *Rules to Govern the Assembling and Presenting of Cost Evidence*, Interstate Commerce Commission Docket 34013, Vol. 2 (April 1965), Exhibit B, p. 31.
　a. Numbers in parentheses indicate standard errors.

Since the firms are too small to obtain all of the long-run economies of scale, they show increasing returns. They seem to be operating close to the long-run cost curve, indicating that their capacity seems to be well used. Thus, to capture the possible economies of scale, they should try to merge or consolidate. (2) The increasing returns associated with the short-run cost functions of the large firms and the constant returns associated with their long-run cost curves indicate the existence of excess capacity on the part of the large firms. Thus, these firms should attempt to abandon some capacity to obtain a more efficient size of plant.

ESTIMATES OF EXCESS CAPACITY IN THE RAIL INDUSTRY. Data on the degree to which capacity is used can be obtained by constructing some crude measures of the utilization of the railroad rolling stock and right-of-way.[27] These are given in Table 4.4. Two measures are given for the utilization of the rolling stock; one assumes that all cars are potentially loaded; the other assumes the existing ratio of loaded-to-empty cars prevails. Of the two, the latter is more meaningful since empty back-hauls are an inescapable part of transportation. Even so, capacity utilization of the rolling stock has never risen above 79 percent and has remained at approximately 75 percent throughout the postwar period.

Data on the use of the right-of-way in Table 4.4 indicate a falling ratio of freight-train miles per mile of track, but a fairly steady ratio of

27. The use of the rolling stock was estimated by calculating the potential ton-miles that the railroads could carry and comparing them with the actual ton-miles carried. The potential ton-miles were estimated by multiplying the number of freight cars by the average load carried and by the average miles traveled per year. By comparing this to the number of revenue ton-miles carried, some measure of the use of the rolling stock was obtained. Although these figures are obviously crude and based on gross averages, they are suggestive.

TABLE 4.4. Rail Capacity Utilization, United States, 1941–64

Year	Millions of actual revenue ton-miles per mile of track	Thousands of actual freight train miles per mile of track	Actual revenue ton-miles as percentage of potential	
			Average load per car	Loaded cars only[a]
1941–45	1.73	1.75	48	78
1946–50	1.61	1.50	48	78
1951–55	1.65	1.33	47	77
1956–60	1.64	1.18	46	74
1950	1.58	1.38	48	78
1951	1.74	1.42	49	79
1952	1.66	1.36	48	77
1953	1.64	1.33	46	76
1954	1.49	1.21	46	74
1955	1.70	1.30	47	76
1956	1.77	1.30	47	76
1957	1.70	1.23	46	74
1958	1.53	1.11	45	73
1959	1.60	1.15	46	75
1960	1.60	1.13	45	74
1961	1.58	1.09	46	75
1962	1.68	1.12	47	76
1963	1.77	1.14	47	76
1964	1.88	1.19	47	76

Source: Association of American Railroads, *Yearbook of Railroad Facts* (1965), pp. 8, 24, 34, 82, 83.
a. Assumes that empty cars are eliminated from back-haul and that the current ratio of loaded-to-empty cars prevails.

ton-miles per mile of track. Since freight trains are carrying increasing loads, the latter figure is the more relevant one. Nevertheless, the average traffic density at no point approaches the estimated optimum level of density of 3 million ton-miles per mile of track required for efficient operations.[28]

Aggregate data on the density of traffic on the existing track are not very useful since they include the highest and the lowest densities. From a study made by Conant,[29] it is possible to obtain more information on the nature of the roadway utilization. For example, in 1953, the density

28. See Kent Healy, "The Merger Movement in Transportation," American Economic Association, *Papers and Proceedings of the Seventy-fourth Annual Meeting, 1961, American Economic Review,* Vol. 52 (May 1962), p. 438.
29. Michael Conant, *Railroad Mergers and Abandonments* (University of California Press, 1964), p. 7.

on only 10.1 percent of the lines could be classified as heavy (14.044 million ton-miles per mile of track, annually), while the density on 60.1 percent of the lines could be classified as medium (2.272 million ton-miles per mile of road), and the density of the remaining 29.9 percent of the lines was light (0.192 million ton-miles per mile of track). The lines with the heavy and medium traffic densities accounted for 98 percent of all the traffic volume. This would indicate that the light-density lines were superfluous and could be abandoned.

Moreover, using several different estimates Conant has shown that the main-line track and secondary-line track are considerably underutilized. One estimate was based on the above figures for 1953 and assumed that the 110,000 miles of main-line track could support the average density carried by the high-density lines while the 112,000 miles of secondary track could support the average density carried by the medium-density lines. Thus, in 1953 a total potential capacity of 1,799 billion ton-miles existed, while only 632 billion ton-miles of freight were carried. This implies a rate of capacity utilization of approximately 35 percent. Similar estimates were made for 1962 based on the number and type of track existing at that time. The potential capacity was estimated to be 5.7 million train miles per day, which was approximately 3.5 times the actual total train miles per day.[30]

Because of the seasonal nature of many rail operations and geographical differences in demand, gross figures such as those given here can be highly misleading. Nevertheless, if some lines utilize their capacity reasonably fully, this implies that the remaining lines must be even more subject to excess capacity than the figures indicate. In general, the large eastern lines and those with a heavy-traffic density seem to be exploiting most of the economies available in railroad operations.[31] Since these lines account for some 50–70 percent of all rail traffic, the bulk of rail traffic would seem to be carried quite efficiently. However, it would also seem to be implied that a large number of lines are not efficiently used and should be discontinued or consolidated to reduce capacity.

EXCESS CAPACITY IN THE TRUCKING INDUSTRY. Data on excess capacity in the other transport industries are virtually nonexistent. Nevertheless, it is possible to argue that regulation has also encouraged the excessive expansion of capacity in the regulated trucking and water industries. In these cases, excess capacity can be laid to the maintenance of value-of-

30. Ibid., pp. 8–11.
31. See Borts, "Estimation of Rail Cost Functions."

service pricing in general and to the regulatory constraints on rate cutting in particular. This is especially true with regard to the trucking industry, which has the same rate structure as the railroads. The previous section indicated that if the railroads were free to cut rates, they could take considerable traffic away from the trucks. In the short run, this would generate substantial excess capacity in the trucking industry. In the long run, it would lead to the abandonment of a large number of trucking runs. Since rate competition is not permitted, however,[32] competition centers on the service sphere, both between trucks and rails and between competing truckers. This encourages trucking firms to purchase enough equipment to be able to satisfy the needs of the shipper as quickly as possible.

Although the Commission would argue that it has prevented excess capacity from developing in the trucking industry, its argument is largely fallacious. The Commission's argument is based on the standard model of monopolistic competition, in which equilibrium only occurs when each firm is producing on the falling portion of its average cost curve.[33] Since total social costs could be lowered by reducing the number of firms, limits upon entry and the number of competitors in any one market should lead to social savings. However, regulation only controls the number of firms, not the number of vehicles used by any one firm. Thus the Commission has failed to limit trucking capacity in any meaningful sense.

Rough measures of truck capacity utilization can be constructed in a manner similar to the estimates of rail capacity utilization given in Table 4.4. The trucking figures are given in Table 4.5 and indicate considerable excess capacity. Even when the empty backhauls are taken into account, the level of capacity utilization of the rolling stock remains below 50 percent. Although these figures are crude and rely on gross averages, they are suggestive.

32. The case *New Automobiles in Interstate Commerce* indicated that on occasion the ICC will permit rate competition (259 ICC 475 [1945]). Nevertheless, it is significant that the "three shall-nots," which would have explicitly permitted rate competition and prohibited umbrella rate making, did not become part of the Transportation Act of 1958. Thus, one must infer that some umbrella rate making is still practiced. For a full discussion of this, see Henry J. Friendly, *The Federal Administrative Agencies* (Harvard University Press, 1962), pp. 131–36.

33. For a full discussion of equilibrium under monopolistic competition, see Edward H. Chamberlin, *The Theory of Monopolistic Competition: A Reorientation of the Theory of Value* (7th ed., Harvard University Press, 1956), pp. 81–100.

TABLE 4.5.   Trucking Capacity Utilization, United States, 1940–63

Year	Actual revenue ton-miles as percentage of potential revenue ton-miles: average load per truck	Percentage carrying loads	Actual revenue ton-miles as percentage of potential revenue ton-miles: empty backhauls eliminated
1940	0.29	65.9	0.43
1941–45	0.25	58.7	0.43
1946–50	0.24	52.7	0.45
1951–55	0.25	54.7	0.45
1956–60	0.29	58.4	0.50
1950	0.24	53.9	0.45
1951	0.24	55.1	0.44
1952	0.25	54.0	0.46
1953	0.25	54.6	0.46
1954	0.25	55.1	0.45
1955	0.25	54.8	0.45
1956	0.26	57.0	0.45
1957	0.30	59.1	0.51
1958	0.30	58.5	0.50
1959	0.30	58.8	0.51
1960	0.30	58.7	0.51
1961	0.30	57.9	0.52
1962	0.28	58.4	0.48
1963	0.28	57.5	0.48

Sources: Automobile Manufacturers Association, *Motor Truck Facts* (1965), pp. 54, 56; U.S. Department of Transportation, Bureau of Public Roads, *Highway Statistics, Summary to 1965* (1967), p. 23. The percentages in the last column are calculated from unrounded data.

Technical Change

The evaluation of the performance of an industry with respect to technical change is difficult because there is no operational standard against which performance can be judged. Since performance can be judged only in terms of opportunities to exploit technical change and innovation, it can be judged only good or bad with regard to the rate at which potentials are exploited. However, the potential for innovation is by its very nature a nonoperational concept. The existence of cost-reducing innovations or technology is not an adequate substitute, since a firm will not profit by scrapping its existing equipment and introducing new equipment unless the average total cost of the new technology is less than the average variable cost of the old technology. Moreover, even if an innovation would lead to short-run cost savings, a firm might hesitate to adopt it if the firm felt the innovation might lead to a long-run increase in costs because of bottlenecks in required inputs. Thus, comparisons of the rate of innovation and technical change between industries mean little, because of differences in their potentials. Consequently, in assessing the performance of the transport industries with respect to innovation and technical change, it is necessary to determine whether performance could have been better in some sense.[34]

R&D EXPENDITURES IN THE TRANSPORT INDUSTRIES. Research and development (R&D) expenditures of an industry are one indication of the resources devoted to innovation and technical change. In this connection, the expenditures of the transport industry appear to be extremely low. While industries in the United States as a whole devoted 4.2 percent of their revenues to R&D expenditures in 1960 and the growth industries devoted between 8 and 9 percent, the transport industries devoted only 0.7 percent to R&D.[35]

Wohl has estimated that in 1960 total R&D expenditures for transportation activities totaled some $700 million. Of this, $600 million was spent on highway transport, with the automotive producers spending $580 million on equipment development. Thus only $20 million was spent on planning, design, operations, and maintenance technology for the highways. Of the remaining $100 million, $70 million was spent on R&D for aircraft technology; only $30 million was spent by the rail and water industries.[36]

Wohl's estimates include expenditures made by the suppliers to the transport industries, which are in the manufacturing sector. In 1960 only $62 million was spent on R&D activities by the nonmanufacturing industries. Even if all of this money had been spent by the transportation industries, which is not likely, this would have represented less than 0.3 percent of their 1960 operating revenues. Thus the equipment suppliers

34. For a full discussion of the problems associated with assessing performance see Bain, *Industrial Organization,* pp. 460–62; and Carl Kaysen and Donald F. Turner, *Antitrust Policy: An Economic and Legal Analysis* (Harvard University Press, 1959), pp. 52–56.
35. Martin Wohl, "Transportation—Technology—The Future," in *Private and Unregulated Carriage,* pp. 3–4.
36. *Ibid.*

TABLE 4.6. Research and Development Expenditures for Railroad Transportation, 1962

(Dollar items in millions)

Type of research	Railroad operators		Railroad equipment suppliers	
	Expenditures	Percentage	Expenditures	Percentage
Basic	$0.1	0.5	$ 0.3	1.8
Applied	2.7	39.0	4.0	26.4
Development	3.3	48.5	10.2	67.4
Operations	0.8	12.0	0.7	4.4
All types	$6.9ᵃ	100.0	$15.2ᵇ	100.0

Source: "Science and Technology in the Railroad Industry," A Report to the Secretary of Commerce by the Committee on Science and Technology in the Railroad Industry of the National Academy of Sciences-National Research Council (processed, August 1963), pp. 58–61.
a. Represents 0.07 percent of revenue.
b. Represents 1.70 percent of revenue.

provide the vast majority of the R&D money devoted to transportation technology.[37]

The railroads are a good case in point. In 1960, 1961, and 1962 the railroads themselves spent respectively 0.07 percent, 0.06 percent, and 0.07 percent of their operating revenues on R&D activities. For these same years, the railroad suppliers spent respectively 1.4 percent, 1.9 percent, and 1.7 percent of their sales revenue on R&D. In absolute terms, the railroads spent a low of $5.3 million and a high of $6.9 million; the suppliers spent a low of $14.8 million, a high of $15.2 million.[38]

Table 4.6 indicates that most of the funds devoted to R&D in the railroad industry are used for development and applied research. The railroads spent relatively more for operations research than the suppliers. Nevertheless, the figure of 12 percent or approximately $800,000 on operations research is not a substantial sum, particularly in consideration of the great service disadvantage the railroads face with respect to trucks.

The relative magnitudes of R&D funds spent by the railroad carriers and

37. Richard J. Barber, "Technological Change in American Transportation: The Role of Government Action," *Virginia Law Review,* Vol. 50, No. 5 (June 1964), p. 846.

38. "Science and Technology in the Railroad Industry," A Report to the Secretary of Commerce by the Committee on Science and Technology in the Railroad Industry of the National Academy of Sciences-National Research Council (processed, August 1963), pp. 48, 49.

suppliers indicate the extent to which the carriers rely on the suppliers for research. Although this dependence reduces the R&D costs to a particular company, it also makes the carriers captives of the equipment vendors. In the railroad industry, any supplier tends to be confined to a narrow area of production, such as wheels, brakes, or undercarriages. Consequently, its research outlook tends to be narrow, and improvements tend to remain within rigidly defined engineering units. Thus for the railroads, cost reductions instead of service improvements have been the major goal. Control and guidance systems, support systems, terminal systems, and loading and unloading systems have virtually been ignored.[39]

ADOPTIONS OF INNOVATIONS IN THE RAILROAD INDUSTRY. That the railroads spend relatively little on R&D and thus on potential innovations is clear. It is not clear, however, that if they devoted more resources to R&D the rate of innovation would increase. All the available evidence suggests that the railroads have been particularly slow in adopting available innovations. For example, it took about 15 years for the diesel locomotive, 25 years for the mikado locomotive, 20 years for the four-wheel trucking locomotive, 25 years for centralized traffic control, and 30 years for retarders to be generally accepted. Although the technology of piggybacking and unit-train operations has been available for at least 30 years, these ideas are only now gaining general acceptance. In general, the time period elapsed between a 10 percent and 90 percent acceptance of an innovation in the rail industry has been 6 years longer than in the steel industry, 2 years longer than in the coal-mining industry, and 14 years longer than in the brewing industry.[40] If innovations are not going to be exploited when they occur, railroads would appear to have little incentive to devote many resources to R&D. Thus the low R&D expenditures and the apparently slow rate of innovation must be connected.

However, the slowness of the rate of innovation in itself does not mean that the performance of the transportation industry has been poor. Poor performance requires evidence that the railroads did not introduce innovations because of monopoly or regulatory constraints. Only if it can be shown that the rate of innovation would have been faster under a dif-

39. See Barber, "Technological Change in American Transportation," for a more complete discussion of specific research and development programs in the transportation industries. Also, the policy of the ICC toward rate cutting has encouraged the railroads to concentrate on cost-reducing technical change.

40. See Edwin Mansfield, "Innovation and Technical Change in the Railroad Industry," in *Transportation Economics* (Columbia University Press for the National Bureau of Economic Research), pp. 185–87.

ferent market structure can it be said that the existing structure has led to inefficient and undesirable performance. Although available evidence is not quantitatively conclusive, it strongly suggests that the rate of innovation in the railroad industry has been stifled by the regulatory process. Thus, with regard to technical change, it is the regulatory process that has performed badly rather than the railroads. As soon as innovations could be exploited profitably the railroads have seemed to exploit them. But the policies followed by the ICC have often delayed the time at which exploitation would be profitable.

Certainly, the joint private-public management that has evolved in the railroad industry has done little to encourage entrepreneurial initiative on the part of the railroads. Since legalism rather than competition has been used to protect the public interest with regard to the railroads, little premium is placed on entrepreneurial aggressiveness and competitiveness. It is interesting to note that among the top railroad management, it is not usually the engineers or scientists who are represented, but the bankers, lawyers, and realtors. As a rule, men who are attracted to these professions are legalistic and tradition oriented and lack strong innovative or entrepreneurial drive.[41]

Nevertheless, it is precisely this legalistic point of view that has enabled the ICC and the railroads to operate the joint management system in relative harmony over the past eighty years.[42] To this extent, it seems fair to blame the lack of entrepreneurial initiatives on the part of the railroads on the regulatory process.

Moreover, even when railroad management wanted to exercise entrepreneurial initiative with regard to innovations, the Commission has often blocked the way. The experience of the Southern Railway System with its Big John cars provides a good case in point.

During the latter half of the 1950s, grain shipments to the southeastern portions of the United States rose from 3.6 million tons to 10 million tons, largely due to the growth of the poultry industry there. The railroads did not share in this growing market, which was largely captured

41. For an interesting discussion of this point, see W. F. Cottrell, "Social Barriers to Technical Change," in R. S. Nelson and E. M. Johnson, eds., *Technological Change and the Future of the Railways* (Northwestern University, Transportation Center, 1961).

42. For an interesting analysis of the interaction of the ICC and the railroads see Samuel P. Huntington, "The Marasmus of the ICC: The Commission, the Railroads, and the Public Interest," *Yale Law Journal*, Vol. 61 (April 1952), pp. 467–509.

by barges (via the Tennessee River and then to point of destination by truck) or by truck (of which as much as 60 percent went by unregulated carriage).[43] Because the ICC does not generally permit major rate reductions without proof of concomitant cost reductions, the Southern Railway developed the large, lightweight, aluminum Big John cars in an effort to regain its share of this market. Each car is divided into four compartments and is easy to load and unload and to clean and maintain; its capacity of 110 tons is twice that of a traditional boxcar, while its weight is 13 tons less. Confident of the success of the cars, the Southern invested $14 million in them.

On August 10, 1961, the Southern announced that it was cutting rates up to 60 percent for minimum five-car shipments of 450 tons, with 90 tons to a car. For example, the rate between St. Louis and Birmingham was reduced from $8.70 a ton to $3.12. The economies that permitted these reductions were due to heavier loads per car, multiple-car shipments, and greater utilization, in which each Big John car was expected to travel up to 60,000 miles a year compared to the annual mileage of 16,425 miles for a typical boxcar. These rates were immediately challenged and suspended. Although the initial suspension is usually only seven months, litigation prevented the Southern from introducing these rates until April 15, 1963, when the Supreme Court ruled that the reduced rates should be introduced. This was twenty months after the initial suspension. Finally, on May 11, 1963, the Southern put the new rates into effect.

On July 1, 1963, however, the ICC ruled that the Southern must raise its rates to a 53 percent reduction, even though it was accepted that the 60 percent reduction covered 102 percent of out-of-pocket costs. The ICC seemed to be motivated by a desire to make sure that the traffic and investment of the water carriers were protected. Meanwhile, the question of the reasonableness of the rates was still under consideration by the courts. Thus the Southern was operating the cars and investing in them without knowing whether the rates on which their profitability was based would ultimately be accepted. Only in September 1965, when the Supreme Court ruled that the proposed rates by the Southern were in fact "just and reasonable," was the railroad able to use the Big John cars freely. This was some four years after their service was first introduced.

The experience of the Southern Railway with respect to the Big John

43. Barber, "Technological Change in American Transportation," p. 863.

cars is a good illustration of the attitude of the Commission toward innovation. On the one hand, the Commission refuses to grant rate reductions in the absence of evidence that these reductions are 'justified in
terms of cost. On the other hand, the Commission often appears to be
unwilling to accept the cost evidence and to permit the requested rate
reductions.[44] Thus, in considering rate reductions, the Commission not
only requires cost evidence, but then may refuse to accept it. This behavior makes sense only if the Commission's main concern is the maintenance of the existing rate structure. Otherwise, it would be difficult to
explain the obstacles placed before a railroad that wants to introduce
rate reductions. At best, the Commission's behavior will distort the investment decision and force the railroads to undertake cost-saving innovations. At worst, it may stifle the innovative initiative of the railroads,
which view the uncertainty created by the Commission's behavior as excessive in terms of the possible returns accruing from the investment.

While the case of the Big John cars is striking in terms of the obvious
obstructionism of the ICC, the case of the introduction of the unit trains
presents a somewhat subtler way in which the introduction of innovation
can be delayed by the regulatory process. In their interesting book,
MacAvoy and Sloss argue that the introduction of unit coal trains in
the East was delayed at least five years by the rate policies required by
the ICC. Briefly the argument they present is this. Unit-train operations
were known and used as early as 1919 when the government adopted
them during the period of government control in the First World War.
However, unit trains were not generally adopted by the railroads because
of the regulatory restrictions placed on rates. In particular, the ICC has
been willing to permit discriminatory rates for similar services or commodities to meet certain competitive situations under existing technology,
but has required that cost savings from innovations be applied nondiscrim-
inately to all shippers using similar services. This means that unless the
savings on the innovation, in this case the unit trains, are sufficiently
great to offset the revenue reductions on the traffic that currently moves
at higher rates, the innovation will not be adopted. Thus the permissible
rate policies to a large extent determine at what time innovations will be
adopted. Consequently, although the eastern railroads could have cut annual costs on their coal traffic by as much as $9 million if they had

44. See, for example, the new automobiles case, in Friendly, *Federal Administrative Agencies*, pp. 131–36, and the ingot molds case, Investigation and Suspension Docket 8038, *Ingot Molds from Pennsylvania to Steelton, Ky.*, 326 ICC
77 (1965).

adopted unit-train operations as early as 1958, they did not introduce these trains until 1963 because the potential revenue losses were greater than the cost savings.[45]

Prior to the introduction of the unit trains, the railroads practiced substantial price discrimination on their coal traffic. The large coastal utilities, which could utilize oil transported by tanker or pipeline, were charged rates considerably less than those charged to inland utilities with no alternative energy sources, even though the cost of transporting coal to these inland stations was less than or equal to the costs of transporting coal to the coastal stations. For example, rates from the coal fields of Pennsylvania to the port cities of Philadelphia, Baltimore, and New York were often 20 to 40 cents less per carload than rates to closer, but inland, cities. Since the elasticity of transport demand on the part of inland utilities was quite low and that of the coastal utilities was quite high,[46] price discrimination that charged high rates to the inland stations and low rates to the coastal stations was profitable for the railroads. Moreover, since the ICC permitted the railroads to reduce rates on their coastal carload traffic while maintaining their rates on their inland carload traffic, the introduction of unit-train service, which would have required reduced rates on all traffic, would have led to reductions in profits. Only in 1962, when demand conditions seemed to be such that the railroads could increase their profits by adopting unit-train operations, were they introduced.

This seems to be a clear case of the regulatory process retarding the adoption of technical change. In particular, the asymmetry with which unit-train rates and carload rates were treated by the ICC postponed the introduction of unit-train operations by at least five years. Because carload rates were permitted to be highly discriminatory while unit-train rates were required to be nondiscriminatory, in the sense that rate variations were only permitted for demonstrable cost variations, the railroads found the maintenance of carload rates and services more profitable than the introduction of unit trains. If, on the other hand, the Commission

45. Paul W. MacAvoy and James Sloss, *Regulation of Transport Innovation: The ICC and Unit Coal Trains to the East Coast* (Random House, 1967), p. 59. Savings of this magnitude in 1958 indicate that unit-train operations could have led to considerable cost savings even earlier. However, data on cost savings prior to 1958 are not available.

46. MacAvoy and Sloss estimate these elasticities to be approximately one-third for the inland stations and about four for the coastal stations. Thus 10 percent reductions in rates would increase the traffic on inland stations by 3 to 4 percent and increase traffic on coastal stations by 40 percent. *Ibid.*, pp. 66–85.

had been consistent and had either required carload rates to vary only with cost differences or permitted the unit-train rate structure to be as discriminatory as the carload rate structure, it seems clear that unit-train operations would have been introduced prior to 1963.

If the goodness or badness of performance with regard to the adoption of technology depends on the exploitation of possible economies when they are profitable, the performance of the railroads must be rated as good, for they introduced unit-train operations when their adoption was, in fact, profitable. However, the performance of the ICC must similarly be rated as bad, for the regulatory constraints imposed by it undoubtedly postponed the introduction of this particular innovation.

While the regulatory process has doubtless hindered technical change in the railroad industries, the peculiar position of railroad labor must also be considered. For the most part, railroad innovations have been labor saving. The introduction of the diesel engine has meant longer trains and consequently lower labor costs per train. The development of the automatic hump yard has meant fewer yard men. Railroad labor is currently dominated by the survivors of these labor-saving innovations, who have seen the level of railroad employment drop by some 60 percent since World War I. But it is precisely because these men are survivors that they are inflexible. The median age of engineers is 59; of firemen, 42; of conductors, 53; of brakemen, 41; moreover, 22.1 percent of all engineers are over 65 years old, while another 23.6 percent are between 60 and 65.[47]

Such an old work force clearly presents problems. Because of their age, such men are hard to place in other areas. Therefore, the engineers and firemen have vigorously opposed any efforts to automate the train operation or to rely on automatic control devices. Moreover, these men have few other alternative occupations. A comparison between the case of the boilermakers and that of firemen is instructive. The adoption of the diesel engine virtually eliminated the need for boilermakers in the railroad industry. However, the change was made relatively easily since boilermakers had a skill readily transferable to other sectors of the economy. Moreover, since they were part of an interindustry union, the union could be used to help place men in other industries. In contrast, the railroad firemen have a skill that is essentially nontransferable and are represented by a union that is solely connected with the railroads.

47. See John T. Dunlop, "Manpower in Operating Classifications on the Railroads," in *Transportation Economics*, p. 425.

Thus the combination of the age of the railroad labor force, the non-transferability of their skills, and the lack of a broad union base makes railroad labor rigid with regard to innovation and technical change. Once a railroad worker loses his job, his chances of finding another one are small. Consequently, railroad labor tends to be hostile to any technical change.

To say that technical change in the railroads is not as high as it should be is not to say that it has been nonexistent. In fact, the rate of productivity change in the railroad and other transportation industries compares favorably with the general growth of productivity throughout the economy. Between 1890 and 1925, productivity (as measured by output per man-hour) went up as rapidly in the railroad industry (2.5 percent per year) as in all transportation industries (2.6 percent per year) and more rapidly than in the economy as a whole (2.0 percent per year). Between 1925 and 1953, productivity rose very fast in the transportation industries as a whole (4.5 percent per year) and somewhat less rapidly in the railroad industry (3.0 percent per year). The railroads' rate of productivity growth was still considerably greater than that of the economy (2.4 percent per year). Between 1890 and 1953 railroad productivity rose by 2.8 percent a year, while that of the entire economy rose by 1.7 percent, and that of the transportation industries rose by 3.1 percent. Finally, it is interesting to note that railroad productivity has risen by 5.8 percent a year since 1953. Thus the technological changes in the rolling stock (three-tiered cars, Big John cars, refrigerated cars), piggybacking, electronic traffic control, and improvements in the maintenance of right-of-way, which permit 15 men to do the work that previously required 60, have improved the productivity of railroad labor tremendously.

Although capital deepening has had some impact on railroad productivity, technological change appears to have had the most impact.[48] Table 4.7 gives some interesting comparisons of productivity changes in the various transport carriers. Railroads are lagging behind airlines, inland waterways, and pipelines, in terms of increased output per employee, but they are considerably ahead of motor carriers. In no sense can the performance of productivity change in the railroads be called bad. Nor, for that matter, can the performance of the transportation industries be called bad. Given the constraints placed on them, they seem to have exploited innovations as rapidly as possible. However, their performance

48. See Mansfield, "Innovation and Technical Change in the Railroad Industry," pp. 171–74, 191–92.

can be called bad in the sense that in the absence of regulation, the rate of technological change might have been greater. This implies poor performance on the part of the ICC rather than on the part of the transportation industries.

TABLE 4.7. Percentage Changes in Output, Employment, and Productivity of United States Transport Carriers, by Mode, 1947–61

Mode of transport	Output	Employment	Productivity (output per employee)
Petroleum pipeline	+147	−25	+17.4
Inland river waterway	+118	−10	+15.6
Airline	+498	+111	+13.1
Railroad	+4	−47	+ 9.7
Motor truck	+188	+105	+ 2.9

Source: Richard J. Barber, "Technological Change in American Transportation: The Role of Government Action," *Virginia Law Review*, Vol. 50, No. 5 (1964), p. 838.

Conclusion

What then are the costs of the present regulatory policies? First is the misallocation of traffic resulting from the continuance of value-of-service pricing. Since railroads and trucks cannot compete for high-density traffic by cutting rates, an area in which railroads have the advantage, competition is concentrated on the service sphere, an area in which trucks have the advantage. Thus a considerable amount of high-density traffic goes by truck that could in fact go more cheaply by rail. Moreover, the use of uniform rate schedules prevents trucks from capturing a good deal of the low-density traffic that currently goes by rail. Because of this lack of rate competition, rates are higher than they would be in a competitive situation. The direct social losses resulting from this misallocation may run about $500 million per year. While this is a small percentage of gross national product, $500 million is not a trivial sum. Moreover, the secondary effects of this misallocation are considerable. Since the transport price structure enters all production costs, the distortions of the rate structure become embodied in all goods. Locational, consumption, and production decisions are distorted. Hence the basic imbalance between bulk and high-value rates leads to repercussions that are felt throughout the economy.

Although more difficult to quantify, the dynamic consequences may be even more important than the short-run allocational losses. The insistence on the notion of a common carrier has encouraged the regulated carriers to maintain sufficient capacity to meet the needs of all the shippers who might want to utilize them. This, coupled with the lack of effective rate competition, which would weed out the less efficient producers, has led to considerable excess capacity in the transport industries. In turn, this has tended to stifle incentives for technological change, modernization, and innovation. Moreover, the regulatory process itself tends to stifle innovation. The criterion of judgment is too often the protection of existing shippers and carriers instead of the future benefits from innovation.

In conclusion then, the costs of the present policies are considerable. Value-of-service pricing leads to misallocation of transport resources, misplaced locational decisions, and distortion of the entire structure of production and of consumption. The regulatory process itself tends to encourage excess capacity and stifle initiative. Whether these costs are too great is difficult to say. Certainly, any change in the status quo will affect certain shippers and carriers adversely. Thus, in considering the merits of the present policies, interpersonal comparisons must be made. Since those who would be adversely affected are vocal and concentrated in a few sectors and since those who would benefit from a change in the present policies are silent and dispersed, the ICC and the political process have tended to weight the losers more heavily than the gainers.

CHAPTER FIVE

The Common Carrier Today

THE IMPORTANCE OF the common carrier in the transport system of the United States has been declining throughout the postwar period. In large part this development can be attributed to the relative decline of the railroads; but regulated motor carriage has also declined relative to private and exempt carriage. The reasons for the erosion of the common carrier's share of intercity freight traffic and the forces at work that may lead to a more rational use of transport resources are discussed in this chapter.

The Declining Role of the Common Carrier

Between 1939 and 1967 the regulated carriers' share of intercity freight fell from an estimated 74 to 67 percent while their traffic grew by 194 percent and that of unregulated carriers grew by 311 percent.[1] Although part of the decline in regulated carriage is due to the reduction of its share within modes, most of it is due to the decline of regulated carriage between modes and, in particular, to the relative decline of the railroads. Within the modes of water, motor, and pipelines, the regulated carriers have grown only slightly less than the nonregulated carriers. However, the railroads have grown considerably less than any of the other modes. Since the railroads are entirely regulated and dominate the ship-

1. In assessing transport trends it is important to choose a prewar year as a starting point because of the distorting effects of war. Since railroads were extensively used during the war, trends that measure the growth of regulated traffic in the postwar period will overstate the relative decline of the railroads. For data see App. C.

ments of regulated carriage, their relative decline has caused all regulated carriage to appear to decline.

The erosion of the position of the railroads is striking. Between 1939 and 1967, the share of the railroads declined from 62.4 to 41.6 percent; the share of motor carriers rose from 9.7 to 22.1 percent; the share of pipelines rose from 10.2 to 20.5 percent; however, the share of inland waterways fell slightly from 17.7 to 15.6 percent. Although air freight grew rapidly, its share of intercity freight is still insignificant. While the intercity ton-miles of freight hauled by railroads grew by 116 percent, the freight hauled by motor carriers grew by 636 percent, by water carriers 185 percent, and by pipelines 549 percent.[2] The relative decline of the railroads is even more pronounced in the postwar period since their traffic has remained virtually constant at its wartime levels.

This decline may be due partly to an increased regional self-sufficiency and partly to a shift in consumption patterns away from commodities and toward services. Nevertheless, it is interesting to note that the ratio of operating revenues to gross national product (GNP) has generally declined much less than the ratio of ton-miles to GNP.[3] This implies that demand is shifting toward higher-valued goods. This would further imply that modes specializing in the transportation of high-value goods should fare relatively better than those specializing in bulk commodities. Table 5.1 corroborates this. The ratio of ton-miles to GNP has risen for air carriers, fallen slightly for motor carriers, and fallen substantially for railroads and water carriers. Interestingly, the ratio of ton-miles to GNP has fallen only slightly for pipelines. This probably reflects the large growth in demand for petroleum products, which are especially suited to pipelines.

Nevertheless, the shift away from railroads cannot be attributed solely to the shift away from bulk commodities, for that does not explain the growth of pipelines and water carriers. Thus, it is necessary to look at

[2] Oi and Hurter corroborate these trends. Using least squares, they estimated the following average annual rates of growth between 1939 and 1959, excluding the war years: all modes, 4.1 percent; railroads, 2.1 percent; motor carriers, 8.8 percent; pipelines, 7.7 percent, and air freight, 22.7 percent. Walter Y. Oi and Arthur P. Hurter, Jr., *Economics of Private Truck Transportation* (William C. Brown Co. for Northwestern University, Transportation Center, 1965), p. 5.

[3] See Table 5.1. Strictly speaking, these data are for all revenues rather than freight revenues alone. Since, however, passenger revenues are small in comparison to freight revenues, the trends shown in Table 5.1 are indicative of the ratio of freight revenues to GNP.

TABLE 5.1. Ratios of Operating Revenues and Ton-Miles to Gross National Product (GNP), by Mode of Transport, United States, for Selected Years, 1940–67

Year	Railroads		Motor carriers		Inland waterways		Oil pipelines		Airways	
	Ton-miles per dollar of GNP	Revenue as percentage of GNP	Ton-miles per dollar of GNP	Revenue as percentage of GNP	Ton-miles per dollar of GNP	Revenue as percentage of GNP	Ton-miles per dollar of GNP	Revenue as percentage of GNP	Ton-miles per dollar of GNP	Revenue as percentage of GNP
1940	3.80	4.47	0.62	0.90	1.18	0.11	0.59	0.23	a	0.08
1945	3.26	4.31	0.32	0.88	0.67	0.08	0.60	0.14	a	0.10
1950	2.10	3.45	0.61	1.31	0.57	0.11	0.45	0.16	0.001	0.20
1955	1.59	2.64	0.57	1.39	0.54	0.11	0.51	0.17	0.001	0.30
1960	1.15	1.94	0.57	1.43	0.44	0.08	0.45	0.15	0.002	0.42
1963	1.07	1.68	0.56	1.45	0.40	0.07	0.43	0.14	0.002	0.46
1967	0.93	1.37	0.49	1.41	0.35	0.05	0.46	0.13	0.003	0.62

Sources: Ton-miles: Appendix Table C.1; revenue, except air; 78th Annual Report of the Interstate Commerce Commission (1964), p. 34, and other issues; air revenue: U.S. Civil Aeronautics Administration, Statistical Handbook of Civil Aviation (1956), p. 79; U.S. Federal Aviation Agency, FAA Statistical Handbook of Aviation (1966), p. 183; Federal Aviation Administration worksheets. GNP: U.S. Department of Commerce, Office of Business Economics, The National Income and Product Accounts of the United States, 1929–1965, Statistical Tables (1966), Table 1, p. 2, Survey of Current Business, Vol. 48 (July 1968), p. 19.
a. Less than 0.0005.

other factors. Some of the erosion of the position of the railroads is due to the maintenance of value-of-service pricing. Although railroads have a clear cost advantage for most shipments traveling more than 200 miles, the previous chapter indicated that trucks carry most of the shipments weighing less than 40 tons. Because the railroads are not permitted to exploit their cost advantage through rate competition, competition is concentrated in the service sphere where trucks have a decided advantage. This has doubtless led to the diversion of considerable traffic from the railroads.

The Issue of Subsidy and Differential Taxation

The railroads have long asserted that part of the erosion of their position is due to government investment policies in other modes of transport. Although there is probably some validity in this assertion, it is for reasons other than those stated by the railroads. Since the period of the initial land grants, the railroads have received virtually no federal aid. Although the Transportation Act of 1958 made low-interest loans available to the railroads, the amount involved was not large.

At no time has the government made direct investments in the railroads. This behavior is in sharp contrast to its behavior with respect to the other modes. The highway system has largely been built by the federal-aid program; virtually all inland waterways are constructed by the U.S. Corps of Engineers; almost all airport construction has been financed with some federal aid. Figure 5.1 and Appendix Table C.4 summarize the total federal expenditures made through 1960 and the projected totals through 1975.

Investment in Highways

A breakdown of the expenditures by mode is interesting. By 1960 a total of $20.7 billion had been spent on the federal highway system. Of this, 37 percent was spent on the primary system, 11 percent on the urban system, 38 percent on the interstate system, and only 14 percent on the secondary system. Since the interstate expenditures are divided roughly equally between rural and urban roads, this means that approximately 55 percent of federal highway expenditures were on primary rural

FIGURE 5.1. Federal Highway Authorizations, Airport Obligations, and Waterway Appropriations; Actual 1940–60, Projected 1961–75

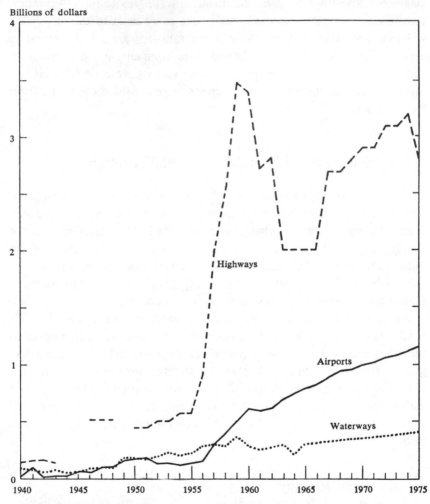

Source: Special Study Group on Transportation Policies in the United States, *National Transportation Policy*, Preliminary Draft of a Report Prepared for the Senate Committee on Interstate and Foreign Commerce, 87 Cong. 1 sess. (1961), pp. 69, 86.

roads and 30 percent were on urban highways. By 1975, of the projected total expenditures of $62 billion, 22 percent are expected to be spent on the primary system, 9 percent on the urban system, 58 percent on the interstate system, and 11 percent on the secondary roads.[4]

It is likely that the federal expenditures on the secondary system did

4. Calculated from data in the Doyle Report.

not affect the railroads adversely. Secondary roads are built in rural areas with so little traffic density that a rail line could not be supported along these routes. Thus, instead of harming the railroads these expenditures probably helped them by enabling unprofitable truck transport to be substituted for unprofitable rail transport.

To varying degrees, however, federal expenditures on the other highway systems have helped undermine the position of the railroads. The urban expenditures have been limited to "the urban extensions" of the federal-aid highway routes and to the urban segments of the interstate highway system. Since their primary goal has been to ease the flow of through traffic, these investments should have made long-haul trucking more attractive. Clearly, the federal expenditures on the federal-aid rural system and the rural interstate system have helped the intercity truckers by making possible higher average speeds and average loads. The federal highway investments have therefore tended to increase the service advantage that trucks hold over rails.

Whether the trucks "pay their full share" of the federal highway expenditures is a source of considerable controversy. As pointed out in Chapter 3, a highway is constructed for and used by automobiles and trucks jointly. Therefore the allocation of the costs between trucks and automobiles must be arbitrary because it is a joint costing problem. The usual procedure is to allocate the cost of the basic roadway suitable for passenger cars between trucks and passenger cars on the basis of their relative use. The incremental costs of building a roadway with sufficient standards to meet the needs of trucks are then allocated among different types of trucks according to their requirements and relative use.[5]

This seems to be a reasonable approach. Trucks should pay for the marginal costs incurred in making the highway meet their specifications. Moreover, since their use causes wear to the basic roadway, they should share in these costs. On the basis of this cost allocation, there is considerable evidence that the heavy diesel trucks do not pay the full costs attributable to their differential wear and relative use of the highways.[6] In

5. See letter from the Secretary of Commerce, Jan. 16, 1961, in *Final Report of the Highway Cost Allocation Study*, H. Doc. 54, 87 Cong. 1 sess. (1961). The wear caused by heavy trucks is considerable. The pavement damage caused by a 16-ton tandem-axle load is 7,450 times as great as the damage caused by a one-ton axle load, which is approximately the load of a typical automobile. See Highway Research Board, *The AASHO Road Test: Proceedings of a Conference, May 1962*, Special Report 73 (1962), p. 422.

6. Letter from the Secretary of Commerce, *Supplementary Report of the Highway Cost Allocation Study*, H. Doc. 124, 89 Cong. 1 sess. (1965).

his message to the Congress in May 1965,[7] President Johnson recommended that user taxes on these vehicles be increased by some 75 percent. Although these heavy trucks account for approximately one-third of all intercity freight travel,[8] the imposition of taxes of this magnitude would not significantly affect the allocation of traffic between rails and trucks. The user charge message estimated that revenues from these taxes would amount to approximately $200 million. Since the diesel vehicles traveled approximately 12.8 billion vehicle miles in 1964, costs per vehicle mile would be increased by 1.57 cents. For a 20-ton high-value shipment, the point at which rails become cheaper than trucks would be reduced from approximately 135 miles to 132 miles. Hence, it is difficult to attribute the relative decline of the railroads' high-value traffic to undertaxation of heavy trucks.

In addition to the federal government, the state and local governments make substantial highway investments.[9] Over the years, these have more than doubled the investment of the federal government. Although their share has been reduced by the acceleration of the interstate highway system, even now state and local governments account for approximately two-thirds of all highway expenditures.

In 1965, expenditures on the United States highway system were $14.3 billion, while expenditures on new highway construction totaled $8.4 billion. State and local governments financed 70 percent of all highway expenditures, but only one-half of new construction expenditures, with the federal government financing the remainder.[10] All states impose user charges, and available evidence indicates that most trucks pay their proper share of the construction costs.[11] Typically, trucks are subject to three types of taxes: motor vehicle registration fees, which are generally

7. Message from the President of the United States, *Proposed Recommendations Relative to Excise and Fuel Taxes,* H. Doc. 173, 89 Cong. 1 sess., May 17, 1965. Specifically, President Johnson recommended increasing the present tax on diesel fuel from 4 cents to 7 cents a gallon; increasing the weight tax on trucks from $3.00 to $5.00 per thousand pounds of gross weight in excess of 26 thousand pounds; increasing the tax on tread rubber from 5 cents to 10 cents per pound.

8. See *Supplementary Report of the Highway Cost Allocation Study,* Table 13, p. 61.

9. See Phillip H. Burch, Jr., *Highway Revenue and Expenditure Policy in the United States* (Rutgers University Press, 1962).

10. U.S. Bureau of Public Roads, *Highway Statistics, 1966,* Table F-2, p. 123, and Table FA-5, p. 177.

11. John R. Meyer and others, *The Economics of Competition in the Transportation Industries* (Harvard University Press, 1959), pp. 77–85.

assessed on a progressive basis in which heavier vehicles pay a higher rate of taxation; motor fuel taxes, in which diesel fuel is taxed at a substantially higher rate to defray the expenses of heavy diesel burning vehicles; and structure taxes, which tax vehicles on the basis of weight and distance. These taxes seem to be structured in such a way that the heavier vehicles pay the marginal construction costs associated with their use. Hence, the main source of possible subsidy is in the federal investment program. However, as pointed out above, it is unlikely that underpayment of heavy trucks has significantly affected the competitive position of the railroads.

Investment in Waterways

Perhaps the most controversial area of federal transportation investment lies in the area of inland waterways. Here the "public subsidy" is the most evident. For many years, government agencies have spent significant amounts on river and harbor developments, general navigational aids, and so on. By 1960 expenditures on navigational aids and improvements totaled about $7.1 billion,[12] and there was another $3 billion of waterway projects in various stages from planning to construction that would extend the waterway network substantially.[13]

There is considerable validity to the charge that water transport has a subsidy advantage over its competitors. This advantage arises from two sources. First, water transport receives a direct subsidy since waterways are provided free of charge. Second, since many waterway projects are approved on the basis of questionable estimates of their potential benefits they often fail to generate sufficient benefits to justify their costs. The questionable estimates arise from the practice of basing estimates of cost savings and future traffic levels on existing rail rates, even though the railroads typically reduce rates in the face of water competition. Although the Bureau of the Budget and the Corps of Engineers have

12. Of this, $5.7 billion was spent by the Corps of Engineers, $219 million by the Tennessee Valley Authority, $1.7 billion by the Coast Guard, and $158 million for charts and other aids by the Coast and Geodetic Survey. Doyle Report, p. 167.

13. Of these, the most important were the Arkansas-Verdigris project and the Trinity River project, costing approximately $1.2 and $1.0 billion, respectively. The Arkansas-Verdigris project is currently under construction and will make 450 miles of the Arkansas and Verdigris rivers navigable into the heart of Oklahoma. The Trinity River project, which has been approved by Congress, will link Dallas and Fort Worth to the Gulf of Mexico.

tried to improve the evaluation of water resource projects by basing the estimates of cost savings on rail costs rather than on rail rates, political pressures have often made the application of this evaluation procedure impossible. In fact, Section 7 of the Transportation Act of 1966 specifies that current rail rates must be used in estimating future waterway benefits.[14]

The subsidy issue is a complicated one, however. First, a subsidy to water carriers is consistent with the ICC's desire to maintain low rates on agricultural products and raw materials, which are suited to barge transport. Establishment of user charges would undoubtedly raise rates on water transport, which might well be followed by increased rail rates. This, of course, would be against the historical pattern of rates and would probably be opposed by the Commission on these grounds. Secondly, water resource and navigational developments have traditionally been based as much (if not more) on political grounds as on economic grounds. Consequently, examples of uneconomic investments are legion. The discussion in the Doyle Report (pp. 95-96) of the Arkansas River project is instructive in this connection.

No evidence was found in the documents examined to indicate that the Arkansas basin area has lacked, now lacks, or in the foreseeable future might lack, adequate transportation services in the absence of this navigational improvement. However, local sponsors of the project stated that they were paying freight rates which were, in general, the highest in the national rate structure, and expressed a belief that development of water transportation on the Arkansas River would relieve this condition. . . .

Inclusion of the navigational features in the Arkansas project will, according to latest estimates, cost the general taxpayers more than $850 million for initial construction, and some $10 million annually for maintenance and operation. One of the principal justifications given the general public for these [operations] . . . is the possible reduction of certain freight rates. This is indeed an exceedingly costly method of obtaining regional freight rate adjust-

---

14. See *Department of Transportation Act,* 80 Stat. 931 (1966), sec. 7. The language of the act is very specific: "The primary direct navigation benefits of a water resource project are defined as the product of the savings to shippers using the waterway and the estimated traffic that would use the waterway; where the savings to shippers shall be construed to mean the difference between (a) the freight rates or charges prevailing at the time of the study for the movement by the alternative means and (b) those which would be charged on the proposed waterway; and where the estimate of traffic that would use the waterway will be based on such freight rates, taking into account projections of the economic growth of the area."

ments in a regulated industry. On this navigation project alone, amortization of the capital investment with interest, coupled with annual charges for maintenance and operation, will be twice as much as the $20 million appropriated to the ICC in 1961 for nationwide regulation of the several forms of transportation under its jurisdiction.

The water carriers have consistently opposed any suggestion that they be made subject to user charges, saying that these charges would lead to substantial losses in traffic. Specifically, the waterway users contend that user charges would result in a shift of petroleum traffic to the pipelines and a shift in water-borne coal movements because steam electric plants would move from their present locations along waterways to mineside sites. Since petroleum accounts for 42 percent of inland waterway traffic and coal for 15 percent, the concern of the waterways is understandable.[15] However, their concern indicates that the social cost of waterway transport may be greater than the social costs of alternative modes for many commodities.

Even though it seems clear that water carriers are receiving a subsidy, its extent is difficult to assess. Waterway investments are typically part of large multiple-purpose investments. Therefore, any estimates of the user charges required to cover investment costs are subject to considerable error, although the figure of 0.7 mill per ton-mile estimated in connection with the social costs of water transport is probably reasonable. The imposition of a toll of this magnitude would do much to remove the advantage of water carriage over rail in a wide range of situations. Since this is spread over all users, however, it seems likely that the users of specific waterway investments would still receive a considerable subsidy.

In assessing the impact of the government's investment policies on the competitive position of the railroads, it is important to distinguish between the pricing policies and the investment program. Although the available evidence suggests that heavy diesel vehicles, which are the main source of railroad competition, are somewhat undertaxed, the full taxation of these vehicles would not diminish the range of efficient trucking operations appreciably. Since water carriers currently pay no taxes, the imposition of user charges to cover current construction and maintenance costs could place barge and rail costs nearer parity on a fairly wide range of shipments. Thus some of the erosion of the railroads' bulk

15. W. A. Connelly, "Statistics on Waterborne Commerce Compiled by the Corps of Engineers, U.S. Army," *Freight Transportation,* Highway Research Record 82 (Highway Research Board, 1965), p. 35.

traffic can probably be blamed on the government's user charge policies.[16]

Nevertheless, it is likely that the government's investment program has had a greater impact on the competitive position of the railroads than the government's user charge policies. The very existence of federal-aid highways and waterways that have been financed out of the general fund enables truck and barge operators to avoid the costs associated with the past construction or maintenance of their rights-of-way. Moreover, since trucks are viewed as the marginal user of highway facilities, their share of new maintenance and construction costs is usually relatively low.[17] Thus trucks are able to avoid the main capital expense associated with highway transport. Similarly, since waterways are often only a small part of large, multiple purpose river developments, barges are often thought to be the marginal beneficiaries and their share of the project costs allocated accordingly. Consequently, they too are able to avoid the main capital expenses associated with barge transport.

In contrast, because railroads are the sole users of their privately provided right-of-way, they must bear the full burden of the capital and maintenance costs associated with it. Moreover, because their right-of-way is privately owned, railroads are subject to property taxes that barge and truck operations can avoid. Although the railroads have long argued that these property taxes are unfair, the taxes should be viewed as a basic cost of railroading in the same way that the capital cost of the roadway should be viewed as a basic cost of railroading.[18] Because of the nature of their right-of-way, it cannot be denied that railroads incur

16. The federal government has also made substantial investments in airports and air facilities. However, the evidence suggests that commercial airlines pay their share of the cost of these investments. (See Meyer and others, *Competition in the Transportation Industries,* pp. 139–44.) Moreover, air freight is such a small percentage of total traffic that the question of the subsidization of air freight can probably be safely ignored. As air freight increases its share of the market, this issue should become more important. Because of its speed, it is likely that air freight will compete primarily with trucks and should not affect rail freight significantly.

17. The most recent cost allocation, which imposes the heaviest burden on intercity trucks, only attributes 21.1 percent of the construction costs and 10.9 percent of the maintenance costs to these trucks. See *Supplementary Report of the Highway Cost Allocation Study,* Tables 47 and 54.

18. There does seem to be some evidence that the railroad property is subject to relatively higher assessments than other forms of property. If so, it would seem desirable to reduce the railroad assessments until they are in line with other assessments. For a full discussion of railroad assessments, see the Doyle Report, p. 487. For an argument in favor of eliminating the property taxes on railroads, see *ibid.,* pp. 445–65, and Dick Netzer, *Economics of the Property Tax* (Brookings Institution, 1966), pp. 72–73.

additional costs relative to those of barge or trucking operations. However, it is important to realize that these differentials are due to the basic structure of the industry and as such are not "unfair" in any way. Consequently, any differential advantage accruing to trucks and water carriers because they use a publicly provided right-of-way should be viewed as part of their "inherent advantage" and not as an artificial differential imposed by discriminatory governmental policies.

Growth of Private and Exempt Carriage

Although the decline of the common carriers can largely be attributed to the decline of the railroads, regulated motor carriers have also shown a decline in their position relative to private and exempt carriage. Since all highway transportation should receive the same benefits from the federal highway program and be subject to the same level of user taxes, the reasons for the relative decline of the motor common carrier must be traced to sources other than the government investment policies. Here, it is probably necessary to look at the nature of the regulatory practices.

Regulation of motor carriers by the Motor Carrier Act of 1935 was based partly on a desire to protect the railroads and to maintain the existing rate structure. It was also based on a desire to limit rate wars and excess capacity in the trucking industry and to assure isolated rural communities of adequate service. By granting certificates of operation, the Commission hoped to control entry, stabilize profits, maintain adequate investment and technical change, eliminate fly-by-night operations, and ensure that isolated shippers received adequate service at "reasonable" rates. Thus the common carrier obligations were supposed to maintain proper standards of service, while the certificates of operation, which imposed restrictions on entry, commodities, routes, and rates, were supposed to give the industry sufficient profits and stability to meet those standards.

These goals have not generally been realized, however. This is partly due to the structure of motor regulation and partly to the economic characteristics of truck transport. The regulatory structure makes it desirable to circumvent the regulatory restrictions imposed on motor transportation. The economic structure of the industry makes it possible to circumvent the regulatory restrictions, since the investment required to engage in private carriage operations or to establish exempt motor transport operations is relatively small.

Regulation of Motor Carriage

By imposing rigid conditions in granting "grandfather" rights to those carriers operating when regulation was imposed in 1935, the ICC pursued a policy of limiting entry into regulated motor carriage. Instead of automatically granting certificates of operation to all motor carriers operating at that time, the Commission required every trucker to show that he had been engaging in bona-fide operations on and continuously since the applicable grandfather date and the date of decision on the application, except for interruptions beyond the carrier's control. Since most of the 90,000 grandfather applications could not be settled until 1941 or later, the Commission's rule of continuous operation led to the denial of numerous rights and consequently served as an effective means of controlling entry.[19]

In addition to limiting entry into the industry, the Commission has also attempted to limit the scope of competition by placing restrictions on the operating rights of regulated truckers. These restrictions are considerable. Every motor common carrier has restrictions on its route and on the commodities it is permitted to carry. The certificates and permits for motor carriers always designate the legal characteristics of the service authorized, that is, common or contract; the routes or territories over which such operations may be conducted; the points to or from which the carrier may render specific service; the commodities or class of commodities which may be transported; and the extent to which the authorized physical movement of trucks is tied to specific highway routes and gateways. Of these, the most significant are the commodity restrictions. A survey taken in 1942 disclosed that 62 percent of the regulated truckers had been limited to specific commodities; that 40 percent of those had been limited to one commodity or type of commodity; and that 88 percent of these had been limited to six commodities or less.[20] There is little reason to believe that these restrictions have been modified in any way.

Moreover, the ICC is very strict in interpreting the commodity classifi-

19. James C. Nelson, "The Effects of Entry Control in Surface Transport," in *Transportation Economics* (Columbia University Press for the National Bureau of Economic Research, 1965), p. 384.

20. Board of Investigation and Research, *Federal Regulatory Restrictions upon Motor and Water Carriers,* S. Doc. 78, 79 Cong. 1 sess. (1945), pp. 304–19; Nelson, "Effects of Entry Control," pp. 390–91.

cations. In various decisions, the Commission has held that "iron and steel rolling mill rolls, finished" are not included in iron and steel products; that "iron and steel and articles made thereof" do not include tractors, tractor engines, or used foundry machines; that "liquid petroleum products" do not include crude oil; that "manufactured or prepared foods" do not include "freshly killed and dressed meats."[21]

The route and territorial restrictions are not much more flexible. Regular route carriers have been granted points on or near their specified highway routes, while irregular route carriers have been given territories in which to operate. The 1942 survey indicated that the principal geographical limitations were on intermediate points and on choice of highway routes. Seventy percent of the regular route carriers possessed less than full authority to serve intermediate points; more than one-tenth had no such authority. Moreover, more than 90 percent of the irregular route carriers were limited to radial service in which their traffic had to be accepted at or delivered to one or more specified points within their territories. Most carriers had to operate through points that they could not legally serve, leap-frogging between noncontiguous points and areas. Regular route carriers were, and still are, required to follow specified highway routes, which often lead to circuitous and inefficient operations. A good example of this was the carrier operating between New York and Montreal via Reading, Pennsylvania, a detour of some 200 miles. Similarly, a carrier operating between the Pacific Northwest and Salt Lake City was permitted to haul commodities eastbound but not westbound.[22] The same survey also found that one-third of regular route intercity carriers had some return restrictions, while about one-tenth had no backhaul privileges.[23]

The ICC seems to have been unwilling to ease these restrictions or to certify new operations. In general, the Commission's rulings show a strong desire to protect the existing carriers. It is up to the applicants for new certificates to show that they will provide a service that is not already available. If the existing carriers can show that they are physically capable of performing a particular service, prospective competitors are usually denied entry, even if they can show that their service is cheaper,

21. Carl H. Fulda, *Competition in the Regulated Industries: Transportation* (Little, Brown & Co., 1961), pp. 102–03.

22. Walter A. Adams, "The Role of Competition in the Regulated Industries," American Economic Association, *Papers and Proceedings of the Seventieth Annual Meeting, 1957, American Economic Review,* Vol. 48 (May 1958), p. 529.

23. Nelson, "Effects of Entry Control," p. 391.

better, or more efficient. The ICC seems to feel that where existing carriers have expended their energy and resources in developing facilities to handle all available traffic, and where the service is adequate, they have a right to protection from new competition.[24]

There are many examples of the failure of the Commission to grant new operating rights in the face of a shipper's desire for that service. An announcement by a shipper that he plans to resort to private carriage should be strong evidence of the inadequacy of the existing service. Nevertheless, in the face of existing carrier protests, the ICC has often refused to grant application for service on just such occasions. In another case, the ICC turned down an application for new service saying that the existing service was adequate, ruling, "the chief dissatisfaction with the existing service is slowness. A further diversion of traffic by the introduction of another carrier does not seem to be the proper solution."[25]

A good example of the difficulties involved with obtaining a new certificate is the Shaffer case of 1951. At that time, W. A. Shaffer Company sought a certificate authorizing it to transport granite from points in South Dakota to points East and from points in Vermont to points in South Dakota and the Midwest. The petition was supported by virtually all of the shippers who preferred the convenience of door-to-door trucking service. Since these shippers usually had to ship in less than railroad carload lots, they had to pay premium prices and suffer slow and unpredictable service. Because of their small size, they could not absorb the costs of storage required for pooling to achieve carload shipments. Moreover, the finished monuments required more crating and handling when shipped by rail. Nevertheless, the ICC refused to grant the certificate on the grounds that while the existing rail service was slow, it was adequate. Although the courts reversed the decision in 1957, by that time Shaffer had gone out of business.[26]

The ICC is not much more flexible in granting alternate routes or through route privileges, even though the circuity and the need for numerous interchanges increase the costs of carriage considerably. Many of the decisions seem to imply that the ICC is unwilling to grant this authority since it would make the applicants too successful and cause undue competition for the other carriers.[27]

24. For a full discussion of these points, see Fulda, *Competition in the Regulated Industries.*
25. *Ibid.,* p. 85.
26. *Ibid.,* pp. 73–75.
27. *Ibid.,* pp. 96, 97.

Unregulated Carriage

In view of the restrictions placed on entry and the extension of operating rights to provide better service, it is not surprising that unregulated motor carriage has continued to be attractive to many shippers. Although regulated carriage grew relative to exempt and private carriage during the war because of various wartime restrictions, in the period between 1939 and 1965 regulated and unregulated carriage shared almost equally in the growth of highway transport. During this period, the relative share of regulated transport in motor traffic fell an insignificant amount, from 37.1 to 36.1 percent.

However, in the postwar period there has been a fairly marked decline in the share of regulated carriage. It fell from its wartime peak of 51 percent in 1943 to just below its 1939 share of 37 percent by 1965. This implies that once the wartime restrictions on unregulated motor carrier use were removed, many shippers turned away from common carrier use and returned to their previous use of private or exempt carriage.

What, then, are the causes of this return to unregulated carriage? There are two primary forms of unregulated carriage: private carriage in which a given firm utilizes its own trucks to perform its own transportation; and exempt carriage in which any firm (regulated trucker, manufacturing firm engaged in private carriage, railroads, or trucking firms specializing in exempt carriage) may carry agricultural commodities that are exempt from ICC regulation. In the first case, the ownership of the vehicle and of the commodities carried determines the exemption; in the second, the nature of the commodity. Consequently, a firm engaging in private carriage typically has the option of utilizing regulated carriage but chooses not to do so for various reasons; a firm engaging in exempt carriage is typically trying to fill an otherwise empty backhaul or is primarily engaged in the carriage of exempt agricultural commodities. Clearly, the possibility of transporting exempt agricultural commodities makes private carriage more viable since it eases the backhaul situation. Since private carriage competes directly with regulated carriage, a discussion of the forces making it more attractive for many firms than regulated carriage is desirable.[28]

PRIVATE CARRIAGE. One would expect private carriage to be profitable in two situations: if rates diverged considerably from costs of transport;

28. Most of the following discussion is based on the findings of Oi and Hurter, *Economics of Private Truck Transportation*.

or if costs of private carriage were less than those of regulated carriage. Since trucking rates are largely based on the structure of railroad rates, it seems likely that truck tariffs would not reflect costs. Unfortunately, data are lacking on the relationship of truck revenues to costs for different commodity types. To the extent that the trucking rate schedule follows the rail rate schedule, the relationship between rail revenues and costs should be fairly close to that of trucks. Thus, it would seem that the higher the ratio of rail revenues to out-of-pocket costs, the greater would be the use of private carriage.

However, a simple rank-order correlation between the ratio of rail revenues to out-of-pocket costs and the percentage of freight shipped by private carriage failed to indicate any relationship of this sort. Either truck rates do not follow rail rates sufficiently closely, or the differences between rates and costs do not vary with commodities but vary with some other factor. By means of rank correlation, it is also possible to test the proposition that private carriage offers better service. If the service associated with private carriage were superior, one would expect high-value goods to use relatively more private carriage than low-value goods. Again, rank-order correlations failed to yield any significant relationships. Thus it appears that service differentials do not vary systematically with commodity type.

Nevertheless, other evidence indicates the importance of rate and cost differentials. Oi and Hurter have analyzed the differentials between regulated trucking rates and the costs of private carriage and found that the greatest divergence between costs and rates occurs on small shipments or on small hauls.[29] Thus firms with many shipping points that require many short hauls seem to be the largest users of private carriage. Their analysis of the nature of the user of private carriage has shown that in general the incidence of private carriage grows with the size of a firm, up to the very large sizes, which rely relatively less on private carriage. This can be explained by the fact that very small firms are unable to utilize private trucks sufficiently to make them profitable, while the very largest firms are able to extract concessions from regulated carriers. Therefore, the medium-size firms with shipments in the range of 4,000 to 20,000 tons annually rely on private carriage the most heavily, with the incidence falling rather sharply on either side.

Within each firm-size class, the use of private carriage is greater for firms that ship a larger proportion of their freight less than 200 miles.

29. *Ibid.*, pp. 182–84.

When the influences of short-haul traffic and number of shipping points are rigidly controlled, however, firm size has only a minor effect on the percentage of privately carried freight. Thus the strength of firm-size effect is largely due to the concomitant variation in short-haul freight and number of shipping points. The larger firms tend to have more shipping points and a higher proportion of small hauls.

Although the large manufacturing firms may adopt private carriage, they rarely divert all of their annual freight tonnage to it. Instead they tend to use private carriage for their regular short-haul traffic and regulated carriers for their peak loads. This tends to increase the unit costs of regulated carriers since they are less able to even out their capacity utilization over the course of a year.

The savings associated with the use of private carriage can be considerable. One Boston paper company was able to cut freight costs by 45 percent by using leased equipment. Another company saved between 25 and 45 percent on freight, even though private carriage cost the firm more than 50 cents per vehicle mile.[30] Since the ICC has estimated costs per vehicle mile to be 41 cents per ton-mile in New England, a wide differential between trucking costs and rates must have existed to enable the firm to achieve such savings.

In general, the costs of common carrier transport should be less than those associated with private carriage because of differences in equipment utilization. Common carriers have full loads in both directions more often than private or exempt carriers. A Highway Research Board study estimated that 52.4 percent of common carrier loadings were in connection with full-load round trips, while only 7.9, 7.3, and 5.2 percent of those by contract, private, and exempt carriers, respectively, were in that category. While only 13.9 percent of common carrier trips had empty returns, 57, 53.8, and 50 percent of private, contract, and exempt carriers respectively, were in that category.[31] Finally, since the loads of common carriers are typically larger than those of private or exempt carriers, the ton-mile cost of the former should be lower than those of private or exempt carriage.

Nevertheless, there is considerable evidence that for short hauls of rel-

30. Kenneth Flood, "Decision Making in Private Carriage," in *Private and Unregulated Carriage* (Northwestern University, Transportation Center, 1963), p. 63.

31. Highway Research Board, *Line-Haul Trucking Costs in Relation to Vehicle Gross Weights,* Bulletin 301 (1961), p. 83, quoted in Nelson, "Effects of Entry Control," p. 410.

atively low shipment weights, both private and exempt carriage cost less than regulated carriage. Part of this is due to the restrictions imposed on regulated carriers. Empty mileage from insufficient commodity or return-haul authority, added mileage from route and gateway restrictions, and idle truck time due to commodity and class restrictions increase excess capacity and unit costs of regulated truckers considerably. Moreover, private carriage should offer better service with regard to flexibility of routes, scheduling, split delivery, speed, and damage to goods. There is also considerable evidence that many firms rely on common carrier service to accommodate peak or residual demands while using private carriage for their normal operations. Since uncertainty of demand will tend to increase capacity and costs, the role of supplier of residual transport demand should increase the costs of regulated carriers relative to private carriage. Thus the cost advantage accruing to regulated carriage because of equipment utilization may be more than offset by service advantages associated with private carriage.[32] This seems to be particularly true for short hauls and small shipment sizes. Consequently, both cost and rate differentials seem to have encouraged the use of private carriage among firms whose shipping is concentrated in high-value, short-haul, low-weight shipments.

EXEMPT CARRIAGE. The evidence relating to exempt carriers is also interesting in connection with the erosion of the position of the motor common carriers. Several U.S. Department of Agriculture (USDA) studies have indicated that the costs of exempt carriers are 10 to 30 percent less than those of regulated carriers, the differential primarily depending on the load factor. The ICC has estimated that in 1960 the costs per vehicle mile in the Middle Atlantic region were 39.4 cents. Since the average load was 10.1 tons a round trip, the cost per ton-mile was 39.0 mills. Although the average capacity of exempt trucks engaged in intercity service is approximately 15 tons, their load factor is usually only 60 percent. For a regulated carrier, the cost of this load per ton-mile is 43.8 mills. However, the USDA has estimated that the ton-mile cost of exempt carriers is 31.7 mills. This implies a vehicle-mile cost of 28.5 cents, some 30 percent less than the common carrier costs. Indicative of these cost differentials was the dramatic reduction in the rates on frozen poultry and frozen fruit and vegetables when these commodities became exempt.

32. In addition, between 1944 and 1958, a tax of 3 percent was imposed on the amount paid for transport services. Since private carriage could avoid this tax, it enjoyed an advantage over other forms of motor transport in this respect.

Within the first year of the exemption, rates on frozen poultry fell between 30 and 35 percent; rates on frozen fruit and vegetables fell between 11 and 29 percent. Significantly, when the exemption was removed
from these commodities in 1958, their rates tended to rise due to the imposition of special service costs.[33]

There are several reasons for these differentials. One is the payment of
drivers on a commission or share of revenue basis instead of a time or
mileage basis. Since exempt carrier operations are usually small, there is
a minimal need for terminals, garages, and office buildings. Moreover,
exempt truckers are able to reduce their costs for administrative and
sales overhead by relying on brokers. This enables them to concentrate
on full-load operations and to eliminate the need to file tariffs. Also, the
exempt truckers are able to avoid the costs of obtaining operating authority. These range from $45,852 for the larger operations to $12,157 for
the smaller ones.[34] Finally, the exempt carriers do not have to maintain
the regular service that leads to considerable excess capacity. Thus even
though the load factor works to the advantage of the common carriers,
the other factors associated with their operations seem to counteract this
load advantage.

Interestingly enough, a USDA survey of poultry processors indicates
that the exempt carriers have a service advantage over the regulated carriers. Although some shippers felt that regulated carriers were more financially responsible and had better insurance coverage, four times as many
poultry processors felt that the service of exempt carriage was better.
They cited the unwillingness of regulated truckers to service off-line
points or to accept less than truckload lots.[35] To a considerable extent,
the advantages cited by the poultry processors were the advantages of
dealing with a small firm. The flexibility associated with willingness to
serve off-line points and to allow multiple stop-offs per load is more
likely to be found in a small, aggressive firm than in a large, well-estab-
lished firm. Thus, the exempt truckers are probably more sensitive to the
needs of the small agricultural shippers than are the large regulated
truckers. In this connection, it is interesting to note the lack of demand
for any form of intrastate transport regulation. Presumably, small ship-

33. See C. Peter Schumaier, "Characteristics of Agriculturally Exempt Motor
Carriers," in *Private and Unregulated Carriage,* pp. 77–95.
34. Nelson, "Effects of Entry Control," p. 413.
35. Clem C. Linnenberg, Jr., "The Agricultural Exemptions in Inter-State
Trucking: Mend Them or End Them?" *Law and Contemporary Problems,* Vol.
25 (Winter 1960), p. 168.

pers in remote rural areas requiring small-lot, short-haul services should be the most in need of the stability and dependability of service that regulation is supposed to provide. The lack of concerted shipper pressures for regulation indicates that regulation generally need not be imposed to achieve these ends. In fact, the evidence suggests that the regulation of trucking may actually hinder their achievement.

In conclusion, then, it seems clear that regulation of the trucking industry has not achieved all of the desired goals. Although regulation may have led to greater stability and profitability of the common carriers, it has not led to the provision of adequate service in many cases. The route and commodity restrictions and the divergence between costs and rates make it profitable for firms to engage in private carriage. And exempt carriage seems to suit the needs of the small-lot shipper more than regulated carriage. The existing regulatory structure makes it desirable to circumvent trucking regulations, and the capital requirements are sufficiently small to make it possible to circumvent them. Thus unless the current regulatory policies are changed, a further erosion of the position of the motor common carrier is likely.

Technological Developments and Innovations

In the past ten to fifteen years, significant developments have taken place that could have a profound effect on the organization and the rate structure of the transportation industry. The growth of certain piggybacking plans in conjunction with the growth of forwarders and shipper associations has tended to undermine the value-of-service rate structure and increase the use of the railroads in essentially a line-haul or wholesaling capacity. The growth of water, pipeline, and recently, extra-high-voltage transport (EHV) transmission has caused the railroads to cut rates on a large portion of their bulk traffic. This has, in turn, stimulated the development and acceptance of cost-saving innovations such as the unit trains or Big John cars. Thus strong competitive forces seem to be at work leading to a more rational use of resources within the transport modes.

Piggybacking

In terms of its effect on the rate structure, piggybacking may well be the most important innovation. In the last ten years, the number of piggyback carloadings has increased by some 500 percent while the annual rate of growth has been in the neighborhood of 15 percent. During this period, piggybacking has grown from 0.5 percent to 3.5 percent of all carloadings.[36]

As pointed out in Chapter 3, the major innovation in piggybacking lies in the division of labor between train and truck. The train provides the line-haul service, while the truck provides the pickup and delivery service. Thus piggybacking is able to exploit the area in which each mode is the most efficient.

Although this division of labor is common to all piggybacking operations, the different plans established by the railroads divide the market into its most profitable areas.

Under Plan I, the railroad deals directly with the motor common carrier which has negotiated with the shipper. Thus the railroad supplies the flatcar and the line-haul service, while the motor carrier negotiates with the shipper, picks up and delivers the shipment, and charges the shipper a motor-carrier rate. The rail rate is usually based on the motor-carrier rate and thus maintains a strong value-of-service element. Despite some animosity on the part of railroad management, which feels that Plan I places trucks in a better competitive position, and the animosity on the part of trucking management, which fears dependence on the railroads, Plan I seems to be reasonably popular.[37] In general, railroads do not offer Plan I service when they feel they can compete with their regular service or other piggybacking plans. However, where the traffic seems to be highly tied to motor carriers or where the railroads find that Plan I service will even out their traffic patterns, they will solicit traffic under that plan. The truckers who use Plan I are usually engaged in long-haul operations and are thus able to capture some of the economies of rail operations on this type of traffic.

Plan V is similar to Plan I in that the railroad deals with a motor common carrier. However, it is truly coordinated service in which a joint rail-motor rate is filed. Under this plan, the railroad may transport a motor carrier's trailer from A to B. Upon delivery to B, the motor carrier may transport the trailer to a more distant point C outside of the railroad's terminal area. This plan is particularly attractive to small truckers

36. See Merrill J. Roberts and Associates, *Intermodal Freight Transportation Coordination: Problems and Potential* (University of Pittsburgh, Graduate School of Business, 1966), p. 62.

37. Eighty percent of the railroads offering piggyback service offer Plan I. *Ibid.*, p. 168.

who are thus able to extend their market area. It is also attractive to railroads because it permits shipments beyond their terminal area. Thus by coordinating their movements, rail and trucking firms assume something of the nature of a transportation company. If extended, this plan should permit the railroads to discontinue some of their inefficient short-haul or low-density service and substitute trucking service for it. However, this step probably requires more trust and cooperation than currently exists between most trucking and rail firms.

Plan II is similar to Plan V in that it permits the railroads to assume some of the characteristics of a transportation company. Under this plan, the railroad deals directly with the shipper, provides the pickup and delivery service in railroad-owned trucks and trailers, and provides the line-haul service between the origin and destination. Because the railroad controls the entire operation, this plan seems to be the most popular with railroad management. It is inferior to Plan V in that the railroad is constricted to its own terminal area. Nevertheless, the success of the New York Central's Flexi-van service indicates that railroads can regain considerable truck traffic through a combination of fast service and low rates.

Plans III and IV are the only plans that provide a flat rate for a ramp-to-ramp service and are thus the most revolutionary in terms of rate making.[38] These plans were instituted to compete with private motor transport and to attract the forwarder traffic. Under Plan III, the railroad furnishes the flatcars while the shipper furnishes the trailers. Under Plan IV, the railroad supplies only the motive power while the shipper provides both the trailer and the flatcar. Because of problems of equipment utilization, this plan seems to be the least used. However, under both plans, the railroads have been known to lease the equipment to shippers if it were available. This has enabled the railroads to use idle equipment and to extend the use of these plans. Although railroad terminal services are not required in either plan, the railroad usually receives the trailer or car at the railhead, transports it, and grounds it.

Since Plan III offers service identical to Plans I and V, its main novelty lies in its rate structure. By citing a flat ramp-to-ramp rate, the railroads have effectively eliminated the value-of-service element in the rate

38. Strictly speaking, this flat rate applies only if no more than 60 percent of the shipment is composed of one commodity. If one commodity comprises more than 60 percent of the shipment, the commodity rate must be applied. This has limited some of the applications of Plans III and IV.

structure and made the supply unit and the demand unit identical. This represents a potential rationalization of the rate structure. Its significance should not be underestimated.

A recent ICC recommendation that Plans III and IV be offered to all shippers or carriers should increase the use of these plans.[39] Although the railroads bitterly opposed this recommendation for fear of its impact on other plans,[40] the Supreme Court ruled in favor of the ICC in early June 1967. Thus the extension of Plan III to all carriers is permitted.

Even in the absence of the Supreme Court ruling, the growth of forwarders and shipper associations in conjunction with Plans III and IV should do much to undermine the value-of-service rate structure.[41] Although forwarders are regulated common carriers, they typically do not own transport equipment (except to service their own terminal area), but consolidate small shipments into truckload or carload lots to be sent by direct common carriers. By taking advantage of the spread between small-lot and carload or truckload rates, the forwarders are able to make a profit, while enabling the carriers and the shippers to obtain the economies of full-lot shipments. Shippers' associations perform the same function, but, as cooperative arrangements between small shippers, they are unregulated and do not attempt to make a profit. However, they are quantitatively not very important at the moment.

Prior to the introduction of Plan III or IV, forwarders were limited to consolidating small shipments into truckload or carload lots and shipping them at the truckload or carload rate.[42] Under Plan III or IV, however, forwarders can consolidate two truckloads and send them by piggyback on a flat carload rate. So long as the flat ramp-to-ramp piggybacking rate

39. Interstate Commerce Commission investigating proceeding instituted June 29, 1962, Ex Parte 230, *Substituted Service—Charges and Practices of For Hire Carriers and Freight Forwarders,* and report, *Substituted Service-Piggyback,* 322 ICC 301 (1964).

40. Plan III rates are considerably less than those under Plan II. Since the costs are also considerably less, it is not clear what impact traffic diversion would have on the railroads' profitability. Since Plans I and V follow the value-of-service rate structure quite closely, Plan III rates should be considerably lower. However, the evidence is quite muddled on this point. See Roberts and Associates, *Intermodal Freight Transportation Coordination,* pp. 186–89.

41. For an excellent discussion of the potential role of forwarders, see Jeffrey S. Wood, "Intermodal Transportation and the Freight Forwarder," *Yale Law Journal,* Vol. 76 (June 1967), pp. 1360–96.

42. In 1964, the average size of the forwarder's shipment was 464 pounds. *Ibid.,* p. 1362.

is less than the comparable truckload or carload rates, forwarders should choose to send shipments by Plan III. Since the carload and truckload rates are based on the value-of-service rate structure while the Plan III rates are not, one would expect forwarders to choose Plan III in many instances. The growth of Plan III indicates that possibilities of this type do exist. Clearly, a significant diversion of truckload or carload traffic to Plan III or IV could undermine the rate structure on high-value commodities.

The recent Supreme Court decision extending the use of Plans III and IV to all carriers should do much to hasten this trend. Although the existing constraints on the use of Plan III should limit its use somewhat,[43] the substitution of Plans III and IV for ordinary truckload or carload service should increase. Sufficient carrier pressures could well end the commodity mixture and route restrictions. In this case, the maintenance of the high-value rate structure would be extremely difficult. Any divergence between the high commodity rate and the flatcar rate would encourage forwarders, motor common carriers, or shippers to use the flatcar rate. Hence the commodity carload or truckload rate would effectively become noncompetitive.

Moreover, piggybacking should enable the railroads to specialize in high-density traffic. The existing blanket rate structure and the long-haul short-haul clause of Section 4 of the Interstate Commerce Act require small, isolated communities to be treated with rate parity, even though the costs of serving these communities may be considerably higher than those of serving major centers. By substituting piggyback for ordinary rail service on their high-density lines and by failing to build piggyback terminals in communities that generate low-traffic densities, the railroads could achieve effective rate differentiation. Because of high levels of utilization, piggyback costs should be quite low on high-density lines. Because ordinary rail service would become concentrated on low-density lines, costs of ordinary rail operations should increase. If these costs become sufficiently high, the substitution of trucking for uneconomical rail services could take place.

Thus the wide acceptance of all commodity piggybacking rates under

43. These are the 60 percent rule described above and the ICC ruling that motor common carriers cannot use piggybacking service if the rail mileage is less than 85 percent of the truck mileage. Although relief may be obtained from this restriction in appropriate cases, the need to petition the ICC imposes additional costs in using piggyback service.

Plans III and IV should lead to a major change in the relationships between rail and truck operations. Under these plans, the railroad primarily performs a wholesaling function in which it provides motive power for flatcar miles, while the motor common carrier, forwarder, or shipper performs the retail function of preparing and soliciting the shipment, picking it up and delivering it. The diversion of ordinary boxcar shipments to piggyback and the substitution of trucking for uneconomical rail service should enable the railroads to minimize their switching and terminal operations, which would then be performed by various transportation retailers. By encouraging trucks to concentrate on distribution activities and railroads to concentrate on line-haul activities, Plans III and IV piggybacking could lead to a division of labor between rail and truck that would represent an efficient allocation of transport resources.

Multiple-Car Shipments

While piggybacking is exerting a profound influence on the shipment and rate structure of high-value goods, other developments are forcing a change in the shipment of bulk commodities. The increased size and competitiveness of barge flotillas, the increased use of pipelines, and the development of EHV transmission as energy sources have put pressure on the railroads' bulk traffic. The response of the railroads to these competitive forces has been the development of the unit train, the Big John cars, and various other forms of multiple car shipments in conjunction with volume rates. The savings from these innovations are enormous and arise from high utilization rates and reduced terminal and switching costs. However, it is in terms of rate making that their impact may be the greatest, for they tend to make the demand unit and the supply unit identical. Hence they do away with arbitrary cost allocations and permit more rational costing and pricing procedures.

The implication of these developments in bulk commodity shipments is simply this: Competition from barge, pipeline, and EHV transmission is forcing the railroads to cut rates on many commodities for which the Commission has traditionally favored low rates. Moreover, innovations in the rail industry have enabled these low rates to be profitable for some railroads. Thus competition may be able to keep these rates low without intervention on the part of the ICC. Moreover, if the railroads can carry these commodities profitably, there is no need for the Commission to maintain high rates on manufactured commodities. Thus the developments in piggybacking in conjunction with the developments in bulk traffic seem to make the elimination of value-of-service pricing both possible and economic. The long-run forces of innovation seem to indicate a railroad rate structure that more closely reflects relative costs.

The picture outlined here is, of course, an oversimplification, which will be expanded in the following chapters. However, it suggests that there are strong economic forces at work that will act to change the existing rate structure and the maintenance of value-of-service pricing. Whether they are desirable is the subject of the remainder of this study. Several alternative policies and their probable impact on the transport industries and on the economy will be analyzed. Only after this analysis will it be possible to determine the transport policy that will lead to the maximization of social welfare.

CHAPTER SIX

Alternatives to Present Policies

AS PREVIOUS CHAPTERS have demonstrated, the basic tenet of current regulatory policies has been the maintenance of rate differentials between low-value bulk commodities and high-value manufactured commodities through value-of-service pricing. This policy made sense in the early days of regulation. The maintenance of low rates on bulk commodities effectively acted as a subsidy to the western farming and mining interests and thus encouraged the development of the West. Similarly, the high rates on manufactured goods effectively taxed the consumers of these goods. Because the demand for manufactured goods was inelastic and because railroads had a virtual transportation monopoly at that time, relatively little distortion occurred in consumption or transportation patterns as a result of these income transfers through the rate structure.

Maintenance of the incomes of agricultural and raw materials producers has been an important aspect of American political life. Farm subsidies and stockpiling procedures are two of the most obvious manifestations of this fact; but continued insistence on the maintenance of value-of-service pricing makes sense only when viewed in this light. The Interstate Commerce Commission (ICC) has repeatedly stressed the need to consider the depressed state of agriculture[1] and has consistently tried to extend the scope of regulation. It apparently feels that the viability of the system hinges on the regulation of the entire industry and on its acceptance of both value-of-service pricing and the dichotomy between bulk and high-value rates. Specifically, if carriers of high-value goods are unregulated, they can cut rates and take traffic away from the railroads. This, however, would make the maintenance of the existing rate differen-

1. For an elaboration of ICC policy, see Chap. 2.

tials impossible. If high-value rates fell, artificially maintained bulk rates would have to rise. Similarly, if water competition forced an excessive decline in rail rates, the losses would have to be made up by increased high-value rates. This could occur, however, only if competing carriers of high-value goods were regulated and could not undercut the railroads.

Thus the maintenance of historical rate differentials relies on an extremely delicate balance. Bulk rates should be kept low, but not so low that they undermine the financial stability of the industry through losses that cannot be covered by the transportation of high-value goods. High-value rates should be kept sufficiently high to enable the railroads to cover their overhead, but not so high as to divert this traffic to alternative carriers.

Faced with strong competition from the water carriers on one side and the motor carriers on the other, the system has been seriously threatened. In the past, the Commission has met such a threat by extending regulation to competing carriers. This was an important factor in the decision to regulate the motor carriers in 1935, and it was probably the prime factor in the decision to regulate the water carriers in 1940.

At the present time, the viability of the regulatory system again appears to be under attack. During the postwar period, barge operations have become increasingly competitive. Technical innovations have resulted in both larger and speedier flotillas, causing barge costs to fall steadily over this period. The response of the competing railroads has been to cut rates and to introduce new cost-saving equipment whenever possible. Nevertheless, most carriers facing severe water competition have fared badly, forcing the burden on high-value traffic to become still heavier.[2] However, as service competition has increased from the regulated truckers and private and exempt carriage, the possibility of maintaining high rates on manufactured goods has been reduced.

Confronted with these developments and the erosion of the position of the common carrier, the ICC has recommended that regulation be extended to the nonregulated carriers. It has recommended the limitation of the agricultural exemptions to the initial farm-to-market movement[3] and the removal of the bulk exemption.

2. This is shown in the increasing ratios of revenues to out-of-pocket costs during the postwar period. For a full discussion of this, see John R. Meyer and others, *The Economics of Competition in the Transportation Industries* (Harvard University Press, 1959), p. 180.

3. Although the ICC has made specific recommendations to end the agricultural exemption in the past, it has abandoned this approach for a more indirect means of limiting the exemption. The Commission's most recent proposal

Even if the exemption were removed from agricultural commodities, railroads and regulated truckers would still encounter competition from private carriage and from air freight. Nevertheless, since the agricultural exemption has cased the backhaul problem of many private trucking operations, its removal could curtail the growth of private trucking and ease competition from this source.

The growth of air freight, which is particularly suited to high-value shipments for which speed is a premium, is another matter. Still in its developmental stage, air freight does not at the moment pose a threat to either the rail or motor common carriers. But its rate of growth suggests an already substantial and rapidly expanding market for this means of transport, a trend which should be accelerated by the development of the super jets.[4] Thus in the next decade, air freight may erode the position of the trucking industry much as the trucking industry made incursions in the rails' markets. Whether the acceptance of the Commission's proposals would enable the value-of-service pricing system to be maintained is, therefore, problematical.

Even if the system could be made to work, however, the desirability of its maintenance must be questioned. Chapter 4 dealt with the inefficiencies created by present policies. Most high-value traffic could go by rail more cheaply than by truck, but is prevented from doing so by the lack of effective rate competition. Excess capacity prevails throughout the transportation industry and the regulatory process seems to have retarded technological change and to have diluted the impact of whatever changes have occurred.

Perhaps it is in this last matter that the potential costs of the Commission's recommendations are greatest. Present competitive forces have caused two dramatic developments in the railroads: the growth of multiple car shipments and the growth of Plans III and IV piggybacking. Multiple car shipments and the accompanying developments in car design have led to a substantial reduction in rail costs. Since these innovations have largely been in response to water competition, it is

is the limitation of the exemption to vehicles with no more than three axles. The rationale of this limitation lies in a belief that the original farm-to-market movement uses small vehicles, while subsequent movements use large ones. See testimony of Rupert L. Murphy, *Transportation Acts Amendments, 1962*, Hearings before the House Committee on Interstate and Foreign Commerce, 87 Cong. 2 sess. (1962), p. 123.

4. The Boeing 747, the Douglas DC-8, and the Lockheed C-5A. Boeing is designing specific cargo planes for automated "straight-in" nose loading and unloading, which can carry over 100 tons of freight in highway-size containers.

questionable whether the rate of technological change would continue at its present pace if the bulk commodity exemption were removed. The effect of the removal of the agricultural exemption on the development of Plans III and IV piggybacking is more difficult to assess. Its direct effect would probably not be great. Nevertheless, insofar as the removal of this exemption would reaffirm the inviolate nature of value-of-service pricing, it is not unlikely that attempts would be made to limit the use of these plans.[5] Thus the acceptance of the Commission's proposals would tend to inhibit the two most important innovations currently taking place in the transportation industries.

Two problems, therefore, are involved in the Commission's recommendations on agricultural and bulk commodities. First, such action may not work; and second, it implies continued traffic misallocation and excess capacity, and a probable stifling of innovation in the railroad and other transport industries. The benefits to be derived are the maintenance of the status quo, and thus relatively little disruption and few losses to the producers, shippers, and consumers who have based their locational, production, and consumption decisions on the existing policies. Whether these benefits are worth the costs is the major question facing freight transportation policy today.

To answer this question, the implications of alternative policies will be analyzed in some detail with regard to their impact on existing production, consumption, and shipping relationships from the point of view of both economic efficiency and economic equity. The specific alternatives that will be considered are cost-based rates under regulation, mergers, the elimination of rate regulation, removal of all specific regulation, the formation of multimodal transportation companies, and agreed charges.

Cost-based Rates

The term "cost-based rates" means different things to different people. To the economist, it implies a traffic allocation based on relative costs

5. The 60 percent rule and the mileage limitation are clear examples of efforts to limit the extensions of these plans. See Interstate Commerce Commission investigating proceeding instituted June 29, 1962, Ex Parte 230, *Substituted Service— Charges and Practices of For-Hire Carriers and Freight Forwarders,* and report, *Substituted Service-Piggyback,* 322 ICC 301 (1964).

and an end to value-of-service pricing. To the ICC, it appears to mean the acceptance of cost evidence in cases involving minimum rates. Since the implications of this policy differ with its interpretation, it is desirable to analyze each of them separately.

The Economist's View

To an economist, cost-based rates imply that relative prices or rates have some direct relationship to relative costs. Practically, this would mean the end of value-of-service pricing or any other form of price discrimination. Rates on high-value manufactured goods would tend to fall, rates on low-value bulk commodities would tend to rise since rates would bear the same relation to costs for all shipments. However, the actual implementation of cost-based rates raises a multitude of problems that bring their feasibility and desirability into question.

Consider, specifically, a proposal to allocate traffic with regard to relative costs.[6] The immediate problems to emerge are the proper definition of costs and their measurement.

In defining costs for policy purposes, the proper costs on which to base rates and the proper horizon of these costs must be determined. There seems to be reasonable agreement on the second point: long-run costs are the relevant costs since they encompass all adjustments in plant and equipment. However, it is not clear whether the appropriate long-run costs are marginal or average costs. Traditional welfare theory says that marginal cost is the relevant cost since it reflects society's valuation of the additional resources required to increase output at the margin. Traditional welfare theory also says that if price does not equal marginal cost in all sectors, it should not equal marginal cost in any one sector. Moreover, setting all prices directly proportional to marginal costs will generally lead to resource misallocation. If the existing divergences between price and marginal cost are known in every sector and can be assumed

6. This was essentially the proposal of the Miller-Wadsworth Amendment, which stated: "The Commission shall permit each type of carrier or carriers to reduce rates so long as rates maintain a compensatory return to the carrier or carriers after taking into consideration overhead and all the elements entering into the cost to the carrier or carriers for the service rendered." (*Congressional Record,* Vol. 84, 76 Cong. 1 sess. [1939], p. 6074; quoted in Robert A. Nelson and William R. Greiner, "The Relevance of the Common Carrier under Modern Economic Conditions," in *Transportation Economics* (Columbia University Press for the National Bureau of Economic Research [1965], p. 365).

constant, the formal relationships between price and marginal cost required for efficient resource allocation can be stated. But these formal relationships have no operational content since the necessary production and consumption relationships are not known. Thus for policy purposes, there is no way to determine the appropriate relationship between prices and marginal costs in any one sector of the economy.[7]

Nevertheless, it seems reasonably clear that rail rates should not be set equal to marginal costs. Since prices are generally greater than marginal costs throughout the economy, setting rates equal to marginal costs in the rail industry would lead to an overutilization of rail facilities and a misallocation of resources in the transport industry. Moreover, since marginal costs always lie below average costs if average costs are falling, setting rates equal to long-run marginal costs would impose permanent losses on all railroads of less than optimal size that operate on the falling portion of the industry's long-run average-cost curve. In the absence of subsidies, these railroads would be forced out of business. The removal of these relatively small railroad companies would probably not represent the proper adjustment in railroad capacity since these firms seem to be using their capacity fairly efficiently.

Although rail rates should ideally bear some relationship to long-run marginal costs, it is impossible to determine empirically what this relationship should be. Thus as an operational matter, if rail rates are to be based on costs, they should probably be based on long-run average costs, or, in the parlance of the transportation industry, fully distributed costs. Since average-cost pricing is generally followed in the United States, relatively few additional distortions should result if railroads also base their rates on average costs. Moreover, since long-run costs reflect the minimum resources required to produce a given level of output, rates based on long-run average costs reflect an efficient utilization of capacity.

On the other hand, if rates were based on long-run average costs, several problems would immediately arise. Because of the large fixed and common elements in rail costs, railroads would face formidable difficulties in estimating the costs of specific services. Cost functions are generalized statements about the relationships between costs and output. They mean relatively little for specific point-to-point movements for which the railroad must charge a specific rate. Suppose for example, the railroad wants to establish a rate for shipping a given commodity between A and

7. For a full discussion of the difficulties associated with marginal-cost pricing when prices diverge from marginal cost in some sectors, see Chap. 4, above.

B over the course of several years in which some adjustment in capacity is permitted. Immediately, the railroad is faced with the problem of allocating its joint and common costs, unless it is totally specialized in the shipment of that commodity between the markets under consideration. This problem goes all the way from allocating the basic management and roadway costs to allocating the specific train costs among the various services and commodities. While statistical cost accounting can give considerable insight into the general behavior of rail-cost functions, it is of little use in determining the appropriate costs at the level of disaggregation under discussion here. Various means of prorating the common or joint costs can be used, but all of them have an arbitrary element and hence are dangerous to use in prescribing rates.[8]

Even if the appropriate costs could be identified and estimated for given rail movements, the interdependence of rates, costs, and output makes it virtually impossible to determine the appropriate rate for the railroad to charge. Existing rail output and costs are based on a demand for rail services that is in turn based on the existing value-of-service pricing structure. Since long-run average rail costs are not likely to be constant, variations in output levels will lead to variations in long-run average costs. Consequently, if rates were set at levels that reflected long-run average costs at existing levels of output, the demand for rail services would very likely react to changes in the rate structure, leading to new levels of output and new long-run average costs. Rates based on the costs associated with the existing levels of output would no longer be appropriate, and a new rate structure would have to be adopted. Only by knowing the cost curves and demand schedules could the equilibrium rates based on long-run average costs be obtained. This information is unavailable. Nevertheless, a rate policy that considered observable costs and ignored the interactions of rates, costs, and output would surely lead to the establishment of improper rates.

Finally, the adoption of rates based on long-run average costs is likely to create problems in capacity adjustment. Since long-run average costs

8. The most usual means of prorating is on the basis of ton-miles. A little reflection will indicate the possible biases involved with this weighting system. For example, commodity shipments requiring specialized equipment that could be used only in one direction would have higher costs than equal shipments that used nonspecialized equipment. Similarly, highly seasonal shipments will typically have higher costs than shipments that are spread throughout the year. In both cases, the use of ton-miles to prorate the common costs will underestimate the costs of the seasonal or specialized shipments.

are based on optimal capacity levels, they must necessarily be considerably less than current average costs if the firm has excess capacity. In view of the large amount of excess capacity prevailing in the railroad industry, rates based on long-run average costs would initially lead to substantial losses. If railroad capacity were easily adjustable, these losses would present no real problems. The railroads would simply divest themselves of sufficient capacity until they found they could earn a normal return at the prescribed rates.

Railroad capacity is notoriously long-lived, however, and the Commission has not shown itself to be particularly sympathetic to abandonments of freight service. Without rapid capacity adjustments, the losses from rates based on long-run average costs would become intolerable. Faced with substantial long-term losses, the railroads would doubtless petition the ICC for rate increases. Thus both the capital structure and the regulatory structure bring the feasibility of this particular rate structure into question. Without the Commission's encouragement of large-scale abandonment, it is unlikely that cost-based rates could be made to work.

In view of the difficulties associated with cost-based rates, the current pricing policies may lead to a more efficient utilization of resources than any prescribed rate structure based on costs. Under present rate policies, the railroads are permitted to practice limited price discrimination in which they charge less than long-run average cost on some commodities, while making up their losses by charging more than average cost for other commodities. So long as the demand is sufficient to cover short-run average variable costs, it will pay the railroad to carry the traffic and thus earn some return on its overhead. Since, however, short-term variable costs will be less than long-run average costs if capacity is not fully used, more capacity will be used under price discrimination as it is currently practiced than under a policy of rates based on long-run average cost. Nevertheless, the railroad will still attempt to scrap its equipment as soon as possible. Thus under the current policies that permit price discrimination, optimal adjustments in capacity should eventually take place without the sudden losses implied by cost-based rates. Although this latter policy would achieve capacity adjustment more quickly, it might well make the capacity adjustment more rapid than is socially desirable.

Against the benefits of greater capacity utilization, however, the "deadweight" losses associated with any form of discriminatory pricing should be considered. Discriminatory pricing is inefficient, and the value-of-service form of price discrimination that is currently followed is particularly inefficient. Consequently, it is difficult to judge whether the social losses of adopting a rate structure based on costs would be greater or less than those caused by the current regulatory policies. Nevertheless, if the railroads were free to pursue a more rational form of price discrimination and abandon capacity accordingly, resources probably would be allocated more efficiently than they would be under a policy of cost-based rates.

Basically, the difficulties associated with any cost-based rates arise because they are cost-based and ignore the element of demand. Thus any effort to implement them would face formidable problems. Since the existing output and cost structures depend so heavily on the existing rate structures, any prescriptive rate structure that failed to recognize this interdependence would fail to reflect the true long-run costs. Rates based on faulty estimates might well lead to more social costs than the existing rate structure. In the face of imperfect knowledge, flexibility in rate making is desirable. Since profits must depend on the nature of costs and demands, it is desirable to permit a rate structure that takes both of these factors into account. For the railroads, which face different demand curves with different elasticities and which have wide divergences between their total and variable costs, this means price discrimination. Commodities with inelastic demands will pay higher rates than those with more elastic demands for comparable services.

The Commission's View

When the ICC refers to cost-based rates, it seems to mean that in minimum rate cases the legality of the proposed rate will be determined by cost evidence instead of other factors, such as the effect of the proposed rate on competing carriers, or established shippers. At least with respect to water carriers, where most of the minimum rate cases occur, the Commission has set out-of-pocket costs as the cost below which rail rates cannot go.[9] Thus in assessing the Commission's policies, the following questions must be answered: (1) From a theoretical standpoint, what costs should set the minimum rate floor? (2) How well do the ICC estimates of out-of-pocket costs approach these theoretically appropriate costs?

---

9. Specifically, the ICC seems to have adopted the rule that rail rates cannot go below out-of-pocket rail costs or fully distributed barge costs, whichever is higher. In rate cases between rail and motor carriers, the ICC seems to have adopted fully distributed costs as the relevant rate floor.

In the normal course of events, short-run average variable cost will set the rate floor for any profit-maximizing firm. So long as demand is sufficient, the firm will always charge a rate greater than average total cost. When demand is insufficient to permit rates to cover average total costs, the firm will still provide the service if the attainable rate is greater than average variable cost. This procedure will enable the firm to obtain some return on its fixed costs and thus minimize its losses and use its capacity as fully as possible. If, however, the only attainable rate is less than average variable cost, the firm will choose to discontinue the service since the losses associated with providing it would be greater than the losses associated with abandonment. Thus it is necessary to ask why any regulatory rate floor should be established and why railroads should be prevented from lowering rates to the level of short-run average variable cost.

In the short run, there seems to be little reason to establish a regulatory rate floor. If faced with a temporary reduction in demand, the railroad will be able to maintain the greatest return by permitting rates to fall to average variable cost. This will permit it to maintain the capacity needed for the expected future increase in traffic. In the long run, however, if faced with a permanent reduction in demand, a rate floor of long-run marginal cost should probably be established. In this case, the firm's existing plant is too large for the traffic volumes, and abandonment of capacity is needed. Without regulatory constraints imposed on it, the firm would continue to provide the service as long as the profit-maximizing rate was greater than average variable cost, and would abandon the service and scrap the equipment only when it wore out. However, when regulatory restraints are imposed on the firm to prevent rates from falling below long-run marginal costs, it will abandon the service and scrap the equipment as soon as the attainable rates fall below this floor. As long as short-run average variable costs lie below long-run marginal costs when the firm is experiencing permanent excess capacity, a rate floor of long-run marginal cost will ensure a more rapid adjustment of capacity to its optimal levels. It should be clear, however, that this rate floor should only be established when a firm is suffering from permanent excess capacity and not when it is suffering from temporary reductions in demand.[10]

10. This distinction creates operational difficulties since the railroad may expect traffic to increase in the future and argue for rates less than long-run marginal cost in the expectation of future traffic increases.

Since long-run marginal costs indicate the social valuation of the resources required to produce an additional unit of service by the most efficient plant, they should be used to establish the rate floor for long-term and continuing services. Consequently, the Commission's practice of using its own estimates of out-of-pocket costs can be defended only if these estimates adequately reflect long-run marginal costs. The biases inherent in the ICC cost estimates are discussed in Chapter 3 and Appendix A, which show that the Commission's estimates of out-of-pocket costs should generally bear little relation to long-run marginal costs. Thus a rate floor based on ICC estimates of out-of-pocket costs has virtually no significance. If the Commission wants to impose a rate floor, it is imperative that it change its costing procedures.[11]

Enough has been said about the use of prescriptive cost-based rates to indicate the dangers in their use. The application of cost-based rates as defined by an economist would tend to create an incorrect specification of the costs, incorrect adjustments in capacity, and excessive losses. But cost-based rates as defined by the ICC have definitely created misspecification of the costs and thus led to misspecification of the rate floors. Basically, the problem lies with a rather mechanistic and simplistic attempt to estimate some subtle cost relationships. While the work of the Canadian National Railways and the Canadian Pacific Railway Company in estimating railroad-cost functions indicates that careful statistical cost accounting can do much to improve knowledge about rail costs,[12] it has not yet reached the level of disaggregation needed in specific rate cases. Thus until the techniques and skills used in rail costing improve considerably, tying rates to costs should be avoided. The probable errors of estimation are so great that the losses involved with the application of the misspecified rates may be greater than the losses associated with the forms of price discrimination currently practiced. If, however, cost-based rates offer no alternative to the existing regulatory practices and policies, what can?

11. For a discussion of the direction in which costing should be changed, see Meyer and others, *Competition in the Transportation Industries,* Chap. 2; John R. Meyer and Gerald Kraft, "The Evaluation of Statistical Costing Techniques as Applied in the Transportation Industry," in American Economic Association, *Papers and Proceedings of the Seventy-third Annual Meeting, 1960, American Economic Review,* Vol. 51 (May 1961); and W. J. Stenason and R. A. Bandeen, "Transportation Costs and Their Implications: An Empirical Study of Railway Costs in Canada," in *Transportation Economics,* pp. 121–38.

12. *Ibid.*

Mergers

Mergers have traditionally been held out as a possible cure for the problems created by excess capacity in the railroads. The Transportation Act of 1920 directed the Commission to prepare a plan to consolidate the railroads into 18 to 20 major lines. Although a plan for a system of 19 railroads was formally adopted by the Commission in 1929, it was never put into operation. In the 1930s the National Transportation Committee advocated the formation of a few large systems on a regional basis in which competition between the railroads would be largely eliminated. More recently, interest in mergers has increased and several proposals have been made for various rail systems.[13]

The argument in favor of mergers is: So long as excess capacity prevails in the railroad system, the railroads will find price discrimination a profitable rate policy. Given the regulatory constraints, price discrimination will take the form of value-of-service pricing. Since this has led to considerable misallocation of resources, a rate structure that reflects costs more closely should increase economic efficiency in the transport sector.[14] However, a rate structure that reflects costs can only be feasible if the railroads reduce their capacity to a more efficient size for their scale of output. Since mergers should permit the railroads to eliminate duplicate facilities, they should enable them to achieve an efficient size. Then a rate structure reflecting costs could be adopted.

Thus in assessing the desirability of restructuring the railroad industry through mergers, two questions must be answered. (1) Will mergers enable the railroads to reach an efficient size? (2) Will this lead to more socially desirable pricing policies?

Chapter 4 indicated that there were two different problems associated with capacity utilization. The small firms seemed to be using their existing plant and equipment reasonably fully, but were of an insufficient size

13. See, for example, Doyle Report, pp. 229–72.
14. It should be stressed that the problems created by value-of-service pricing arise not so much because the rates are discriminatory with respect to different commodities, but because the rate structure assumes low elasticities of demand for rail services on the part of manufactured commodities that do not exist. While competitive rate making would doubtless still have commodity price discrimination, it would take a different form than that currently practiced. This point will be expanded in the following section.

to exploit all of the economies associated with rail operations. While the large firms seemed to be sufficiently large to exploit these economies, they were suffering from some excess capacity. Graphically, this means that the small firms are probably producing at points close to the long-run cost curve where long-run average costs are falling, while the large firms are probably producing at points off the long-run cost curve, but within regions where long-run average costs are essentially constant or rising slightly. Thus, for each type of firm the policy prescriptions are different. The small firms should amalgamate to form firms sufficiently large to reach an efficient level of operation; the large firms should reduce capacity to the point where they are operating on or near the long-run cost curve.

Consolidation of the small firms seems unlikely. Small firms typically are regional, with connecting links to the major trunk lines. Since small firms rarely are contiguous to each other, consolidation could take place only through the connecting trunk line. This does not seem to be a viable form of merger, however, since the consolidated firms would have their various parts connected by trunk lines owned by other railroads. Alternatively, the larger railroads could absorb the smaller ones. Since this would serve to expand the capacity of the larger railroads, which are already suffering from excess capacity, mergers of this type would be desirable only if they could lead to subsequent reductions in capacity. This would depend, in turn, on the possibility that duplicate facilities could be consolidated. The scope of such duplication should be fairly limited since small firms are usually regionally specialized and serve areas that are not served by major trunk lines. Consequently, it is questionable whether mergers of this type would improve the efficiency of resource utilization.

If consolidation of small firms is not feasible and if their absorption by large firms is untenable, the only other possibility of mergers seems to be in the consolidation of large firms. Here mergers can take two forms: end-to-end mergers or side-by-side mergers. The first type of merger occurs when a railroad wants to extend its sphere of influence and its territory. Insofar as this type of merger leads to reduction in interchanges, it should lead to more efficient operations and reduced transport costs. However, it is unlikely that this form of merger would lead to substantial reductions in capacity. Side-by-side mergers of railroads operating in the same territory with duplicate facilities could do much to reduce excess capacity. In this connection, the actual or pending mergers of the Seaboard and Atlantic Coast lines; the Great Northern, the Northern Pacific, and the Burlington lines; the Norfolk and Western and the Nickel Plate lines; the Norfolk and Western and the Virginian lines; and to a lesser extent, the Pennsylvania and New York Central lines would probably achieve the greatest economies and reductions in capacity.[15]

Nevertheless, in view of the large size of most of these firms, it is questionable if the merged companies could reach an efficient size.[16] Although some economies in joint operation could doubtless take place to permit reduction in capacity, unless the Commission adopts greater flexibility in granting abandonments on lightly used lines, it is doubtful that mergers in themselves would lead to the desired reductions in capacity. Consequently, the net effect of mergers may be reduced efficiency in the use of rail resources.[17]

The desirability of mergers should also be questioned to the extent that they reduce rail competition. The list of actual and pending mergers given above indicates that many of the consolidated railroad companies will have enormous economic power. Fear of monopoly power delayed for many years the final consummation of the Penn-Central merger and the ICC approval of the Great Northern-Northern Pacific-and Burlington merger. With the formation of the Penn Central Company, the way seems to be open for a major consolidation of rail lines. In this case, it is likely that each remaining railroad will have considerable monopoly power within its region and that there will be relatively little interrail competition.

Consequently, even if merged railroads were able to reduce capacity sufficiently to reach an efficient size, regulation would have to be continued. No profit maximizing firm with considerable monopoly power will voluntarily choose to charge a rate equal to fully distributed costs as long as the traffic will move at a rate greater than that level. Thus, unless railroads are forced to charge rates equal to fully distributed costs, they will practice much the same forms of price discrimination that they practice now, while being considerably more profitable and having considerably more monopoly power. This does not seem to be the goal of the ICC in permitting mergers; nor should it be.

15. For a full discussion of the economies of specific mergers, see Michael Conant, *Railroad Mergers and Abandonments* (University of California Press, 1964), Chap. 4.

16. Kent Healy has argued that firms of more than 20,000 employees are subject to managerial diseconomies of scale. See Kent Healy, *Economies of Scale in the Railroad Industry* (Yale University Press, 1961).

17. See the summary of the conference of experts below, pp. 184–85, for an elaboration of this point.

But if firms are forced to base their rates on fully distributed costs, the problems raised in the previous section arise. Namely, how can fully distributed costs be made an operational concept in a situation of a multiproduct firm with large fixed costs? Thus, even if mergers would lead to efficiently sized firms (which is questionable) and cost-based rates could be required without severe losses, cost-based rates would require even more stringent rate regulation than currently exists. In view of the difficulties connected with determining costs and the unsatisfactory costing methods employed by the ICC, there is little reason to hope that such a policy would lead to an efficient allocation of resources. In the absence of stringent rate regulation, mergers could create excessive monopoly power.

Obviously, any movements toward reducing regulation will create problems and dislocations for groups that have made past decisions on the existing policies. Nevertheless, the rigidities with regulatory rate making seem to be so great that it is desirable to assess the potential impact of policies leading toward deregulation.

Deregulation of the Common Carriers

What would happen if all common carriers were deregulated and permitted to follow rate and abandonment policies that they thought would maximize their profits? To answer this, the behavior of the various modes should be analyzed with respect to three types of traffic: competitive bulk traffic; high-value traffic; and noncompetitive bulk traffic.

Competitive Bulk Traffic

The behavior of rail rates on water competitive traffic depends on the nature of the demand facing the railroad, which in turn depends on existing water rates and the dynamic behavior of water costs and rates. In the short run, a railroad will determine its volume of traffic by the point where marginal costs equal marginal revenues; this will in turn determine the profit-maximizing rate. Whether this rate is above, below, or equal to the ICC estimate of out-of-pocket costs largely depends on the nature of the railroad's demand curve. The larger the volume of rail demand and the less elastic the demand curve, the more likely is the profit-maximizing rate to be more than out-of-pocket costs. Similarly, the smaller the volume of rail demand and the more elastic the demand curve, the more likely is the profit-maximizing rate to be less than out-of-pocket costs. Because of inventory and other service differentials, barge rates will probably be less than rail rates. If barge operations are sufficiently competitive, barge rates will equal fully distributed barge costs.

As long as costs or demands do not change, there is little reason for the postulated rates to change. However, during the postwar period barge costs have been dropping continuously due to technological changes (and probably government investments). If barge costs drop, the equilibrium is disturbed. The initial reaction of barge operators will be to find the new profit-maximizing point on their demand curve, which must necessarily be a lower rate than the initial equilibrium. Since the relative rate structure has been disturbed, the rail demand curve will probably shift inward while the barge demand curve will shift outward.

The equilibrium rates depend on the demand and cost curves, and it is likely that both rail and barge rates will fall below their initial levels. The relationship between the new barge rates and barge fully distributed costs will depend on the ease of entry into the barge industry in response to the cost-saving innovation. Because there are some costs to entry, it is likely, however, that barge rates will lie above barge fully distributed costs for existing operators. Unless barge rates drop below the short-run variable rail costs, rail rates will still stay above this floor. There is no reason competitive forces should keep them above long-run marginal costs or above out-of-pocket costs as measured by the ICC.

In the short run, as long as rates cover short-run variable costs, the railroad would sustain losses on its water competitive traffic. In the long run, the railroad would be under pressure to do one or both of two things: scrap existing uneconomic plant and/or invest in new cost-saving equipment. Thus while abandonment of a large portion of the equipment devoted to water competitive shipments is a possibility, it is not a probability. Instead, the more likely reaction of the railroad is the scrapping of uneconomic equipment, the abandonment of some marginal service, and investment in new equipment that would reduce its costs to barge levels and enable it to compete more effectively with water transport. Thus water competition seems more likely to lead to technical change in the railroad industry than wholesale abandonment of water competitive routes.

As long as cost-saving technology is available to both barge and rail operations, the probable outcome of competition is excessive investment in both modes. The situation is dynamically unstable. Faced with cost and rate reductions on the part of the barges and ensuing traffic losses, the response of the railroads should be investment in new cost-saving equipment to recapture some of their lost traffic. Hence the railroads would probably alter the nature of their capacity instead of reducing it, as they usually would do in a situation where rates failed to cover average total cost. If the railroads were successful in recapturing the traffic, the barge operators would suffer from excess capacity. If the railroads were not successful, they would suffer from excess capacity. In this event, the process of capacity adjustment would be extremely slow in view of the longevity of rail equipment.

Even if the railroads were successful in capturing barge traffic, as long as new cost-saving techniques were available to barge operators, this success should be temporary. Thus innovations and rates would probably take place in the barge industry that would recapture some of the rail traffic. This, in turn, would create excess capacity in the rail industry and stimulate the railroads to make new investments in cost-saving innovations.

The key element to the instability outlined here is continued technical progress and cost-saving innovations in both the barge and rail industries. As long as the rates of change are approximately equal, an unstable adjustment in capacity should take place. The innovating mode will plan its investments and rates on the assumption that the rates in the competing mode will remain at their previous levels. When faced with rate reductions and loss of traffic, the reaction of the competing mode will probably be rate reductions and similar investments in new techniques. So long as each mode bases its rate and investment decisions on the assumption that the rates and technology in the competing mode will remain static, and so long as technical innovations are available to permit each mode to respond to rate reductions and innovations, the expected outcome should be more or less continual rate reductions, investment in innovations, and excess capacity.

Interdependencies of the sort outlined here exist throughout the economy in any oligopolistic industry marked by relatively few sellers, and, in most industries, stable price and investment policies seem to exist. In the case of barge and rail competition, communication and control are much more difficult since the nature of the firms is so different. Moreover, the problem is compounded because considerable barge traffic is privately operated by large manufacturing companies. Thus, in the absence of regulation, rate competition between the modes seems more likely than the quality of advertising competition that characterizes much of American industry. This implies long periods of excessive investments and rates that fail to cover long-run marginal cost or fully distributed costs. This is precisely the outcome feared by the Commission, which wants to extend regulation to all bulk commodities. In the context of the present regulatory policies where rate competition is limited, the Commission's fears are understandable. If the present rate structure is to be maintained and if service is to be continued, long periods of losses implied by the dynamic interactions outlined here probably would be untenable. Nevertheless, in the context of the present analysis, where rate competition is assumed to prevail, the problems presented by this dynamic instability may not be excessive because of the impact of free rate competition on the railroads' other traffic. This will now be analyzed.

High-Value Traffic

Deregulation and an end to common-carrier obligations should create pressures that will encourage railroads to perform an essentially wholesaling operation and trucks to perform an essentially retailing operation. Although this allocation of traffic would undoubtedly lead to an improvement in the allocation of transport resources, it would also lead to a reduction in the profitability of trucking operations and might lead to a reduction in the welfare of certain communities.

The existing rate structure discriminates in favor of suburban and relatively small, isolated communities. Because of the application of the blanket rate structure and the long-haul, short-haul clause of Section 4 of the Interstate Commerce Act, large-volume shippers in major centers are charged rates identical to those of low-volume shippers in relatively isolated communities. Since costs tend to fall with the volume of shipments and the traffic density on a given route, the existing rate structure tends to discriminate against centrally located and large-volume shippers.[18]

The effect of deregulation on the shippers that have received favorable treatment under the present rate structure is difficult to predict. It is quite

18. Recently the ICC has permitted some rate differentiation for very large volume shipments. See Paul W. MacAvoy and James Sloss, *Regulation of Transport Innovation: The ICC and Unit Coal Trains to the East Coast* (Random House, 1967), and Robert F. Lundy, *The Economics of Loyalty Incentive Rates in the Railroad Industry in the United States* (Washington State University Press, 1963).

possible that the small shippers who are not centrally located have been receiving rail service at less than cost because of the low-traffic density on the lines connecting those shippers with the major consuming centers. Consequently, in the absence of regulation, the railroads could either raise rates sufficiently to cover their costs or they could abandon service. Because rail costs for small-shipment, low-density service are quite high and trucks are inherently better adapted to this kind of small-lot, irregular-route service, it is likely that profitable rail rates would be above profitable trucking rates. Thus abandonment of rail service to these communities would probably take place.[19] Abandonments of this nature would do much to rationalize the structure of rail capacity and ensure that the railroads concentrated on the high-volume, high-density traffic for which they have a clear advantage.

Whether the railroads' abdication of their relatively small-lot, irregular traffic to the trucks would lead to rate increases in this traffic is difficult to say. Certainly, to the extent that rates to these communities have been held down by regulation, rates would tend to rise. However, there is considerable evidence that regulation has caused trucking costs to rise.[20] Consequently, deregulation should cause trucking costs to fall. The net effect of deregulation on rates to the relatively small-lot, isolated shippers depends on the extent to which these shippers have been subsidized under regulation, the potential reduction in trucking costs, and the extent of competition in the trucking industry. However, in view of the rate reductions of 20 to 30 percent that followed the deregulation of frozen poultry, it is unlikely that deregulation would lead to rate increases unless these shippers had received substantial subsidies under regulation.

In conclusion, deregulation of rates and services to small-lot, irregular-route shippers should have the following effects: (1) substitution of truck for rail services; (2) relatively small changes in rates; (3) increased rail profitability due to the abandonment of this service; (4) to the extent that entry does not vitiate the savings accruing to a given firm, increases in the profitability of trucking firms due to cost reductions and possible rate increases.

The situation with regard to high-volume, high-value traffic is some-

19. In this connection, it is interesting to note that the president of a large midwestern railroad was quoted as saying that he would like to abandon almost a third of his rail capacity. See summary of conference of experts, p. 184, below.

20. For a full discussion, see Chap. 5, above.

TABLE 6.1. Shipments Weighing 30 Tons or More as a Percentage of All Shipments, by Shipper Group, United States, 1963

Shipper group	All shipments		Shipments weighing 30 tons or more			
	Total tons	Total ton-miles	Tons shipped by all modes	Tons shipped by rail	Ton-miles shipped by all modes	Ton-miles shipped by rail
Meat and dairy products[a]	4.1	4.7	—	—	—	—
Other processed foods	11.8	11.2	44.8	42.8	56.0	54.4
Candy, beverages, tobacco products	3.7	3.9	29.0	26.2	48.9	46.5
Textile mill and leather products[a]	1.3	1.7	—	—	—	—
Apparel and related products[b]	0.4	0.6	—	—	—	—
Paper and allied products	5.7	6.5	36.2	30.3	51.4	45.5
Chemicals, plastics, and related products	6.1	6.7	64.6	52.5	72.8	57.0
Drugs, paints, and related products	6.2	6.5	43.0	39.3	59.4	54.8
Petroleum and coal products	16.1	13.3	75.2	14.7	83.2	17.4
Rubber and plastic products[a]	1.0	1.4	—	—	—	—
Lumber and wood products except furniture	7.5	13.1	58.6	54.2	77.2	74.8
Furniture and fixtures[c]	1.0	1.4	—	—	—	—
Stone, clay, and glass products	14.7	6.9	45.5	34.1	52.5	45.3
Primary iron and steel products	9.5	7.4	53.2	46.5	62.8	56.2
Primary nonferrous metal products	1.5	2.1	41.0	34.1	54.7	51.8
Fabricated metals except cans and miscellaneous products[a]	1.3	1.5	—	—	—	—
Metal cans and miscellaneous fabricated metal products[a]	1.4	1.5	—	—	—	—
Industrial machinery except electrical[a]	0.6	0.8	—	—	—	—
Machinery except electrical and industrial[a]	1.6	2.6	—	—	—	—
Communication products and parts[c]	0.3	0.4	—	—	—	—
Electrical products and supplies[d]	1.1	1.7	—	—	—	—
Motor vehicles and equipment	2.7	3.5	25.0	23.5	24.8	24.1
Transport equipment, except motor vehicles[a]	0.3	0.4	—	—	—	—
Instruments, photographic equipment, watches and clocks[c]	0.1	0.2	—	—	—	—
United States total	100.0	100.0	—	—	—	—

Source: U.S. Bureau of the Census, *Census of Transportation, 1963*, Vol. III: *Commodity Transportation Survey*, Pt. 3, Shipper Groups, Tables B and 3. a. Maximum shipment size given was 15 tons. b. Maximum shipment size given was ½ ton. c. Maximum shipment size given was 5 tons. d. Maximum shipment size given was 10 tons.

what different. These shipments represent the so-called "cream" of the traffic and are highly profitable for both rail and trucking operations. A large proportion of these shipments currently go by truck. However, because current regulatory policies prevent the railroads from exploiting their cost advantages, the current shipments carried by the railroads essentially reflect the demand of the residual traffic for which trucks cannot compete because of length of haul, shipment size, and so forth. Once rates were deregulated, railroads would be able to exploit their cost advantage fully; and shippers should be sufficiently sensitive to the potential rate reductions that the demand curves facing the railroads would be quite elastic in a deregulated environment. Thus the reaction of railroads to deregulation should be sizable rate reductions and the capture of a wide range of medium-size, medium-haul shipments that currently go by truck.

More specifically, rate competition and the resulting stimulus to technological change should cause the rail demand curve to be quite elastic for all shipment sizes up to forty tons. On larger loads, the railroads can still exploit some monopoly power since their costs are significantly below those of either trucking or piggyback operations. At least for manufactured goods, this represents a fairly small proportion of freight traffic as Table 6.1 shows. Since competitive traffic dominates rail shipments in high-value goods, it is likely that rail rates will be pushed down to trucking costs on most high-value traffic of shipment sizes less than forty tons.

In the longer run, the elastic range of the rail demand curve should be even greater since trucking costs should fall over time. Part of this should arise from the increasing size of trucks; part from the cost reductions created by the utilization of the interstate highway system; part from a reduction in service competition which seems to cause trucking costs to rise dramatically; and part from a reduction in the restrictions that currently increase trucking costs.[21] Thus the level of trucking costs should fall over time, increasing the area of effective competition between rail and truck. In response to reduced trucking costs, the railroads should be further stimulated and encouraged to introduce piggybacking operations. Once rail rates fall to trucking variable cost, however, intermodal pres-

21. For a full discussion of this see James C. Nelson, "The Effects of Entry Control in Surface Transport," in *Transportation Economics,* and Walter Y. Oi and Arthur P. Hurter, Jr., *Economics of Private Truck Transportation* (William C. Brown Co. for Northwestern University, Transportation Center, 1965), Chap. 5.

sures will cease to exert any downward pressure on rail rates. Below this point, trucking firms should choose to go out of business rather than meet the reduced rail rates. Since a given railroad typically faces a wide range of trucking operations with different cost curves, this minimum profitable rate may appear at fairly low levels. The extremely low markup that railroads obtain from animal products that are subject to exempt carriage and the viability of the firms specializing in exempt commodities indicate that this point of minimum trucking costs may be quite low for many firms. Nevertheless, the railroads will gain little additional traffic by reducing rates below this point. Therefore, in the absence of interrail competition, rail rates will tend to settle at the out-of-pocket costs of the most efficient trucking firms.

It is unlikely that interrail pressures will force rates to fall below this level. Rate bureaus have legitimized collusive rail pricing to such an extent that there is currently virtually no price competition among the railroads. With deregulation, rate bureaus would presumably be abolished. However, the history of collusive pricing in the railroad industry is sufficiently long so that tacit collusion would probably be substituted for overt collusion. Moreover, the behavior of other industries characterized by a few sellers indicates that price competition would be an unlikely course for the railroads to adopt. Thus to the extent that rail costs (including any service differential) lie below trucking costs, the railroads should be able to obtain a monopoly profit, and the shippers will fail to receive the full benefits of possible rate reductions.

Rate competition for the high-value, high-volume commodities should cause rail profits to increase and trucking profits to fall. Since current regulatory policies prevent the railroads from following profit-maximizing pricing policies, the rate reductions stemming from deregulation should reflect increased profitability. To the extent that deregulation may induce reductions in trucking costs, the increased profitability of the railroads may be somewhat vitiated. Nevertheless, it seems unlikely that trucking costs will fall sufficiently to offset all of the potential increase in rail profits. Because regulation enables the trucking operators to enjoy an artificial degree of monopoly power, deregulation would almost certainly lead to a reduction in trucking profits. Competitive pressures from the railroads and other trucking operators would probably cause the less efficient trucking operators to go out of business and ensure that the remaining trucking operators would receive no more than a "normal" return.

Noncompetitive Bulk Commodities

Probably the traffic with the most inelastic demand is in the noncompetitive bulk commodities. Since these commodities have no alternative to rail transportation, their elasticity of demand for rail services is determined by the importance of rail costs in the final-goods price and the elasticity of the final-goods demand. It is given by the product of the elasticity of demand for the commodity and the percentage of rail costs in the final-goods price.[22] Thus the more elastic the final demand for the commodity and the more important rail costs are in the final-goods price, the more elastic should be the demand curve facing the railroads. As long as the rail elasticity is less than one, the railroad will gain revenue by raising rates. If the percentage of rail costs in the final-goods price is known, it is possible to define a critical elasticity of demand for the commodity that will make the rail elasticity equal to one. So long as the actual elasticity of demand falls below the critical elasticity, rail rates will tend to increase.[23] Table 6.2 gives these critical elasticities for the major bulk commodities. Although data on elasticities are not generally available, the few studies that have been made indicate elasticities of less than two in absolute value.[24] Since this is considerably less than most of the critical elasticities listed in Table 6.2, rather large rate increases could be expected on noncompetitive bulk traffic.

These conclusions should be modified by the existence of market competition, which arises from the existence of alternative sources of supply. Market competition should be particularly significant for energy fuels and for agricultural products and should limit the range of potential rate increases. In particular, as petroleum and extra-high-voltage (EHV) transmission become increasingly used by utilities, the elasticity of demand for coal as an energy source should increase considerably. Small price increases in coal should lead to more than proportional reductions in volume. Since rail costs play such an important part on delivered coal

22. For a discussion of this point, see Chap. 3, note 38, above.
23. This conclusion should be qualified because it ignores the cost element. With a linear demand curve and zero marginal costs, the profit-maximizing rate will occur at the point where the elasticity of demand is equal to one. With positive marginal costs, the profit-maximizing price will be at a point on the demand curve where the elasticity is greater than one. Thus, the critical elasticities are somewhat understated since rail rates would be at levels where the elasticity of the rail demand would be greater than one.
24. Meyer and others, *Competition in the Transportation Industries*, p. 198.

TABLE 6.2. Freight Costs as Percentage of Wholesale Value at Destination, and Critical Demand Elasticity, Selected Commodities Transported by United States Railroads, 1959

Commodity	Rail freight cost as percentage of wholesale value at destination	Critical demand elasticity of commodity (absolute value)
Wheat	10.07	9.9
Corn	12.18	8.2
Flour	7.48	13.4
Sugar beets	9.51	10.5
Anthracite coal	30.45	3.3
Bituminous coal	41.96	2.4
Coke	18.47	5.4
Iron ore	19.67	5.1
Gravel and sand	54.92	1.8
Crushed stone	54.79	1.8
Slurry stone	57.25	1.7
Phosphate	27.94	3.6
Pulpwood	24.11	4.1
Lumber	20.74	4.8
Fertilizers	18.88	5.3
Manufactured iron and steel	6.16	16.2
Cement	17.77	5.6
Animal feed	6.42	15.6

Source: First column, Interstate Commerce Commission, Bureau of Transport Economics and Statistics, *Freight Revenue and Wholesale Value at Destination of Commodities Transported by Class I Line-Haul Railroads*, 1959, Statement 6112 (1961), App. A, pp. 16–20; second column, calculated from first column by defining a critical elasticity of demand for the commodity that makes the rail elasticity equal to one.

prices, the area for potential rate increases in the rail-coal traffic should be limited. In fact, market competition could well force rates down on coal.[25] Since coal accounts for a major portion of the revenues on bulk commodities, competition from other energy sources should curtail a wide area of potential rate increases.

The effect of market competition with regard to agricultural products is more difficult to predict. Agricultural products from any given source typically compete with those from other sources in the consuming market. Since the prices of agricultural goods are usually determined by a

25. This has already happened in the East Coast where competition from petroleum has forced rail rates down drastically. For a full discussion, see M. A. Adelman, "American Coal in Western Europe," *Journal of Industrial Economics*, Vol. 14 (July 1966); MacAvoy and Sloss, *Regulation of Transport Innovation*; and Lundy, *Economics of Loyalty Incentive Rates*.

competitive bidding mechanism, the market price must be taken as given by both the railroads and the farmers. In the short run, a railroad in a monopoly position can charge a rate greater than the difference between the market price and the cost of production, since the farmer will get no return on his crop unless he can move it to the market. In the longer run, however, the difference between the market price and the cost of production will tend to set a limit on the rate the railroad can charge. Because of market competition, the delivered price cannot rise above the market price; because of sensitivity of production to income, the farmer's received price cannot fall below his costs of production for an extended period of time.

Within the range of market price and producers' costs, the rail rate should be determined by competitive conditions. In the absence of pipelines to carry agricultural and other non-petroleum products, the rail rates should be determined by the extent of rate competition existing among the competing railroads. The collusive pricing behavior of railroads under the sanction of rate bureaus makes the likelihood of effective rate competition remote, even in the absence of these rate bureaus. Moreover, in view of the relatively high markups over cost on many bulk and agricultural commodities currently transported from the West, it appears that the railroads are able to exploit a considerable amount of their potential monopoly power in spite of the existing regulatory constraints.[26]

In the absence of rate regulation, the behavior of rates on noncompetitive agricultural commodities depends on the existing spread between market prices and the received producers' prices. If this spread just equaled the existing rail rates, there should be little scope for rate increases. If this spread is greater than the existing rates, rate increases should be expected. However, if existing rail rates were less than the difference between market prices and production costs, farmers should be earning more than a normal return; farm incomes should be relatively high. The fact that farm incomes are chronically depressed indicates that farmers are not obtaining any of the differentials between market prices and producers' prices. Thus the railroads appear to have little untapped monopoly power with respect to rates on noncompetitive agricultural

26. For example, the following ratios of revenues to out-of-pocket costs on goods transported within the western territory are significant: wheat, 193; corn, 159; sorghum grain, 134; soybeans, 145. Interstate Commerce Commission, Bureau of Accounts, *Distribution of the Rail Revenue Contribution by Commodity Groups, 1961*, Statement 6–64 (1964), Table 7.

commodities. This implies that rate deregulation would probably not lead to a marked increase in rates, which seem to be currently close to their profit-maximizing levels. Although some rate increases would probably take place, it seems unlikely that rate deregulation would lead to large-scale rate increases and consequent reductions in producers' incomes. Therefore, although producers of noncompetitive bulk commodities would probably not benefit from rate deregulation, they probably would not lose very much.

What then is the probable outcome of deregulation of rates on the competing modes, the consumers, and the shippers or producers?

An end to rate regulation would tend to increase rail profits on high-value goods and on noncompetitive agricultural traffic. Its impact on rail profits associated with water competitive traffic is difficult to assess and depends on the nature and extent of technological change available to barge and rail operations. As long as cost-saving innovations are available to both modes, it is likely that each mode will experience periods of expanding traffic followed by periods of contracting traffic and excess capacity as each mode gains a temporary advantage over its competitor. Since competitive pressures should push rail rates down to marginal costs, it is likely that even while expanding their water competitive traffic, the railroads would fail to cover overhead and would suffer losses on this traffic. At the point when the cost savings are exploited sufficiently to bar further cost reductions, the low-cost carrier should carry the bulk of the traffic while the high-cost carrier should be saddled with considerable excess capacity. Although pure conjecture, it is likely that the railroads will ultimately become the high-cost carrier because of the inherent cheapness of water transport.

Thus the probable eventual outcome of rate competition for the railroads is increased profitability on their high-value and noncompetitive bulk commodities, and losses on their water competitive bulk commodities, preceded by a period of increased investment and reduced rates. Although the railroads should attempt to divest themselves of plant and equipment built to carry water competitive bulk commodities, the period of capacity adjustment should be quite long. During this period, the rail lines that were heavily involved in water competitive traffic would probably suffer considerable losses. However, as long as they were not too specialized in this traffic, they should be able to obtain enough revenues from their other traffic to permit an orderly downward adjustment in capacity.[27] Clearly railroads that are not subject to water competition would enjoy increased profits as a result of rate competition.

Although deregulation of rates would probably have an initially adverse effect on water carriers, its long-run effect would probably be to increase their profitability. This follows from the analysis of the impact of rate competition on rail traffic. Thus during the period of investment and rate reductions, the water carriers would probably be subject to fluctuating profits and periods of losses. Once an equilibrium was established in which the water carriers had a decided cost advantage, their profitability should increase. Thus on the whole rail and water carriers are likely to benefit from increased rate competition. It should be pointed out, however, that if rail operations turned out to have a long-run cost advantage over barge operations, water carriers would suffer and many would be forced out of business.

Since motor carriers are now protected from intermodal and intramodal rate competition, deregulation and its concomitant competitive pressures would almost certainly reduce trucking profits substantially. On the one hand, because of the cost advantage enjoyed by rail operators with respect to much of the traffic that currently goes by truck, it is likely that trucking carriers would suffer considerable losses from rail competition. On the other hand, because of the ease of entry into trucking, profitable trucking operations on noncompetitive traffic would attract new entrants and concomitant reductions in profits. Thus trucking firms would not only be forced into the relatively unprofitable short-haul, small-size, irregular-route traffic by rail competition, but would find that their rates would be pushed down to costs by trucking competition. The result would be a sharp reduction in trucking profitability.

Since the resulting rail-truck allocation represents an improvement in the allocation of transport resources, society as a whole should gain from rail-truck competition. However, to the extent that free entry into the trucking industry leads to increased excess capacity in that industry, society will suffer some losses. Nevertheless, the gains resulting from improved rail-truck allocation will likely exceed any losses from increased excess capacity in the trucking industry. It is important to realize that

27. Railroads in the southern territory should be the most susceptible to water competition because of the large number of waterways in this territory. However, most of the railroads here derive the bulk of their revenue from manufactured goods. Thus their dependence on water competitive traffic does not seem to be particularly marked.

while society as a whole should gain from deregulation, the truckers will lose. Thus the hostility of the trucking industry to any form of deregulation is understandable and must be countered if a change in policy is to be made.

Consumers should gain as a group from an end to regulation. Rates on high-value manufactured goods in major consuming centers should tend to fall, thus leading to reduced delivered prices. The impact of deregulation on rates to more isolated consuming centers is more difficult to predict. The reduction in trucking costs and increased competition between truckers resulting from deregulation should offset any upward pressure on rates that would arise from the removal of subsidies that shippers in these communities might have enjoyed under regulated rates. Because of increased water-rail competition, rates on water competitive bulk traffic should fall, leading to reduced delivered prices. Although the rates on noncompetitive bulk traffic might rise, market competition should prevent any rate increases from being reflected in consumers' prices. Thus the impact of rate competition on delivered prices should be stable prices or price reductions. Consequently, the consuming public as a group would benefit from rate competition.

Similarly, producers would tend to benefit from deregulation. Reduced transport costs on manufactured goods and competitive bulk traffic and the resulting reductions in market prices should act to increase sales and profits.[28] However, a lack of competitive pressure would probably preclude producers of noncompetitive bulk commodities obtaining any benefits from rate competition. Nevertheless, in view of the rail profits currently earned on bulk agricultural commodities and the low level of farm

---

28. This conclusion should be modified somewhat by the likelihood that certain producers who had made their locational decision on the existing rate structure would find themselves at a disadvantage if the rate structure changed significantly. This is particularly true of the millers. One of the major aspects of the grain-rate structure has been the granting of transit privileges under which a single rate was quoted from point to point, even though the grain had been processed into flour en route. This has meant that mill locations have not been responsive to transport costs and have tended to be established nearer the sources of supply than they might have been in the absence of this equalizing procedure. Since most of the contested multiple-car grain rates do not grant transit privileges, the millers fear that increased rate competition would upset their locational equilibrium and cause their present locations to become unprofitable. For an expression of this opinion, see testimony of D. H. Wilson, *Transportation Act 1963*, Hearings before the House Committee on Interstate and Foreign Commerce, 88 Cong. 1 sess. (1963), Pt. 1, pp. 558–70.

income, it appears that the railroads are already exploiting considerable monopoly power. Thus, it is questionable whether rate deregulation would lead to higher rates and reduced farm incomes. It is unlikely that rate deregulation would lead to rate reductions and increases in income. Thus producers of noncompetitive agricultural commodities should be no better or worse off under a policy of rate deregulation than they currently are. Producers of other noncompetitive bulk commodities would probably lose from rate deregulation since increased rates would tend to be pushed back on them. Consequently, their received incomes might well fall while those of other producers were rising.

In conclusion then, the main losers from deregulation would be the railroads facing severe water competition, trucking firms, producers of noncompetitive bulk commodities, consumers and producers in small, isolated areas insofar as any existing subsidy they receive is greater than the potential trucking cost reductions caused by deregulation, and society as a whole insofar as the dynamics of rail and water competition create excessive investment and inefficient capacity adjustments. The gainers would be the consumers and producers in the major population centers, most railroads, most water carriers, and society insofar as resources were allocated more efficiently, excess capacity was reduced, and innovations stimulated. In assessing the desirability of ending all rate regulation and common carrier obligations, the gains must be weighed against the losses. Before attempting to do this, however, other alternatives will be analyzed to see if they would yield the same benefits while producing fewer costs.

Transportation Companies

The discussion of the previous section implicitly assumed that the existing separate ownership of modes would continue. By removing this restriction and permitting the formation of transportation "department stores" or integrated transportation companies, the same benefits, at a lower cost to society, might be achieved as those stemming from simple deregulation.

Transportation companies are multimodal by nature and would typically engage in rail, water, trucking, and possibly air operations. Although not a necessary occurrence, railroads would probably form the nucleus of these companies and acquire barge and trucking lines. It is precisely this possibility that has prevented their formation. Because of the disparity in size between railroads and barge or trucking companies, it was feared that railroads would neglect barge or water services or innovations, leading to an overall reduction in transport services. At an early stage, therefore, railroads were forbidden to engage in other transport services, and the legal separation of modes has continued to the present time.

There are several advantages to establishing transportation companies, however. Such companies should be able to coordinate intermodal services and provide a more efficient package of transport services to the shipper than could be achieved under the existing separation of modes. Moreover, by permitting the substitution of trucking for rail services, transportation companies should enable the railroads to achieve a more efficient scale of operation and thus eliminate one of the major costs of current regulatory policies. Although this substitution and capacity adjustment should also take place under deregulation, transportation companies should be able to coordinate rail and trucking services better than could rail and trucking operations acting independently. Transportation companies should also be less subject to the dynamic inefficiencies inherent in rail-water competition. Because a transportation company would supply both rail and water transportation, it should be able to take the interdependencies of cost and demand into account and plan its rate and investment policy accordingly. Thus periods of excessive investment and the social costs associated with excess capacity would be less likely to occur. Because they would maximize rail and water profits jointly, transportation companies should not be subject to one of the main sources of losses arising from deregulating rates alone.

The impact of transportation companies on competing modes is somewhat difficult to assess. Since the railroads are the corporate giants of the industry, it is likely that a relaxation of the rule prohibiting intermodal firms would be met by railroad acquisitions of firms in other modes. Thus trucking firms that might be forced into bankruptcy by competitive rail operations should be bought by the railroads. Since the railroads would probably purchase only the more profitable trucking firms, the less profitable firms would have to fend for themselves, and would likely be forced into the short-haul, small-lot, irregular-route traffic. But they would probably be no worse off than under a policy of deregulation.

Because of the economies that can be obtained by offering coordinated rail-truck service, the capitalized value of the trucking firms purchased by rail companies should increase. Therefore, the owners of the trucking firms that were purchased by the railroads would probably be better off than they would be under a policy of simple deregulation. Nevertheless, because trucking firms would no longer receive the regulatory protection that currently inflates the profitability of trucking operations, truckers would still be worse off than they would be under the current regulatory policies.

Barge lines would probably be better off than they would be in the case of rate deregulation. The formation of transportation companies should remove the competitive instability between rail and water operations, and therefore increase the capitalized value of the barge lines. Thus, whether barge lines were purchased by railroads, barge companies should be better off under a system of transportation companies than in an environment where rate competition prevailed alone.

The impact of transportation companies on consumers and producers depends on the extent to which competition is able to operate. If each region were served by one transportation company, that company would be in a position to operate as a complete monopoly. Even if this monopoly power were not exploited, its mere existence would be intolerable. Thus monopolistic transportation companies would have to be treated as public utilities and regulated accordingly. However, as long as each region is served by several railroads, it should also be served by several transportation companies.[29] The market structure would be oligopolistic, which is accepted in many other sectors of the economy as leading to reasonably acceptable economic behavior.

Whether oligopolistic transportation companies would produce acceptable economic behavior is difficult to say and depends on the extent of competition that would exist in the industry once these companies were formed. The performance of most tight-knit oligopolies of three or four sellers has not been particularly good in terms of economic efficiency. In general, most tight-knit oligopolies are characterized by a lack of price competition, the maintenance of excess capacity to forestall entry, and an unwillingness to introduce technical change and innovations that may make existing plant or equipment obsolete or that may reduce costs and encourage price reductions.[30]

29. The present trend in mergers may negate this statement in the relatively near future. The implications of this development will be discussed in the following chapter.

30. For a full discussion of oligopolistic behavior see Joe Bain, *Industrial Organization* (2d ed.; John Wiley and Sons, 1968), and Carl Kaysen and Donald F. Turner, *Antitrust Policy* (Harvard University Press, 1959).

The implications of such behavior for transportation companies would be the substitution of service for rate competition, expansion of each firm's capacity to increase its competitiveness with respect to service, an unwillingness to introduce cost-saving innovations for fear of upsetting rate relationships and a relative neglect of piggybacking or barge innovations that might make existing investments in rail or trucking facilities obsolete.[31] In this case, transportation companies would not provide a reasonable alternative to current regulatory policies.

There is reason to believe that transportation companies would not be able to operate as tight-knit oligopolies. Because of the low barriers to entry in trucking and barge operations, any monopoly profits arising from noncompetitive pricing or investment behavior on the part of the transportation companies would likely be a signal for entry. If unexploited innovations in water transport exist, entrants should be attracted to develop them. In this respect, the relatively large numbers of private water carriers should do much to ensure relatively competitive behavior on the part of the transportation companies. Similarly, if transportation companies set bulk or high-value rates at noncompetitive levels, independent water or trucking operators could enter the industry and undercut these rates. Thus the threat of entry should do much to force transportation companies to behave competitively.

However, the possibility of truck or water competition should force rates down only to the level of the costs of an all-water, an all-truck, or a combined water-truck shipment. To the extent that the costs of a shipment by a transportation company lie below the costs of nonrail shipments, transportation companies should reap some monopoly profits. But the previous section pointed out that this limit to rate reductions was equally true in the absence of transportation companies. Whether transportation companies are permitted in conjunction with deregulation, intermodal competitive pressures will only force rates to fall to the variable costs of a nonrail shipment. Whether rates fall below this will depend on

31. In general, firms will introduce new technology only when the long-run average total cost of the new technology is less than the short-run average variable cost of the old technology. Since short-run average variable costs of rail operations are quite low, transportation companies would probably be unwilling to introduce barge innovations unless the resulting cost savings are quite large. The same problem probably exists for piggybacking, although to a lesser extent. As long as piggyback costs are less than the short-run variable costs of trucking operations, transportation companies should be willing to introduce piggyback innovations.

the extent of interrail or intertransportation company competition. Given the structure of the rail industry, rates are unlikely to fall below this point whether transportation companies were formed. In terms of economic efficiency, the rate structure that would exist under transportation companies would be no better or no worse than the rate structure that would exist under deregulation alone.

On balance, deregulation accompanied by transportation companies may be preferable to deregulation alone. The costs to the trucking and barge lines should be less under integrated transportation companies than under deregulation alone. Transportation companies should reduce the social costs inherent in water-rail competition by permitting a company to take the interdependencies of the two modes into account and adjust capacity and rates accordingly. In addition, the rate structure should be similar under both policies, with the effective rate floors set by the cost of nonrail shipments. In both cases, the impossibility of entry into rail operations enables the railroads to obtain some monopoly profits. However, these profits might be higher under transportation companies because of the economies obtained by coordinated movement. In conclusion, then, as long as effective competition could be maintained, the benefits arising from transportation companies would probably be the same as those arising from deregulation alone, while the costs may be somewhat less. Thus deregulation in conjunction with the formation of transportation companies should be considered as an alternative to the policy of deregulation and the continued separation of modes.[32]

Agreed Charges

The least radical change in present policies would likely be the permission of agreed charges. Under this arrangement, rail companies would

32. The impact of transportation companies on government investment and pricing policies should be mentioned. Currently, each mode receives differential benefits from public investments. Because transportation companies would benefit equally from government investments, their formation would do much to end the conflict over public investment policy. However, to the extent that the current policies lead to inefficient use of resources, criticism of them is desirable. Although there is little reason to think that rate competition would lead to a more efficient pricing policy with respect to public transportation investments, there is considerable reason to think that the formation of transportation companies would diminish the existing pressures for change. This then should prob-

be able to negotiate with a shipper to transport 80 to 90 percent of his annual volume on the railroad for a year to eighteen months, with the charge to be renegotiated at the end of that period. The agreement would be public, and once a railroad had made this agreement with a given shipper, it would have to extend the same terms to all shippers who were willing to ship the specified percentage of their freight by the railroad. For example, if a shipper with an annual volume of 5 million tons made an agreement to ship 90 percent of his freight with the railroad in question for a reduced rate, the railroad would have to extend this same rate to a small shipper with an annual volume of 5,000 tons if he also shipped 90 percent of his freight by the railroad.

It is questionable whether this policy would be desirable. As was indicated in Chapter 3, there are substantial economies associated with large-volume shipments. With an assured annual volume of 3 to 4 million tons, unit trains can reach costs of 4 mills per ton-mile. It is doubtful that these costs could be achieved for annual volume much less than this, however, for the economies associated with unit trains derive from extremely high levels of utilization. The past policy of the ICC to insist on equality of rates for shippers of vastly different shipment sizes has meant the continuation of uneconomic and inefficient coal mines that have been able to compete effectively with larger, more efficient mines because of the freight-rate parity. The removal of this parity by permitting special unit-train or volume rates was a large step toward economic rationality. Since agreed charges would maintain this parity, they would tend to reduce economic efficiency in this area. The result of this parity would either be higher rates on very large-volume shipments or losses on the smaller-volume shipments. Because of competitive pressures from water and other energy sources, the railroads would probably follow the latter course to minimize their losses. Whether such a subsidy to small shippers is desirable is questionable.[33]

The impact of agreed charges on high-value manufactured commodities is somewhat difficult to assess. The relative lack of private trucking

---

ably be treated as an additional social cost associated with the formation of transportation companies.

33. Nevertheless, the political power of the small shipper is considerable. During the hearings on the Kennedy bills, the small coal operators testified vigorously against the deregulation of bulk commodities and attacked the unit-train developments. See testimony of Robert Holcomb, *Transportation Act, 1963,* Hearings before the House Committee on Interstate and Foreign Commerce, 88 Cong. 1 sess. (1963), Pt. 2, pp. 581–90.

operations in the largest manufacturing firms indicates that these firms may already be obtaining substantial rate concessions from the railroads.[34] The imposition of agreed charges would bring these concessions into the open and would extend the reduced rates to smaller firms with less monopoly power. Since the current level of rail rates encourages an uneconomic diversion of traffic to trucks, any rate reductions would be desirable. However, it seems unlikely that agreed charges themselves could create as competitive a rate structure as that resulting from free rate competition or transportation companies.

In fact, there seems to be considerable fear that agreed charges would limit intermodal competition. This arises from the extended nature of the contract and the penalties connected with breaking contracts. If a contract is established for a period of twelve to eighteen months, competitive rate reductions are effectively barred for this duration. At best, this characteristic of agreed charges would lead to slow and sticky rate adjustments. At worst, it could serve to tie shippers to their contract carriers and tend to exclude competing carriers. This tying should last only for the latter portion of the contract, and it is unlikely that it would necessarily continue through the period of renegotiation. Nevertheless, competitive reactions must be slower under agreed charges than under the other policies being considered.[35]

Moreover, instituting agreed charges would create considerable problems of implementation in the field of high-value goods, because of "the most favored nation" aspect of the agreed charges. Under agreed charges, the rate treatment offered to the most favored shipper is extended to all similar shippers. The difficulty arises precisely in defining "similar" shippers. Since goods are not usually identical, problems would arise in determining what characteristics constitute similar. A liberal interpretation would tend to end commodity price discrimination, while a stricter one would tend to maintain it. It seems clear, however, that considerable litigation and resources could be engaged in this question.

Finally, agreed charges should do little to help the dynamic problems of capacity adjustment inherent in rail and water competition. Although the tying aspect of the agreement should enable the railroads to plan their traffic volume with a fair degree of certainty for a period of a year to

34. Oi and Hurter, *Economics of Private Truck Transportation,* p. 192.
35. This slowness in competitive adjustments has troubled the ICC, which has barred all agreed charges arrangements to date. For a full description, see Lundy, *Economics of Loyalty Incentive Rates.*

eighteen months, once the agreement is over, the shipper is free to rene-
gotiate with a competing water carrier. Thus under agreed charges the
competitive reactions should be slowed, but not ended. Consequently, rail
and water carriers should still be subject to the process of traffic losses,
investments in cost-saving equipment, rate reductions, subsequent traffic
gains, and eventual losses as the competing mode reacts with new investments and rate reductions. As long as rail and water operations are independent, it is impossible for them to take the interdependencies of the
two modes into account. Thus excess capacity and dynamic inefficiencies
are likely to result.

Agreed charges seem to have relatively little to recommend them.
They are subject to the same inefficiencies as free rate competition. In
addition, they create further inefficiencies by failing to permit rate differentials to reflect cost differentials. Although the rate structure under
agreed charges should be more competitive than it currently is, both free
rate competition and transportation companies would lead to an even
more competitive rate structure. The stickiness of reactions and the contract nature of the charges should act to limit competitive forces. Hence,
agreed charges appear to lead to only marginal improvements over the
current regulatory policies while creating new sources of inefficiencies.

CHAPTER SEVEN

What Course for Regulation?

OF THE VARIOUS courses of action considered, the following require further consideration: (1) continued and increased regulation as proposed by the Interstate Commerce Commission (ICC); (2) free rate competition and an end to common carrier obligations; (3) formation of transportation companies and complete deregulation; (4) continued regulation with relaxation of existing rules with regard to piggybacking and minimum rates.

Present Regulatory Policies

The discussion in earlier chapters has indicated the problems created by present regulatory policies: inefficient traffic allocations, excess capacity, stifling of technological change and innovation. These are social costs of considerable magnitude. There are, however, strong forces supporting present policies. The negative reaction to the Kennedy bills, which were aimed at deregulating rates on bulk commodities, on the part of the ICC, the water carriers, the trucking firms, and the adversely affected producers was sufficient to kill the bills in spite of administration and railroad support.

The advantages of the present regulatory policies are the very real ones of the maintenance of the status quo. Any change in them would alter the traditional rate relationships and thus disturb the structure on which past consumption, production, and transportation decisions have been made. A rationalization of the rate and transportation structure would doubtless divert considerable traffic from trucks, increase rail and

163

water competition, and make some production locations unprofitable; it might also cause rates to increase to small-lot, small-volume shippers and lead to a reduction of farm and mining income in the West. In the past, specific losses suffered by producers, consumers, and carriers have been thought sufficiently great to outweigh the social benefits arising from a rationalization of the transport industry.

Any new transportation policy must be able to counteract the criticisms of potentially adversely affected groups. Changes in regulatory policies will not be made unless either the losers can be adequately compensated or their numbers and their losses restricted. Although the benefits to be derived from rationalization of the transportation structure are enormous, the specific gains resulting from a more efficient allocation of transportation resources are too diffused to count much. The costs, however, are concentrated in a few highly vocal groups who believe they will suffer substantial income losses if any changes are made. In this situation, the articulate losers will always be given more weight than the dispersed, apathetic gainers.[1]

An End to Rate Regulation

In terms of economic efficiency alone, a policy that ended all rate regulation and common carrier obligations would create benefits far in excess of costs. Although rate competition might lead to excessive investments and rate reductions in connection with rail and water competition, it should also lead to an efficient allocation of traffic between the competing modes, increased innovation and technological change, and a more efficient utilization of transport capacity. The direct benefits to the users of transport services from a rationalization of the rate structure would

1. In this connection, the testimony on the Kennedy bills is interesting. The first time the bills came up for consideration in 1962, some forty-three people testified. Of these, only six represented shipping groups in favor of the bills. Of the more than sixty who testified the following year, only 8 additional shipping groups spoke in favor of the bill. Thus over the course of both hearings, only fourteen out of the more than one hundred people who testified represented favorable shipper or consumer interests. In contrast, sixteen representatives of the water industry and eighteen representatives of the trucking industry testified against the bills. *Transportation Acts Amendments, 1962,* Hearings before the House Committee on Interstate and Foreign Commerce, 87 Cong. 2 sess.; *Transportation Act, 1963,* Hearings before the House Committee on Interstate and Foreign Commerce, 88 Cong. 1 sess. (1963).

probably be on the order of $500 million a year. Since the rate structure affects pricing relationships throughout the economy, its rationalization would generate benefits considerably in excess of this figure. Unfortunately, the benefits from increased innovation and technical change cannot be quantified; nor can the benefits from increased capacity utilization. Nevertheless, these benefits may well be greater than those arising from a rationalization of the rate structure. Thus $500 million must represent a minimum estimate of the social costs of the current regulatory policies. While unquantifiable, the total costs must be far in excess of this figure.

Although rate competition and abolishing common carrier obligations would do much to rationalize the structure of the transportation industry, the analysis of the previous chapter indicated that this policy would fail to meet the objections of the potentially adversely affected groups.

Trucking firms would be particularly hard hit, since rail rates would tend to fall to the variable costs of the most efficient trucking firms. At best, many trucking firms would be forced into the relatively unprofitable short-haul, small-size, irregular-route service; at worst, many would be forced out of business.

Although water carriers would probably enjoy an eventual long-run competitive advantage over railroads, the immediate consequences of rate competition between rail and water carriers would probably be an extended period of intensive rate competition, excessive investment, and reduced profitability for both modes. Thus for what might be the relevant time horizon of many water carriers, rate competition would likely lead to losses rather than gains. Moreover, since there is some evidence that water carriers are currently protected by "umbrella rate making," competition would still tend to reduce their profitability in the absence of the dynamic inefficiencies outlined here.

To the extent that regulation prevents railroads from exploiting their potential monopoly position with respect to noncompetitive bulk commodities, deregulation should lead to increased rates and concomitant reductions in the incomes of the producers of these commodities. This would particularly affect the western farming and mining interests. Furthermore, insofar as rate competition would end the existing discriminatory pricing policies on which many past locational decisions have been based, additional producers would probably be hurt. The millers and small coal producers are especially vulnerable in this respect. Since the present blanket rate structure tends to discriminate in favor of rural and suburban areas, deregulation might also lead to rate increases in these areas unless competitive pressures were sufficiently great to offset rate increases arising from the removal of any subsidy the areas might receive under current regulatory policies.

Thus a policy aimed at deregulating rates alone creates considerable problems with regard to income distribution. Although the affected income groups have doubtless received differential benefits and gains as a result of the existing regulatory policies, by now they have come to view these benefits as their proper due. Moreover, they have received considerable support for this view from the ICC, which has consistently stressed the specific losses arising from a given decision or policy change rather than the more general social benefits. In the past, the combined opposition of the ICC and the adversely affected income groups has been sufficient to block any change in policy. Consequently, in the absence of a marked change in attitudes regarding the importance of these potential losses, it is likely that the same forces will be able to block future policy changes that do not take these income claims into account.

Formation of Transportation Companies

If a reasonable degree of competition among integrated transportation companies could be assured, a policy permitting the formation of transportation companies could possibly satisfy most of the claims of the adversely affected groups while permitting even greater gains in terms of economic efficiency than those provided by rate deregulation alone. In particular, as long as two or three transportation companies operate in a region with a competitive fringe of barge and trucking firms, the resulting rate and transportation structure should be quite similar to that envisaged under deregulation. Under both policies, the rate floor would tend to be set by the costs of an all-motor or a joint truck-water shipment in the absence of interrail or intertransportation company price competition. Because transportation companies can take intermodal interdependencies into account, however, capacity and rate adjustments would likely be more orderly if transportation companies were permitted than under a policy of simple deregulation.

Hence, the social benefits in terms of economic efficiency should be greater under transportation companies than under rate deregulation. Moreover, the social costs in terms of income distribution should be less since many trucking and barge firms would be compensated directly through absorption by the transportation companies. However, transportation companies would probably still have an adverse effect on the producers of noncompetitive bulk commodities and those who have based their locational decisions on the existing rate structure. Consequently, whether or not transportation companies were permitted, some means would have to be found to compensate the adversely affected producers.

So long as complete deregulation and the formation of transportation companies could ensure adequate rate competition, this policy would be preferable to one that permitted only rate deregulation. But the maintenance of effective price competition is always difficult in industries dominated by a few firms, and without vigorous and effective competition transportation companies could lead to even more monopolistic inefficiencies than the current regulatory policies.

The previous chapter indicated that effective competition depends on the creation of at least two and preferably more transportation companies serving a given region and the existence of a fringe of competitive trucking and barge firms. In conjunction with the competition inherent in two or more firms vying for increased market shares, the existence of the independent barge and trucking lines should be able to keep rates at their competitive levels. Any efforts at price leadership that resulted in monopolistic rate making would be met by entry and rate cutting on the part of the independent firms.

Although the oligopolistic market structure outlined in the previous paragraph could probably ensure a reasonably competitive rate structure, a monopolistic market structure in which one transportation company dominated a region probably could not. The economic power inherent in such a company would probably be sufficient to forestall any effective competition from independent operation and would, in any case, be socially and politically intolerable.

In view of the present merger policies pursued by the ICC, the likelihood of monopolistic transportation companies seems greater than that of competitive companies. The Penn-Central merger and the Atlantic-Seaboard merger have created virtual railroad monopolies in the entire Northeast and Middle Atlantic States and most of Florida. The pending Great Northern-Northern Pacific-Burlington merger would create a virtual railroad monopoly in most of the Northwest. While such monopolies may be acceptable in the highly regulated transportation environment of today, they would not be acceptable in the environment of deregulation and the creation of transportation companies. Thus the final Supreme Court approval of the Penn-Central merger has probably foreclosed the option of deregulation in conjunction with the formation of transportation companies. Now that a company with the potential monopoly power of the Penn Central has been formed, it is inconceivable that it would be permitted to acquire competing trucking and water lines to ensure a virtual transportation monopoly. However, it is unlikely that the Penn Central Company could be dissolved to form competing transportation companies.

Thus as a practical alternative, a policy of deregulation and the formation of integrated transportation companies seems to be unreasonable. Moreover, in view of the costs it imposes on specific income groups, a policy of rate deregulation and an end of common carrier obligations does not seem to be a feasible alternative to current regulatory policies. Does this then mean that the inefficiencies created by the present regulatory policies will be continued indefinitely? Here the answer is probably yes and no.

Relaxation of Some Existing Rules

The outlook for radical changes in policy is not particularly bright, but the outlook for some improvement is considerably better. Chapter 5 discussed the competitive forces currently at work in the transportation industry and concluded that developments in piggybacking and multiple-car shipments could do much to rationalize the rate and transportation structure. The opening up of Plans III and IV piggybacking to all potential customers should undermine the value-of-service element in the rate structure. By offering a flat ramp-to-ramp rate for a container or flatcar, the railroads provide an alternative to the inflated commodity rate. Any differences in the commodity and the piggybacking rates greater than forwarder and/or trailer costs should divert traffic to piggyback and thus generate pressures to reduce the commodity rate.

If Plans III and IV are to be truly competitive with other forms of transport, however, the rule limiting the piggybacking container rate to shipments in which one commodity comprises no more than 60 percent of the shipment weight and the rule forbidding the use of piggybacking by motor common carriers if the rail distance is less than 85 percent of the highway distance must be abolished.[2] Removing these restrictions on the use of piggybacking would do much to rationalize the structure of transportation and could be done immediately within the existing regulatory framework.

The following example illustrates the way in which Plan III piggybacking could serve to rationalize the transport structure. Suppose the ICC permits railroads to quote a flat ramp-to-ramp container rate for a given haul that is freely open to all potential users regardless of the contents of the container. If the piggybacking rate and the costs of getting the shipment to and from the piggybacking site are less than the common carrier trucking costs, the motor common carrier will choose to send his shipment by piggyback instead of over the road. Under the existing rate structure, trucking firms should find themselves more profitable. In a nonregulated environment, the increased profitability of trucking firms would tend to attract new firms which would reduce their rates to piggybacking levels. Thus competition would effectively create a rate structure that approximated costs.

In the regulatory environment, competitive pressures can work only in an indirect fashion. Since trucking rates and the number of trucking firms are not easily adjusted, the usual competitive forces created by freedom of entry are not operative. Here is where the role of the private shipper or the forwarder enters. Faced with piggybacking savings that are not passed on to him, a shipper could choose to purchase or lease his own trailers and deal directly with the railroad. As long as the sum of the piggybacking rate, the trailer costs, and the costs required to move the trailer between the points of origin and destination and the piggybacking ramp was less than the quoted trucking rate, the shipper would divert his traffic from the regulated trucking firms and engage in a combination of private trucking and piggybacking operations.

Similarly, forwarders should be able to undermine the position of regulated trucking firms by consolidating truckload lots into piggybacking shipments. If the truck rate were greater than the sum of the piggybacking rate, trailer costs, and pickup and delivery costs, a competitive forwarder should be able to solicit truckload shipments, provide pickup and delivery service, and then consolidate them into piggyback shipments. However, the ability of forwarders to exert competitive pressures of this type is currently limited by several restrictions imposed by the ICC. Of

2. Although the ICC will waive this rule in appropriate circumstances, its existence undoubtedly places restrictions on the free use of piggybacking.

these, the most important are the restrictions on entry, on the ability of forwarders to provide their own motor service outside of their terminal area, and on the size of shipment a forwarder may handle.[3]

Under current regulatory policies, the Commission requires evidence that existing forwarder service is inadequate before it will issue certificates of operation to forwarders. This means that existing forwarders are essentially free of the threat of entry as long as they provide "adequate" service. Consequently, under existing policies, the exploitation of any rate spread between trucking and piggybacking services must depend on the competitiveness of the forwarders operating within a given terminal area. Nevertheless, lack of threat of entry eliminates one of the major competitive pressures. Therefore, noncompetitive pricing among forwarders is possible, whereby any differences between piggybacking rates and trucking rates would accrue to the forwarders who would receive monopoly profits. A sufficient number of forwarders usually operates within any given terminal area to provide reasonably competitive behavior; but the threat of entry is needed to ensure fully competitive behavior and to guarantee that forwarders will exploit any rate spread between trucking and piggybacking operations and pass the savings along to the shippers.

Even if entry were free, the ability of forwarders to undermine the trucking rate structure by using Plans III and IV would be limited by the ICC's rule that they cannot provide direct services for traffic that lies outside of their terminal area, which is usually quite small. Although the sum of the piggybacking rate, the trailer cost, and the pickup and delivery costs might be less than the trucking rate, a forwarder would be unable to exploit the differentials if the pickup and delivery rate charged by a trucker were sufficiently high. Thus the ability of a forwarder to undermine a monopolistic trucking rate by providing alternative service is somewhat limited.[4]

Finally, the Commission's policy toward the size of shipments limits the forwarders' competitive ability. If a forwarder is primarily engaged in the handling of truckload or carload lots without assembly or consolidation, the Commission will presently rule that he is operating outside the limits of his authority. The Commission has also ruled that it is permissi-

3. For a full discussion, see Jeffrey S. Wood, "Intermodal Transportation and the Freight Forwarder," *Yale Law Journal*, Vol. 76 (June 1967), pp. 1360–96.

4. Section 409 of the Interstate Commerce Act permits motor common carriers to give special contract rates to forwarders for distances up to 450 miles. For a full discussion of the implications of this policy, see *ibid.*, pp. 1381–85.

ble for a forwarder to consolidate truckload shipments into piggyback shipments. Nevertheless, it is not clear whether the Commission would permit a forwarder to engage primarily in consolidations of this type. Without a clear sanction to perform consolidations of this type, the forwarders' ability to exploit Plans III and IV is somewhat constrained.[5]

If forwarders are to be able to take full advantage of Plans III and IV and provide the competitive benefits implied by their utilization of these plans, it is imperative that the ICC take a more permissive stand toward forwarder operations. In particular, the Commission should permit the following: (1) free entry into forwarding, provided the applicant meets certain minimum standards of service; (2) freedom of forwarders to provide direct motor pickup and delivery service outside of their terminal areas; (3) freedom of forwarders to handle any shipment size. These changes would require no legislation and would ensure that shippers of all sizes and resources could take full advantage of the cost savings implied by Plans III and IV.

Even though free competition might be limited with regard to the regulated motor carriers, the possibilities of private, forwarder, and shipper association carriage should enable effective entry to undermine the position of the regulated motor carrier. Faced with a loss in traffic and profits, the reaction of the regulated trucking firms should be to reduce rates. Thus even in the regulatory environment, unrestricted use of Plans III and IV piggybacking in conjunction with the removal of certain forwarder restrictions should force the rail and trucking rate structure to come close to the competitive rate structure.

The growth of piggybacking should also have important implications for the utilization of transport capacity. Because of the blanket-rate structures and the economies associated with high utilization of railroad equipment, the railroads are forced to perform a large amount of low-density service that is probably uneconomical at existing rates. The Commission has been unwilling to permit the railroads to abandon this service or to raise rates sufficiently to make the substitution of truck service attractive.

By concentrating their high-density traffic in piggybacking and their low-density traffic in ordinary boxcar service, the costs of this service might increase sufficiently to justify rate increases that would attract competitive truck service. Since trucks are better suited to low-density traffic, the

5. For a full discussion, see *ibid.*, pp. 1377–81.

substitution of truck for low-density rail service and the abandonment of low-density rail capacity would represent an improved allocation of resources.

Once the railroads discontinued their low-density service, average rail costs would fall. This should then justify reductions of rail rates on the high-density traffic. Thus further forces should be set in motion to correct the misallocation of transport resources in the high-value, high-density traffic.

The widespread use of Plans III and IV piggybacking should lead to a rate structure that reflects relative costs and a traffic allocation in which railroads concentrate on the wholesaling service of the line-haul operation and trucks concentrate on the retail service of the distribution operation.

More flexible attitudes toward railroad abandonments on the part of the Commission would hasten these trends. Trucks have shown themselves to be more than an adequate substitute for rail service on low-density, small-size, short-haul service. Railroad abandonments that ensured adequate trucking service would benefit the railroads, the trucking firms, and the shippers whose traffic is often better suited to trucks.

Just as Plans III and IV piggybacking are creating pressure toward a competitive rate structure in the high-value goods, the existence of aggressive water competition and alternative energy sources for coal have forced the railroads to develop new cost saving techniques and to reduce rates accordingly. The railroads have shown themselves to be very responsive to competitive pressures and have consistently tried to adjust rates down to costs in the face of severe water or market competition. However, the experience of the Big John cars, the unit trains, and the constant litigation concerning minimum rates indicates that the Commission views these developments with considerable suspicion. Although part of the Commission's reluctance to permit rate reductions may arise from a fear of the possible dynamic inefficiencies of free rail-water competition, a greater part of it probably arises from a desire to permit the water carriers to maintain their existing competitive position or to protect producers that might be adversely affected by volume rate reductions.[6] Nev-

6. For example, in the recent *Ingot Molds* case the Commission tried to prevent the railroads from reducing rates on ingot molds shipped between Pittsburgh, Pa., and Steelton, Ky., to capture the traffic that currently goes jointly by truck and barge. Since the proposed rail rate is well above out-of-pocket costs, one can only infer that the Commission is attempting to protect the barge and trucking carriers in preventing the railroads from reducing their rates down to the

ertheless, it is likely that the Commission could permit considerably more freedom in granting rate reductions while guarding against excessive losses that might arise from competitive pressures.

Thus a policy of more relaxed regulation with regard to piggybacking, forwarders, abandonment, and minimum rates would seem to be the least disruptive and the most easily adopted. Failure to relax piggybacking or forwarder restrictions and rigidity with regard to abandonment and minimum rates would effectively prevent any rationalization of the transport structure and maintain the gross inefficiencies that currently exist in providing transportation services. Therefore the greatest opportunity for a rationalization of the transport structure probably lies with the Commission itself, which must recognize the magnitude of the social costs connected with the maintenance of the present regulatory policies.

By ending all restrictions on the use of Plans III and IV piggybacking, by removing all restrictions on forwarders with respect to entry, control of motor carriers, and size of shipment, and by permitting abandonments that would ensure substitution of truck for rail services, the Commission could set competitive forces in motion that would in themselves tend to create an efficient allocation of transport resources with respect to high-value goods. Although the slowness of the projected changes might seem to be an undesirable consequence of the regulatory process, by mitigating the effects of competition on the trucking firms, slowness may in fact be desirable. By being more flexible with respect to innovations and rate reductions on competitive bulk traffic, the Commission could quite rapidly permit a competitive rate structure to be established with respect to these commodities, while limiting the competitive excesses that could develop. Finally, by preventing mergers that could substantially lessen competition, the Commission could hold open the option of establishing transportation companies if the more marginal policy changes outlined in the past few paragraphs did not prove to be effective.

Although these changes require no legislation and are feasible within the existing regulatory framework, there is some question whether they are feasible within the existing regulatory climate. The Commission was primarily established to protect certain groups from monopoly exploitation by the railroads and has consistently stressed issues of economic equity rather than economic efficiency. Losses to a particular carrier or

joint barge-truck rate. In a recent decision, the Kentucky District Court ruled in favor of the railroads. Investigation and Suspension Docket 8038, *Ingot Molds from Pennsylvania to Steelton, Ky.,* 326 ICC 77 (1965); U.S. District Court for the Western District of Kentucky at Louisville, Civil Action 5227 (April 1967).

producer have generally been given more weight than the social losses resulting from the inefficiencies created by the rate structure. Thus unless the Commission recognizes the magnitudes of the social costs associated with the present regulatory policies, even marginal changes will not be made.

If any changes are to be made in the current regulatory policies, two truths must be recognized: the existing regulatory framework and policies have led to inefficiencies and social costs arising from a misallocation of transport resources that must be corrected; the losses accruing to specific income groups from such a correction must be minimized. Thus any new transportation policy must have the dual goals of economic efficiency and maintenance of the income levels of the adversely affected groups. The first and foremost requirement for any change in policy must be a recognition and acceptance of these two not entirely consistent goals on the part of the Commission, the legislators, and the economists concerned with transportation problems. The problem then becomes one of devising a policy that will satisfy both goals.

Any policy change is unambiguously desirable only if every person is at least as well off after the change as he was before it. However, virtually no change is possible that fulfills this criterion, for there will always be gainers and losers. In this situation, the gains must be weighed against the specific losses; if the losses are relatively small and if the gains are sufficiently large, the change is usually thought to be desirable. Obviously, value judgments must be made. An infinite weight on any losses would preclude any change, while a zero weight could lead to excessive hardships.

Unfortunately, there are no "proper" weights to use. Nevertheless, the policy changes proposed here with respect to piggybacking, forwarders, abandonments, and minimum rates should lead to social benefits far in excess of any costs to specific income groups. Thus, unless it is believed that the relatively small specific losses should be given sufficient weight to offset the considerable social gains, the existing transportation policy should be changed in the proposed directions. The fiction should be ended that a policy applicable to the market and transportation structure of the late nineteenth century is also applicable to the market and transportation structure of the latter half of the twentieth century. Efforts should be concentrated instead on the way in which this policy can be changed to apply to current conditions while minimizing the costs of this change.

CHAPTER EIGHT

Summary of Conference Discussion

DESPITE THE TASK FORCE reports, studies, and governmental messages on transportation policy in recent years, consensus on appropriate courses of action remains elusive. Economists, government administrators, and transportation management fail to agree not only with one another but also among themselves about the extent to which regulation is desirable and about the form it should take. To discuss the issues raised by current and alternative regulatory policies, a two-day conference of experts on the subject was held at the Brookings Institution in December 1967. Its purpose was not to obtain a consensus, but rather to afford the participants an opportunity systematically to lay out their reactions to the crucial issues confronting freight transportation policy.

Discussion at the conference revolved around two basic issues: What are the costs associated with current regulatory practices? Are any alternative policies or practices preferable?[1]

Costs of Current Regulatory Policies

In discussing the costs of current regulatory policies, the participants stressed the overall losses in economic efficiency and distinguished between static and dynamic costs. Although never explicitly defined in the

1. Indication of general agreement in the material which follows is my own assessment of the discussion, for no effort was made at the conference to establish a formal consensus. This summary represents what I consider to be the most significant points made at the conference, without any attempt to reflect all individual comments.

discussion, static costs seemed to mean the total resource savings that would accrue to society if all transport shipments were reallocated so that each was made at minimum social cost and if all other production relationships were reallocated accordingly. By dynamic costs, the participants seemed to have in mind the potential increase in the flow of income that would accrue to society if the existing and future stock of capital in the transport sector were utilized as efficiently as possible.

Static Costs

With vigorous dissents on the part of industry representatives, there seemed to be general agreement that considerable misallocation exists in commodity shipments. For the most part, the participants felt that a large number of trucking shipments could go more cheaply by rail, and that some rail shipments could go more cheaply by water. No participant, however, was willing to state that a given point-to-point commodity shipment went by the high (social) cost mode. The participants felt that subtle differentials in service and problems associated with estimating social costs made such quantification impossible.

By and large, the participants treated the figures on the relative costs of the different modes cautiously. While they generally agreed that these figures were reasonably accurate as averages, all stressed their inapplicability to specific situations. Several participants pointed out that unmeasurable characteristics of service can have an important impact on relative costs in many cases. Reliability of shipment, costs of loading and unloading, differences in free time, and the ability of a shipper to control the arrival of a shipment can all have important impacts on relative rail or trucking costs in particular cases. Moreover, the participants were dubious about the relevance of the Interstate Commerce Commission (ICC) cost data, which they believed of little use in assessing relative costs. Consequently, they were wary of making any general statements, for example, to the effect that shipments weighing more than 20 tons and going more than 200 miles should go by rail.

In spite of the doubts expressed by the participants concerning the specific cost estimates, it was generally agreed that the thrust of the analysis was correct: a large number of high-value shipments that currently go by truck could, in fact, go by rail at considerably less social cost. Because of their doubts concerning the specific cost and demand estimates, however, the participants were skeptical of the estimated static cost of the current regulatory policies of $300 million to $500 million a year. They felt that these figures might slightly overestimate the costs of misallocation within the transport industry, but underestimated the static costs within the entire economy and grossly underestimated the total static and dynamic costs arising from current regulatory policies. Many of the participants feared that these estimates would be identified as the total costs of regulation. In fact, a few of the participants did just that. They considered it a rather low cost, comparing favorably with costs of misallocation in other sectors of the economy. One participant pointed out that while this might appear to be a low cost, it was not so small when considered as a recurring cost. If these annual costs were discounted, their present value was probably on the order of $10 billion; and this figure should be compared with the once and for all costs of changing current regulatory policies. This notion was attacked on two grounds: there might be some benefits arising from current policies that had not been estimated; and the costs of altering them might not in fact occur once and for all and might therefore also require discounting.

Dynamic Costs

It seemed to be generally agreed that although they were not quantifiable, the dynamic costs associated with regulation were greater than the static costs. In particular, regulation was thought to contribute to poor investment decisions, excess capacity, and excessively high costs of service. The discussion of the impact of regulation on investment was far-ranging and highlighted the difficulties faced by the railroads in obtaining adequate capital, the distortion of the railroad investment decision, the stifling of innovation, and—although this was not blamed on regulation—the misallocation of investment funds in waterways.

The problem of railroad investment was discussed at some length, and it seemed to be generally believed that the industry had trouble obtaining funds. One participant singled out the recently instituted rent-a-train service as an example of the lengths to which railroads will go to avoid making capital investments. However, there seemed to be agreement that the railroads could find external funds to finance investment in rolling stock—if at a very high price—even though, it was stated, investment in road and structures had to be financed internally. In the course of this discussion, the hostility of the railroads to the 1958 transportation act, which made federal loans available to them, was explained in terms of (1) the railroads' relatively high liquidity at that time; (2) restrictions imposed on the loans, which made them an expensive form of capital; and (3) management's fear of dependence on government funds. Although corporate liquidity was said to be dangerously low, the current attractiveness of such a loan program was not discussed.

Four possible reasons were given for the railroads' difficulties in obtaining capital for modernization: First, management is inept. Second, regulatory constraints inhibit the exploitation of existing possibilities for profitable innovation. Third, few profitable investment possibilities exist in the railroad industry. Fourth, interdependencies among railroads make it difficult for any one railroad to capture the benefits of its investments in the absence of similar investments on the part of other railroads.

The ineptitude of railroad management was generally conceded. Top management in the railroad industry, it was agreed, usually consists of men who can write good tariffs or get along with the regulatory authorities rather than men skilled in management or innovation.

The regulatory process was also held responsible for the lack of rationalization in the railroad industry. Delay in the introduction of unit trains and Big John cars was cited as an example of how the regulatory process explicitly repressed innovation; but there was general agreement that regulation in more subtle ways both prevented railroads from rationalizing their capital structure and forced uneconomic debt-equity structures under current market conditions. Moreover, several participants stated that, by curbing freedom to maximize profits, regulation dulled managerial aggressiveness. As evidence, the unwillingness to invest in aluminum cars was blamed on regulation, for it prohibits rates that would ensure the intensive utilization required to make such equipment profitable.

Many participants thought that regulation tended to distort the investment decision. Several participants believed that the need to justify rate reductions in terms of cost reductions demonstrable on the ICC's rail form A tended to channel investments into areas where the railroads could demonstrate cost savings to obtain desired rate reductions. Trilevel cars, aluminum cars, and development of the trailer on flatcar as opposed to the container on flatcar were cited as instances in which regulation influenced the nature of the investment. Although some participants believed that the need to demonstrate cost savings tended to stimulate innovation, most seemed to find the distortions undesirable. One participant stated that he found it hard to believe that the railroads should thank the ICC for stimulating their investments in this fashion.

In addition to the restraints regulation places on railroad management and innovation, the participants stressed its impact on the amount of rail capacity. The enormous opportunities to rationalize the industry through disinvestment and abandonments, currently forbidden by the ICC, were generally recognized. In conjunction with this, it was pointed out that in forcing the railroads to perform low-density service, the ICC made them act like retailers, when in fact their relative advantage lay in acting as wholesalers of transportation services. Because of this, rail costs tended to be higher than they would be if the desired rationalization could take place.

Although the problems associated with trucking regulation were not extensively discussed, several nonacademic participants expressed concern over the agricultural exemption and thought it should be reduced. More generally, many participants seemed to feel that trucking regulation was extremely inefficient and acted to raise trucking costs substantially as a result of the route and gateway restrictions and the emphasis on service competition, which encourages common carriers to maintain excess capacity.

Finally, virtually all of the participants felt that the federal investment program in waterways represented serious misallocation of scarce federal funds. The specific criteria used to measure the costs and benefits of navigation investments were thought to inflate the estimated benefit-cost ratio. Many navigation investments were held to be absurd in terms of economic efficiency. While there was less discussion of the highway program, some participants seemed to feel that some highway investments were carried to the point where marginal social costs were greater than marginal social benefits.

In conclusion, it was generally agreed that the costs of current regulatory practices were substantial, even if they cannot be precisely measured. Misallocation of resources, stifling or distortion of investment and innovation, prevention of needed rationalization of railroad capital, increased transport costs, and inefficient investment policies were all singled out as costs of current regulatory or government policies. What is more important, most of the participants felt that the benefits obtained from these policies were not worth their costs.

Alternatives to Present Policies

While there was virtual unanimity that the present regulatory policies do not work well, there was less agreement concerning the desirability of adopting alternative policies. Many participants worried about the transitional losses that substantial changes in policy might impose on some producers and shippers and thought that many would find adjustments to new policies painful. Concern was expressed for injustice in changing the rules at this point, when many shippers and producers had made commitments and locational decisions on the assumption that current regulatory practices would continue.

Participants felt that without adequate compensation for groups that would be adversely affected changes in current regulatory policies were unthinkable. Nevertheless, most thought that noneconomic goals (such as income transfers) could be more efficiently achieved by direct policies and that economic goals were not well served by regulation. Although the discussion only touched on practical alternatives to achieve noneconomic goals, the distributional implications of changes in current regulatory policies were brought up in connection with virtually all alternatives.

Attention focused on the following alternatives to current regulatory policies: cost-based rates; termination of minimum rate regulation; total deregulation and an end to common carrier obligations; mergers; and formation of multimodal transportation companies.

Cost-based Rates

In discussing cost-based rates, the participants distinguished between tying all rates to costs (presumably fully distributed) and permissive pricing that would let rates fall to marginal cost (presumably long-run, but some participants seemed to have in mind short-run). None of the participants favored a rate structure rigidly tied to relative costs. Numerous reasons were cited: (1) Because of the highly questionable costing procedures followed by the ICC, tying rates to costs as measured by the Commission would lead to even greater misallocation of resources than currently exists. (2) Even if costing procedures were to improve, the administrative burden placed on the ICC by such a policy would be awesome. (3) Since average-cost pricing is often used as a means of cartelizing an industry, this procedure might lead to more rather than less cartelization of transport. (4) In view of the excess capacity prevailing in the railroad industry, any effort to tie rates to long-run average costs would require subsidies until capacity could be adjusted downward. Since railroad capacity is notoriously long-lived, subsidies would probably be required for the foreseeable future. But subsidies are politically infeasible. Therefore, discriminatory pricing would have to be pursued to make up the burden, thus contradicting the notion of cost-based rates.

In addition to doubting the feasibility of cost-based rates, several participants raised the question of their distributional implications. It was generally believed that many agricultural products and shipments over 2,000 miles currently travel at less than full cost. While no one was willing to speculate on the ultimate distributional impact of cost-based rates, it was felt that they would lead to rate increases on many agricultural and bulk commodities shipped to the East from the West. In addition, several participants expressed concern for the impact cost-based rates would have on distant cities which now enjoy parity with nearer cities in a single-rate district. In this connection, one participant thought that the impact of cost-based rates would be greater on trucking than on rail shipments. In view of the current parity that small-lot shippers in small towns and suburban areas enjoy with large, central-city shippers, several participants believed that cost-based rates in the trucking industry could seriously affect their competitive position. While none of the participants who raised the question of distributional impacts was willing to comment on whether they were "good" or "bad," all felt that they must be weighed in assessing a change.

There was considerably more sentiment among the participants for a permissive policy that would permit rates to fall to marginal cost when such reductions could be justified on grounds of costs. While they did not explicitly state this, most seemed to have in mind an extension of current ICC policies that would let rates fall to long-run marginal cost. Nevertheless, the discussion seemed to indicate that some of the participants had short-run marginal costs in mind. This would explain most of the reservations voiced against this policy. Several participants were worried that larger shippers could use monopsony power to force rail rates down excessively. They cited cases of railroads, because of shipper power, handling commodities at what were agreed to be ridiculously low prices and accepting unfavorable divisions of the revenues from joint rates when shipper-owned switching railroads were involved. However, some participants felt that such potential problems were overstated. There was also some concern over predatory pricing on the part of the railroads. Although, as was pointed out in the discussion, predatory pricing is an expensive way to drive out a competitor and the Sherman Act should prevent it, the possibility remained a source of concern to many participants. Again, the problem of potential losses to shippers and carriers caused by substantial rate changes was raised by several of the experts.

Minimum Rate Deregulation

There seemed to be general agreement that ending minimum rate regulation was not feasible because of the interdependence of all rail rates. Most participants seemed to feel that so long as rate bureaus remained, it was inconceivable that railroads could price competitively in one area while colluding in another. In general, to the extent that the participants were referring to short-run marginal cost in permissive pricing, the arguments against minimum rate deregulation were the same as those listed above. Thus there was widespread belief that unless some safeguards were imposed to prevent excesses of monopoly and monopsony power, minimum rate deregulation would not work. Specific safeguards suggested ranged from strengthening the powers under the Clayton Act to limit price discrimination by railroads to permitting competing carriers to impose injunctions against rate reductions if they anticipated being unduly hurt.

As a partial answer to these problems, one participant suggested that railroads be permitted to reduce rates up to 10 percent a year at their discretion, but be required to show cause for larger reductions. Several others agreed this was worth trying. Another participant suggested that instead of ending minimum rate regulation as such, carriers be prohibited from protesting rates. This procedure would eliminate 90 percent of all rate cases before the ICC, while still protecting the shippers. Although some thought that this suggestion might solve the problem, others were skeptical.

Total Deregulation

In discussing the problems associated with significant changes in the rate structure, several participants stressed its complex nature and the often uncomprehended trading relationships built on it. One participant likened the rate structure to a giant balloon that would bulge in unforeseen places when poked. Although the rate structure looks complicated, the point was made that industry has built up delicate trading relationships that would be disrupted by any changes in the rate structure. One participant cited an industry in which salesmen needed only to carry the railroad rate structure to enable them to quote prices to their customers. Another cited a railroad that cut rates on a commodity shipment that it thought was noncompetitive with shipments of other railroads only to find vigorous opposition on the part of other railroads and shippers. Citing these interrelationships, some of the nonacademic participants felt that the trading relationships in the economy were in a sufficiently fine equilibrium that a major change in the rate structure would lead to chaotic developments. Although this view was not widely held, many appeared to be wary of making major experiments with the rate structure because of their unpredictable consequences and their irreversibility.

In addition to the problems associated with ending minimum rate regulation, total deregulation of rates raised other questions among the participants. Many were worried about possible increases in discriminatory pricing. Moreover, several wondered about the compatibility of coordinated through shipments with intramodal price competition. The role of the rate bureaus concerned some, and there was general feeling that they were incompatible with rate competition. Again, several participants raised the question of transitional losses caused by a restructuring of rates and stressed that compensation must be paid to those hurt in the process.

While the conference tended to focus on the implications of rail-rate deregulation, the implications of ending common carrier obligations and rate regulations on trucking also received attention. Some participants felt that deregulation might lead to less investment and innovation because of increased uncertainty. Moreover, the problem of the trucker who paid a large sum for operating rights in a certain area, on the assumption that trucking regulation would continue, troubled them. While there was general agreement that the present form of trucking regulation was singularly inefficient, it was also realized that deregulation could impose substantial losses on many truckers and shippers.

One participant suggested adoption of the policy followed in most of the European countries: issuance of medallions to all private and for-hire truckers per ton of capacity while ending all other restrictions on trucking operations. Presumably, by controlling the number of medallions, the government could dictate capacity and thus to some extent profitability and rate levels. A free market in medallions would be permitted, and when their price went above some upset limit, the government would put more on the market until the price fell to the desired level. The lower the medallion price, the more trucking capacity and, presumably, the more competitive the industry. The upset price would be a matter of government policy. All existing truck capacity would be granted medallions at the initiation of such a plan, thus protecting their capital investment.

This proposal was greeted with interest and enthusiasm on the part of most of the participants, and it was generally agreed that it should be studied more fully. One participant questioned its viability in view of the many problems associated with increasing the number of taxi medallions in most large cities. While there was some concern for the service that would be provided to outlying areas, in general, the participants seemed to believe that competitive pressures would ensure adequate service. There was also agreement that the isolated, small-lot, irregular-route shipper, who is currently subsidized by common carriage, would find that his shipping costs increased substantially under this proposal.

Mergers

Several participants stated that if present merger trends continued, the possibility of any form of deregulation would become academic. By and large, the participants viewed the present merger trend with concern, because they believed: (1) the effects of inefficient and unaggressive management would be magnified in larger enterprises; (2) in the absence of regulation, the potential economic power of the merged companies would be excessive; (3) given the present attitude of the ICC toward abandonment, mergers would fail to solve the problems of excess capacity.

The participants seemed to agree generally that rationalization of the rail industry required massive abandonment. The Chicago-Omaha lines were singled out as having excessive duplication of lines and facilities. Stressing the need for abandonment, one participant quoted the president of a large midwestern railroad, who said that if he had the freedom he would get rid of one-third of his miles of track. To show that abandonment need not impose hardship on shippers, this same railroad had successfully substituted trucking for rail service along several low-density lines. In this connection, it was pointed out that an important benefit of rate deregulation could lie in the ability of a railroad to price itself out of an unprofitable market. While this view was greeted with some sympathy, participants seemed to agree that substitute service was preferable.

Transportation Companies

The attitude of the participants toward integrated transportation companies was ambivalent. On the one hand, they agreed that transportation companies offered great potential for rationalizing the transport industry. By offering integrated service, transportation companies had the potential to rationalize the capital structure of the industry; to eliminate excess capacity and abandon facilities as required; to offer better service; and to reduce transport costs by coordinating and integrating the various modes. On the other hand, participants raised the following problems associated with transportation companies. First, with little faith in railroad management's ability to take advantage of current possibilities for rationalization, they were dubious that it could realize the potentials offered by integrated transportation companies. Second, since railroads would presumably form the basis of these companies, there was concern that they would dominate and neglect potential developments and innovations in other modes. Third, there was general doubt that transportation companies would offer their integrated services to trucking or barge firms that were not subsidiaries, and none of the participants could think of ways to ensure that independent firms would be treated with parity and thus could remain competitive. Fourth, in the light of the recent merger movement, the potential power of these companies worried the conference participants. The possibility of nontransport acquisitions was also troublesome and raised specters of giant conglomerates of economic power. Fifth, there was considerable doubt that the companies would in fact act competitively and thus rationalize the transport structure.

In answer to these criticisms, it was pointed out that the low barriers to entry into trucking and barge operations should enable competitive pressures from independent operators to force integrated transportation companies to act competitively. Moreover, by stimulating a reorganization of management, the formation of integrated transport companies would almost certainly lead to rationalization of the transport structure. Nevertheless, most of the conference participants remained troubled by the implications of establishing integrated transport companies.

As an alternative to such companies, several participants raised the possibility of developing companies that would act as transport brokers

and integrate various transport services without owning any transport facilities. It was felt that, with relatively few changes in regulatory constraints, freight forwarders could become an effective force to integrate
transport services. One participant thought that United Parcel Service
might offer a good model on which to base the development of transport
brokers, although several others thought that its services were too limited.
While it was generally agreed that the development of transport brokers
or forwarders would be desirable insofar as they would offer better service and thus function as a transportation department of a large corporation to a great many small shippers, there was some feeling that their impact would be too marginal. Insofar as the participants believed that a
major reorganization of the transport rate and capital structure was
needed, they thought that transport brokers or forwarders were an inadequate solution.

Conclusion

Three basic views toward regulatory policy seemed to be expressed at
the conference. At one end of the spectrum was a group of economists
who believed that regulation was working badly, that its costs were excessive, and that major changes in the transport regulatory structure were
desirable. By and large, this group favored rate deregulation, the end of
common carrier obligations, and formation of integrated transportation
companies. They seemed to believe that the problems caused by transitional losses were not very great and could probably be ignored. At the
other end of the spectrum was a group of representatives of industry and
the ICC who found the present regulatory structure to be working fairly
well, and who favored extending regulation to the exempt water carriers
and truckers. They were suspicious of instituting major changes in the
rate structure, which they thought would lead to chaotic adjustments.

Somewhere between these two extremes lay what appeared to be the
majority view. These participants were unhappy with the impact of current regulatory policies which, they agreed, created both static costs of
resource misallocation and dynamic costs of excess capacity and poor investment decisions. But they could not agree on any desirable change in
policy. Although they felt that any distributional goals of regulation
could be better served by direct policies, they were worried about the
losses sustained in transition to a new policy. And in view of the political

structure of Congress, they saw no obvious mechanism for compensating such losses, although they thought the Trade Expansion Act of 1962 might point the way. Most of them supported experiments with deregulation, although they were apprehensive about the irreversible nature of this policy. Some favored experimentation with integrated transportation companies, although they voiced concern about the ways in which the potential monopoly power of these companies could be controlled. They all viewed favorably regulatory changes that would give freight forwarders more scope for action, and all favored substituting the medallion system for current forms of truck regulation.

In spite of the range of views presented at the conference, there seemed to be a nearly unanimous agreement that present regulatory policies are very costly to the United States economy and that present merger policies are rapidly closing out options on alternatives. Since the participants represented a wide spectrum of views and attitudes, this consensus implies that, at the very least, implications of proposed mergers should be carefully studied and that the impacts of alternative policies be quantified to see if the social costs of producing transport services can in fact be reduced.

Conference Participants

NATHANIEL A. BACK *U.S. Army Corps of Engineers*
PAUL H. BANNER *Southern Railway System*
BURTON N. BEHLING *Association of American Railroads*
GEORGE H. BORTS *Brown University*
WILLIAM M. CAPRON *Brookings Institution*
ANN F. FRIEDLAENDER *Boston College*
AARON GELLMAN *The Budd Company*
KERMIT GORDON *Brookings Institution*
EDWIN T. HAEFELE *Resources for the Future*
BEN W. HEINEMAN *Chicago and North Western Railway Company*
J. W. HERSHEY *American Commercial Lines, Inc.*
GEORGE W. HILTON *University of California at Los Angeles*
HOLLAND HUNTER *Haverford College*
EDWARD V. KILEY *American Trucking Associations*
A. SCHEFFER LANG *Department of Transportation*
LESTER B. LAVE *Carnegie-Mellon University*
EDWARD MARGOLIN *Interstate Commerce Commission*
JOHN R. MEYER *Yale University*
EDWIN S. MILLS *Johns Hopkins University*
SAMUEL H. MOERMAN *Wynn & Moerman*
DENNIS C. MUELLER *Cornell University*
GORDON MURRAY *Department of Transportation*
JAMES R. NELSON *Amherst College*
ROBERT A. NELSON *Department of Transportation*
JOSEPH A. PECHMAN *Brookings Institution*
MERTON J. PECK *Yale University*
JOHN E. TILTON, JR. *Brookings Institution*
ERNEST WEISS *National Transportation Safety Board*
GEORGE W. WILSON *Indiana University*

APPENDIX A

A Critique of Interstate Commerce Commission Costing Procedures

Most problems associated with cost estimates of the Interstate Commerce Commission (ICC) arise from its estimation and use of the percent variable, which is supposed to measure the percentage of total costs that are variable with output. Out-of-pocket costs are assumed to be the same constant percentage of total costs for all railroads. Therefore, in estimating costs the ICC not only assumes that all cost curves are linear, but that all railroads produce with precisely the same degree of increasing returns to scale.

The ICC cost concepts can be related to those of economists by considering Figure A.1, which shows the short-run cost curve of a given firm, given by fTC. At point of production C', total costs are given by OC, fixed costs are given by Of, and variable costs are given by fC. At the point of production C', the percent variable is given by the ratio of fC/OC. At different points of production the percent variable will be different. Along the cost curve fTC, the percent variable can take on values greater or less than 100.

The marginal costs of production are reflected by the slope of the tangent FC' drawn at the point of production C'. The intercept (OF) of this tangent represents what the ICC calls constant costs which are those costs that do not vary with output. Under the Commission's estimating procedure, variable cost would by given by FC, and the percent variable would be given by FC/OC, which is less than the true percent variable. Along the tangent line (FC'), the percent variable will always be less than 100, indicating that the firm is operating under increasing returns to scale. Only if the cost function is linear will the economists' and the Commission's definitions of constant or fixed costs and the percent variable coincide. These differences in definition form a major source of confusion in interpreting the Commission's cost estimates and arise from its insistence on treating all cost curves as linear.

To derive the percent variable, the ICC fits a least-squares regression line to the observed points to estimate a linear cost function in the form $C = a + bX$.[1] It then estimates the percent variable at the average values and

---

1. Specifically, it fits the line $C/M = a + bX/M$ where C = total cost, X = ton-miles, and M = miles of road. For a critique of this method of costing, see John R. Meyer and others, *The Economics of Competition in the Transporta-*

FIGURE A.1. Relation between Linear and Nonlinear Short-Run Total Cost Curves for a Given Plant and Equipment

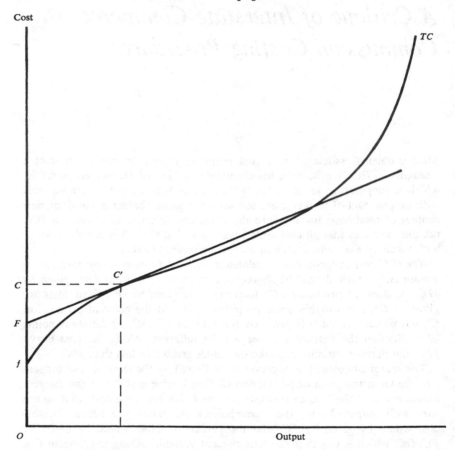

applies this to all cases. The problems associated with this procedure are two: first, the estimated percent variable will only be correct for one level of output and will tend to overestimate the percent variable for small firms and under-

tion Industries (Harvard University Press, 1959), Chap. 2; John R. Meyer and Gerald Kraft, "The Evaluation of Statistical Costing Techniques as Applied in the Transportation Industry," in American Economic Association, *Papers and Proceedings of the Seventy-third Annual Meeting, 1960, American Economic Review,* Vol. 51 (May 1961), pp. 313–34; G. H. Borts, "Production Relations in the Railway Industry," *Econometrica,* Vol. 20 (January 1952); G. H. Borts, "The Estimation of Rail Cost Functions," *Econometrica,* Vol. 28 (January 1960); and verified statements of George H. Borts, Zvi Griliches, and Gerald J. Glasser in *Rules To Govern the Assembling and Presenting of Cost Evidence,* Interstate Commerce Commission Docket 34013, Vol. 2 (April 1965).

FIGURE A.2. Biases Associated with Estimating Rail Cost Curves

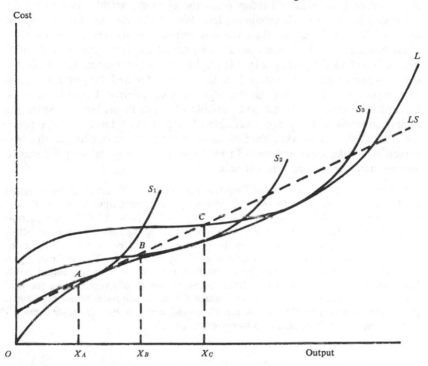

estimate it for large firms; second, the estimated marginal cost may bear little relation to the actual long-run marginal cost.

These problems can be seen in Figure A.2 which portrays a long-run cost function L and three short-run functions S_1, S_2, and S_3, representing increasing levels of capacity. Since relatively more excess capacity seems to prevail among larger than smaller firms,[2] the points of production A, B, and C are drawn to reflect declining levels of capacity utilized as the size of plant increases. If these three points constituted a cross section sample, the broken line fitted to them would look like LS in Figure A.2. Its estimated slope would be greater than the actual slope of either the long-run or the short-run cost curves at the relevant points of output. Thus the estimated marginal cost would be greater than the true marginal cost.

The percent variable is estimated to be equal to $(b)(\overline{X}/\overline{C})$ and is therefore equal to the estimated marginal cost divided by the average cost *at the average level of output*. In this example, output level B is assumed to be equal to the average level of output of the railroads in the sample. Thus, for railroad B the estimated percent variable only differs from the true percent variable insofar as the estimated marginal cost differs from the true marginal cost.

2. See Chap. 4, above, pp. 83–84.

However, for the other railroads, an additional bias occurs because the estimated percent variable will differ from the percent variable implied by the regression line. For roads producing less than B, the percent variable applied by the ICC will be higher than the one implied by the regression line; for roads producing more than output B, the percent variable applied by the ICC will be less than the percent variable implied by the regression line. Since the true long-run marginal cost is less than the estimated long-run marginal cost, errors introduced through the regression equation will tend to increase the overestimation of the percent variable of small firms, but to reduce the underestimation of the percent variable of large firms.[3] Thus for large firms, the estimated percent variable may overestimate or underestimate the true percent variable, while for small firms the estimated percent variable should overestimate the true percent variable.

3. Formally, let b be the true long-run marginal cost assumed to be constant for the relevant range. Then the true percent variable at output levels A, B, and C is given by $(b)(X/C)_{A,B,C}$. Since $(X/C)_A < (X/C)_B < (X/C)_C$, the percent variable must necessarily increase with output. If a least-squares line is fitted, the estimated long-run marginal cost is b', which is greater than b. Then, under the ICC formula, the percent variable is given by $b'(X/C)_B$. This estimated percent variable will clearly overestimate the true percent variable for output levels less than B. However, for output levels greater than B, b' overestimates the true marginal cost, while $(X/C)_B$ underestimates the true reciprocal of average costs. Hence the direction of the bias is not clear and depends on the relative magnitudes of the errors associated with using b' and $(X/C)_B$.

Derivation of the Costs of Transporting High-Value Goods

Rail Costs

Basic rail costs were obtained from the Interstate Commerce Commission (ICC),[1] with the costs of a boxcar operating in the official territory (eastern district plus Pocahontas region) taken as representative. These costs were then adjusted for inventory differentials. Since goods in transit are a form of working capital, differences in size and speed of shipment give rise to differences in inventory costs.

Smaller shipments make it possible to hold smaller inventories and thus lead to reduced inventory costs. Because the optimal boxcar load is at least twice that of the optimal truck load, rail operations should suffer from an inventory disadvantage with respect to trucks due to these differences in shipment size. However, against these inventory costs must be weighed the additional costs that arise from the greater frequency of ordering associated with small loads. As the value of the commodity rises, as the annual storage costs rise, and as the size of rail shipments rises relative to the size of trucking shipments, inventory costs associated with rail operations will rise. They will fall as ordering costs increase, as annual volume of freight handled increases, and as the size of the trucking shipments increases relative to the size of rail shipments.

Specifically, the inventory costs associated with rail operations arising from differences in shipment size can be given by the following formula:

$$\left[\frac{CI + K}{2Y}\right](Q_r - Q_t) + S\left(\frac{1}{Q_r} - \frac{1}{Q_t}\right)$$

where Y = the expected yearly sales in physical units, assumed to be 5,000 tons;
Q_r = the most economical shipment size for rail (in tons);
Q_t = the most economical shipment size for truck (in tons);
K = the annual storage cost per unit, assumed to be \$30.00 per ton;
S = procurement costs of a single order, assumed to be \$1.00 per order;
I = cost of interest, risk, and obsolescence as a percent of value, assumed to be 10 percent per year;
C = the value of the merchandise per ton.[2]

1. Interstate Commerce Commission, Bureau of Accounts, *Rail Carload Unit Costs by Territories for the Year 1963*, Statement 5–65 (March 1965), Table 3.

2. See John R. Meyer and others, *The Economics of Competition in the Transportation Industries* (Harvard University Press, 1959), pp. 348–53, for a full discussion of this formula.

TABLE B.1. Inventory Costs Resulting from Size Differentials between Rail and Truck Shipments for Selected Commodity Groups, by Value and Size of Shipment, United States, 1963

Commodity group	Value per ton (dollars)	Difference in inventory cost (cents per ton) if							
		Truck shipment is 10 tons and rail shipment is					Truck shipment is 20 tons and rail shipment is		
		15 tons	20 tons	30 tons	40 tons	50 tons	30 tons	40 tons	50 tons
Cutlery, hand tools, and hardware	1,942.78	7.88	17.43	38.20	59.79	81.72	20.76	42.36	64.29
Tires and tubes	1,508.65	5.72	13.09	29.52	46.77	64.36	16.42	33.68	51.27
Motor vehicles and equipment	1,283.46	4.59	10.84	25.02	40.02	55.36	14.17	29.18	44.52
Plastics and related materials	1,181.62	4.08	9.82	22.98	36.96	51.28	13.15	27.14	41.46
Paints, varnishes, and kindred products	593.00	1.14	3.93	11.20	19.29	27.72	7.26	15.36	23.79
Beverages and flavoring extracts	339.75	-0.13	1.40	6.14	11.70	17.60	4.73	10.30	16.20
Paper and paper products	297.49	-0.34	0.98	5.30	10.44	15.92	4.31	9.46	14.94
Industrial chemicals	202.68	-0.82	0.03	3.40	7.59	12.12	3.36	7.56	12.09
Iron and steel castings	190.01	-0.88	-0.10	3.14	7.20	11.60	3.23	7.30	11.70
Steel and rolling mill products	176.72	-0.94	-0.23	2.88	6.81	11.08	3.10	7.04	11.31
Products of petroleum refinery	59.50	-1.53	-1.40	0.54	3.30	6.40	1.93	4.70	7.80

Source: Estimated from formula on p. 195. Value data are based on Interstate Commerce Commission, Bureau of Transport Economics and Statistics, *Freight Revenue and Wholesale Value at Destination of Commodities Transported by Class I Line-Haul Railroads, 1959*, Statement 6112 (October 1961), App. A. Interstate Commerce Commission classifications used for the respective groups are hardware, tools and parts; tires and tubes; passenger, freight, and knocked down automobiles and autotrucks, other motor and military vehicles; plastics, cellulose articles; paint, paint material, putty, and varnish; malt and alcoholic liquors, other beverages, syrup and molasses; newsprint, printing, and wrapping paper, paper bags, other paper and paper articles; chemicals, sulphuric acid, acids, sodium products, alcohol, blacks; cast iron pipe and fittings; pig iron, iron and steel (billet, bloom, ingot, bar, rod, slab, nails, wire, manufactured), pipe and fittings; gasoline, road fuel, petroleum residual oils, lubricating oils and greases, refined petroleum products and other gases. A weighted average was taken for each group, based on millions of tons of revenue freight carried by the railroads. The appropriate component of the wholesale price index was used to inflate the weighted averages from 1959 to 1963 values. *Economic Report of the President, January 1965*, Table B-43, pp. 240-41.

Table B.1 shows that for a high-value commodity carried in carload lots of 40 tons, the service differential can be as much as 60 cents a ton. Since the terminal costs for shipments of this size are in the order of $1.50 a ton, this imposes a considerable extra cost on rail operations. For low-value commodities, however, these differentials are insignificant and are in the order of 6 or 7 cents a ton.

The service differentials due to time in transit must also be considered. Rail shipments are slower than truck shipments for the following reasons: (1) the average moving speed of trains is lower than the average speed of trucks; (2) freight trains get shunted off on sidings to permit faster trains to pass; (3) rail interchanges require more time than trucking interchanges; (4) freight trains must be switched through terminals; (5) rail operations require more time for pickup and delivery. Given the time differentials between trucking and rail operations and the value of the commodity, the costs associated with delaying a shipment one hour can be calculated.

The actual inventory costs depend on the time differential between shipments by truck and by rail. This can be approximated by the formula

$$T = \left(\frac{M}{20} - \frac{M}{33}\right) + 0.1\left(\frac{M}{20}\right) + \frac{M}{230}(6 - 3) + \frac{M}{140}(8) + 48$$

where $T =$ time differential in hours between rail and trucks;
       $M =$ miles of haul.

The first term represents the difference in the average freight car speed of 20 miles an hour and the average truck speed of 33 miles an hour. The second term represents the time lost as a train is placed on a siding to permit other trains to pass and states that approximately one-tenth of time in transit represents time lost on sidings. The third term represents the time differential of three hours between truck and rail interchanges, which take place approximately 230 miles apart. The fourth term represents the average 8-hour switching time that takes place at rail terminals placed approximately 140 miles apart. The final term indicates that it usually takes a train 48 hours longer to perform the pickup and delivery service than a truck owing to the additional time required to load and unload and switch a boxcar. Multiplying this expression by the cost of delaying a ton an additional hour yields the inventory cost associated with the slower rail speeds.[3]

3. See *ibid.*, pp. 192–93, for a full discussion of this formula. Specifically, the inventory time costs associated with time in transit were estimated by the following expression:

$$\frac{CI}{H}\left[\left(\frac{1}{20} - \frac{1}{33} + \frac{0.1}{20} + \frac{3}{230} + \frac{8}{140}\right)M + 48\right] = \frac{CI}{H}[0.095M + 48]$$

where $I =$ the rate of discount, assumed to be 10 percent a year; $C =$ the value of the commodity, per ton; $H =$ the number of hours in a year (8,760); $M =$ length of haul. Thus CI/H is the cost of delaying one ton of a given commodity one hour; $0.095M + 48$ is the number of hours the shipment is delayed.

In deriving Table 3.1 all inventory costs that vary with length of haul were treated as additional line-haul costs, while those that do not vary with mileage were treated as additional terminal costs.

TABLE B.2. Inventory Costs Resulting from Speed Differentials between Rail and Truck Shipments for Selected Commodity Groups, by Value and Length of Haul, United States, 1963

Commodity group	Value per ton (dollars)	Total cost of delay (cents) if shipment is carried					Unit cost of delay (cents per ton-mile) if distance is				
		100 miles	200 miles	500 miles	1,000 miles	1,500 miles	100 miles	200 miles	500 miles	1,000 miles	1,500 miles
Cutlery, hand tools, and hardware	1,942.78	128.64	150.82	217.36	328.26	439.16	1.286	.754	.435	.328	.293
Tires and tubes	1,508.65	99.88	117.10	168.76	254.86	340.96	.998	.585	.338	.255	.227
Motor vehicles and equipment	1,283.46	84.97	99.62	143.57	216.82	290.07	.850	.498	.287	.217	.193
Plastics and related materials	1,181.62	78.24	91.73	132.20	199.65	267.10	.782	.459	.264	.200	.178
Paints, varnishes, and kindred products	593.00	39.27	46.04	66.35	100.20	134.05	.393	.230	.133	.100	.089
Beverages and flavoring extracts	339.75	22.50	26.38	38.02	57.42	76.82	.225	.132	.076	.057	.051
Paper and paper products	297.49	19.72	23.12	33.32	50.32	67.32	.197	.116	.067	.050	.045
Industrial chemicals	202.68	13.40	15.71	22.64	34.19	45.74	.134	.079	.045	.034	.030
Iron and steel castings	190.01	12.59	14.76	21.27	32.12	42.97	.126	.074	.043	.032	.029
Steel rolling mill products	176.72	11.72	13.74	19.80	29.90	40.00	.117	.069	.040	.030	.027
Products of petroleum refinery	59.50	3.94	4.62	6.66	10.06	13.46	.039	.023	.013	.010	.009

Source: Estimated from formula given in note 3, p. 197. See Table B.1 for source of value data.

Table B.2 shows that the inventory costs arising from the speed differentials between rail and truck can be substantial and are particularly sensitive to the value of the commodity and the length of haul. For high-value commodities being shipped 500 miles or over, these costs range between 3 and 4 mills a ton-mile. As the length of the journey diminishes, the costs rise rapidly, and for a trip of 200 miles can be as high as 7 to 8 mills. However, for low-value goods the costs are insignificant and can be ignored.

Trucking Costs

Trucking costs were estimated for vehicles in the Middle Atlantic region in 1964. Table B.3 shows that terminal costs drop dramatically with shipment size up to 5 tons, and then continue to fall at a smaller rate up to shipments of 20 tons. Since shipments greater than 20 tons require an additional truck, the functions relating terminal costs to shipment size typically have a discontinuity at 20 tons. There are two main sources of the economies of trucking operations: First, since the pickup and delivery and billing costs are fixed for any given trip or shipment, these costs will drop per ton as the load increases. Second, as the size of shipment increases, it is more likely to be consolidated at a terminal instead of a platform, and thus requires smaller handling costs.[4]

TABLE B.3. Trucking Terminal Costs, by Cost Component and Weight of Shipment, Eastern-Central United States, 1964

(Costs in dollars per ton)

Weight of shipment (tons)	Pickup and delivery cost	Platform handling cost	Billing and collecting cost	Total terminal cost
1	10.04	10.42	0.82	21.28
5	5.84	3.26	0.14	9.24
10	4.08	0.82	0.08	4.98
15	3.32	0.26	0.04	3.62
20	2.92	0.16	0.04	3.12

Source: Interstate Commerce Commission, Bureau of Accounts, *Cost of Transporting Freight by Class I and Class II Motor Common Carriers of General Commodities by Regions and Territories for the Year 1964*, Statement 7–65 (August 1965), pp. 42–43.

4. Almost 90 percent of 1-ton shipments, but only 45 percent of 5-ton shipments, 15 percent of 10-ton shipments and virtually no 20-ton shipments must be platform handled (central region data). See Interstate Commerce Commission, Bureau of Accounts, *Cost of Transporting Freight by Class I and Class II Motor Common Carriers of General Commodities by Regions or Territories for the Year 1964*, Statement 7–65 (August 1965), p. 31.

For any given truck, the line-haul costs can be divided into running and fixed costs. Included in the running costs are maintenance, tires and tubes, fuel, and the driver's pay. Included in the fixed costs are insurance, depreciation, and overhead (indirect administrative expenses, fringe benefit payments to employees, property taxes, and interest). Since the costs associated with any given truck are typically a small percentage of the total costs of a firm, the relevant unit of operation is the truck instead of the vehicle-mile. The firm typically adjusts the number of vehicles to its scale of operation instead of the use of its vehicles. Therefore line-haul costs per vehicle-mile can be taken as constant, given the average use of the vehicle.[5] While the costs per vehicle-mile are constant and independent of the load carried, the ICC has estimated that some line-haul costs do increase with the load. Consequently, line-haul trucking costs do not vary inversely with the size of shipment, although they fall until the capacity of the truck is reached.

Piggyback Costs

Estimates of piggyback costs are made somewhat difficult by the abundance of plans available. Under Plan I, the railroad simply carries the truck trailer and negotiates with the trucker. Since the shipper still negotiates with the trucker, he obtains none of the economies associated with piggybacking operations. Under Plan II, the railroad offers door-to-door service and negotiates directly with the shipper. However, the use of this service is limited to areas served directly by the railroad. Plans III and IV are similar, and were devised to attract forwarder and private carriage. Under these plans, the shipper provides the pickup and delivery service and the trailer (Plan III) or the trailer and the flatcar (Plan IV), while the railroad provides the ramp and a flat rate per container. Plan V is essentially a combination of Plans I and II, in which interchanges between rail and truck take place to permit the effective area of the piggybacking operations to be extended. This is the only really coordinated movement between rail and truck.

Of these plans, Plan II seems to incorporate the total costs of piggybacking best. It includes all of the pickup and delivery, terminal, and line-haul expenses. Thus its costs will be analyzed to indicate the nature of the social costs of piggyback operations.

Terminal costs associated with Plan II include the usual trucking costs of pickup and delivery plus the additional costs required to fasten the trailer onto the flatcar, to make it ready for shipment, and to make up the piggyback train. Since trucking terminal costs have already been analyzed, it is necessary to consider only the additional costs associated with piggybacking operations. These include billing and collecting costs, the costs associated with tying and untying the loaded and empty trailers onto the rail car, special service costs

5. See Meyer and others, *Competition in the Transportation Industries*, pp. 91 and 92, for an elaboration on this point.

TABLE B.4. Terminal Costs Associated with Piggyback Operations, 1963

Type of cost	Amount (dollars)
Station clerical expense, per trailer	4.24
Tiedown and untie, per trailer	9.00
Special service cost, per trailer	1.07
Trailer cost (investment and operation), per trailer	7.80
Switching cost, per trailer	8.68
Total cost per trailer	30.79
Total cost per flatcar (1.7 trailers per car)	52.34

Sources: For station clerical, special service, and switching costs: Interstate Commerce Commission, Bureau of Accounts, *Rail Carload Unit Costs by Territories for the Year 1963*, Region V, derived from Table 3, p 22, and Table 16, p. 56. For tiedown and untie: the ICC has estimated these costs at $18 (*ibid.*). This is considerably higher than the estimates of Meyer and his associates—$3.50 (John R. Meyer and others, *The Economics of Competition in the Transportation Industries* [Harvard University Press, 1959], p. 105). Since the Meyer estimates were based on the most efficient equipment, they are probably not relevant to most piggyback operations. To be conservative, a figure of $9 was taken here. Trailer cost: assumes cost of $2.60 per day and three days spent in terminals.

applicable to trailer on flatcar (TOFC) traffic, and switching costs at one-half those assigned to regular flatcar switching operations at the origin and destination. The cost of the trailers must also be considered, which for purposes of the analysis can be assumed to be provided by the railroad.[6]

Terminal costs associated with one trailer are $30.79 and with one flatcar, $52.34 (Table B.4). To this must be added an additional terminal cost of $0.006 per ton for all shipments, which makes a basic terminal cost of $52.35 per car for piggyback shipments. This should be compared with the basic rail terminal costs of $66.18 per car plus $0.10 per ton. Hence the terminal costs associated with piggybacking operations are at least 20 percent less than those associated with ordinary boxcar operations, but the actual savings involved are greater than this because of the higher inventory costs associated with ordinary boxcar operations.

The basic line-haul costs associated with piggyback operations are

6. These costs of ownership are $2.60 per day and can be derived as follows. (See National Academy of Sciences–National Research Council, Highway Research Board, *Line-Haul Trucking Costs in Relation to Vehicle Gross Weights*, Bulletin 301 [1961], p. 69.) The costs of a trailer are approximately $4,500. To this must be added the costs (approximately $250 to $300) of the attachment required to enable the trailer to be fastened to the flatcar (see Meyer and others, *Competition in the Transportation Industries*, p. 107). Thus assume that the total trailer cost is $5,000, a 10 percent rate of interest, a nine-year life under straight-line depreciation, and annual costs of repairs, insurance, and licenses of $375 (R. E. Clancy, "Growth, Economics and the Future of Piggybacking," [Master's thesis, Massachusetts Institute of Technology, 1963], p. 74), then the annual cost of a trailer is $930 which comes out to $2.60 per day.

somewhat larger than those associated with ordinary boxcar operations. While a boxcar can carry a 40-ton load at 6.7 mills a ton-mile, a piggybacking flatcar can carry this load for 7.3 mills a ton-mile. Similar differentials prevail for lower loads; a boxcar can carry a 10-ton load for 20.6 mills a ton-mile, a piggybacking flatcar can carry the load for 23.0 mills a ton-mile.[7] Since piggybacking operations require an additional cost for the trailers in transit, the boxcar cost differentials should be even greater.[8] For a 10-ton shipment, the additional trailer cost would be 1.7 mills a ton-mile; for a 40-ton shipment these costs would fall to approximately 0.4 mill a ton-mile.

Offsetting these higher basic costs are the lower inventory costs associated with piggybacking operations due to shorter times in transit.[9] While the inventory costs accruing to boxcar operations due to time in shipment were 3 to 4 mills a ton-mile for shipments of 500 miles, comparable piggybacking costs are only in the order of 2 mills a ton-mile. Thus the reduced inventory costs offset the higher line-haul costs associated with piggybacking operations. The net result is piggybacking line-haul costs that are roughly similar to the line-haul costs of ordinary boxcar operations.

7. Tables 3.1 and 3.2.

8. Since the use of a trailer costs $2.60 a day, each day a TOFC flatcar is engaged in service costs the railroad $4.42 for the use of a flatcar in transit or $0.18 an hour. For a given haul of M miles, the time in transit (T) can be given by the following expression:

$$T = \frac{M}{20} + \frac{3M}{230} + \frac{4M}{140}.$$

This expression is developed from the previous section and implies that the average speed of the train is 20 miles an hour, that switching takes 3 hours and occurs every 230 miles and that terminal interchanges occur every 140 miles and take 4 hours. Multiplying the time in transit by the hourly cost of the flatcar yields an additional cost of 1.65 cents per flatcar-mile.

9. A reasonable approximation of the time differential between trucking and piggybacking operations can be given by

$$T_t - T_P = \frac{M}{20} - \frac{M}{33} + \frac{4M}{240} + 24$$

where T_t = trucking time, T_P = piggybacking time, and M = length of haul. This assumes that rail switchings are reduced in half and that pickup and delivery times associated with piggybacking operations are one-half of those associated with ordinary train operations. Thus the inventory costs are given by

$$\frac{CI}{H}\left[(M)\left(\frac{1}{20} - \frac{1}{33} + \frac{4}{140}\right) + 24\right]$$

where C = the value of the commodity, per ton;
   I = the rate of discount, assumed to be 10 percent per year;
   H = the number of hours in a year.

APPENDIX C

Statistical Tables

TABLE C.1. Intercity Freight Traffic in the United States, by Mode of Transport and by Percentage Federally Regulated, 1939–67[a]

(In billions of ton-miles)

Year	Airways	Rail-roads	Inland waterways			Motor carriers			Oil pipelines		
			Total	Regulated		Total	Regulated		Total	Regulated	
				Total	Percent-age		Total	Percent-age		Total	Percent-age
1939	0.012	338.9	96.2	n.a.	n.a.	52.8	19.6	37.1	55.6	n.a.	n.a.
1940	0.014	379.2	118.1	n.a.	n.a.	62.0	20.7	33.4	59.3	n.a.	n.a.
1941	0.019	481.8	140.5	n.a.	n.a.	81.4	26.8	32.9	68.4	n.a.	n.a.
1942	0.034	645.4	148.6	n.a.	n.a.	59.9	28.1	46.9	75.1	n.a.	n.a.
1943	0.053	734.8	141.7	n.a.	n.a.	56.8	28.8	50.7	97.9	n.a.	n.a.
1944	0.071	746.9	150.2	n.a.	n.a.	58.3	27.3	46.8	132.9	n.a.	n.a.
1945	0.091	690.8	142.7	n.a.	n.a.	66.9	27.3	40.8	126.5	n.a.	n.a.
1946	0.093	602.1	124.0	7.4	6.0	82.0	30.4	37.1	92.5	73.1	79.0
1947	0.158	664.4	146.7	8.8	6.0	102.1	37.7	36.9	104.2	82.3	79.0
1948	0.223	647.3	150.5	9.0	6.0	116.1	46.7	40.2	119.6	94.5	79.0
1949	0.235	534.7	139.4	8.4	6.0	126.6	47.9	37.8	114.9	91.4	79.5
1950	0.318	596.9	163.3	9.8	6.0	172.9	65.6	37.9	129.2	102.1	79.0
1951	0.379	655.4	182.2	10.9	6.0	188.0	72.3	38.5	152.1	120.2	79.0
1952	0.415	623.4	168.4	10.1	6.0	194.6	70.8	36.4	157.5	124.4	79.0
1953	0.413	614.2	202.4	12.1	6.0	217.2	76.5	35.2	169.9	134.2	79.0
1954	0.397	556.6	173.7	10.4	6.0	214.6	72.3	33.7	179.2	141.6	79.0
1955	0.481	631.4	216.5	13.0	6.0	226.2	82.9	36.6	203.2	160.6	79.0
1956	0.563	655.9	220.0	13.2	6.0	253.8	83.0	32.7	230.0	179.8	78.0
1957	0.572	626.2	231.8	13.9	6.0	244.9	78.3	32.0	222.7	173.7	78.0
1958	0.579	558.7	189.0	11.3	6.0	247.0	79.1	32.0	211.3	167.8	78.0
1959	0.739	582.0	195.0	n.a.	n.a.	275.0	n.a.	n.a.	225.0	n.a.	n.a.
1960	0.778	579.1	220.3	n.a.	n.a.	285.5	n.a.	n.a.	228.6	n.a.	n.a.
1961	0.895	567.0	209.7	n.a.	n.a.	296.5	n.a.	n.a.	233.1	n.a.	n.a.
1962	1.289	600.0	223.1	n.a.	n.a.	309.4	111.9	33.8	237.7	205.4	86.4
1963	1.296	629.3	234.2	n.a.	n.a.	331.8	120.6	36.3	253.4	217.2	85.7
1964	1.504	666.2	250.2	n.a.	n.a.	349.8	125.1	35.8	268.7	229.5	85.4
1965	1.910	708.7	262.4	n.a.	n.a.	388.4	140.3	36.1	306.4	263.5	86.0
1966	2.252	750.8	280.5	n.a.	n.a.	380.9	n.a.	n.a.	332.9	285.9	85.9
1967	2.592	731.2	274.0	n.a.	n.a.	388.5	n.a.	n.a.	361.0	n.a.	n.a.

Sources: Motor carriers, 1939–45: Walter Y. Oi and Arthur P. Hurter, Jr., *Economics of Private Truck Transportation* (William C. Brown Co. for Northwestern University, Transportation Center, 1965), p. 14. Airways, 1939–56, and all other data, 1939–45: U.S. Bureau of the Census, *Historical Statistics of the United States, Colonial Times to 1957* (1960), p. 427. Other data (except airways), 1946–59: Special Study Group on Transportation Policies in the United States, *National Transportation Policy*, Preliminary Draft of a Report Prepared for the Senate Committee on Interstate and Foreign Commerce, 87 Cong. 1 sess. (1961), p. 50, Airways, 1957–67, and all other data, 1960–67: *73rd Annua lReport of the Interstate Commerce Commission* (1959), p. 11, and subsequent reports. Percentages may be based on data before rounding.

n.a. Not available. a. All airway and railroad transport carriers are federally regulated.

TABLE C.2. Indices of Federally Regulated and Unregulated Intercity Freight Traffic in the United States, by Mode of Transport, 1939–67[a]

Year	Airways 1946 =100	Railroads 1939 =100	Inland waterways			Motor carriers			Oil pipelines		
			Total 1939 =100	Reg- ulated 1946 =100	Unreg- ulated 1946 =100	Total 1939 =100	Reg- ulated 1939 =100	Unreg- ulated 1939 =100	Total 1939 =100	Reg- ulated 1946 =100	Unreg- ulated 1946 =100
1939	12.9	100	100	n.a.	n.a.	100	100	100	100	n.a.	n.a.
1940	15.1	111.9	122.8	n.a.	n.a.	117.4	105.6	124.4	106.7	n.a.	n.a.
1941	20.4	142.2	146.0	n.a.	n.a.	154.2	136.7	164.5	123.0	n.a.	n.a.
1942	36.6	190.4	154.5	n.a.	n.a.	113.4	143.4	95.8	135.1	n.a.	n.a.
1943	57.0	216.8	147.3	n.a.	n.a.	107.6	146.9	84.3	176.1	n.a.	n.a.
1944	76.3	220.4	156.1	n.a.	n.a.	110.4	139.3	93.4	239.0	n.a.	n.a.
1945	97.8	203.8	148.3	n.a.	n.a.	126.7	139.3	119.3	227.5	n.a.	n.a.
1946	100.0	177.7	128.9	100.0	100.0	155.3	155.1	155.4	166.4	100	100
1947	170.0	196.0	152.5	118.9	118.3	193.4	192.3	194.0	187.4	112.6	112.9
1948	239.8	191.0	156.4	121.6	121.4	219.9	238.3	209.0	215.1	129.3	129.4
1949	252.7	157.8	144.9	113.5	112.3	239.8	244.4	237.0	206.7	125.0	121.1
1950	341.9	176.1	169.8	132.4	131.6	327.5	334.7	323.2	232.4	139.7	139.7
1951	407.5	193.4	189.4	147.3	146.9	356.1	368.9	348.5	273.6	164.4	164.4
1952	446.2	183.9	175.1	136.5	135.8	368.6	361.2	372.9	283.3	170.2	170.6
1953	444.1	181.2	210.4	163.5	163.2	411.4	390.3	423.8	305.6	183.6	184.0
1954	426.9	164.2	180.6	140.5	140.1	406.4	368.9	428.6	322.3	193.7	193.8
1955	517.2	186.3	225.1	175.7	174.5	428.4	423.0	431.6	365.5	219.7	219.6
1956	605.4	193.5	228.7	178.4	177.4	480.7	423.5	514.5	413.7	246.0	258.8
1957	615.1	184.8	241.0	187.8	186.9	463.8	399.5	501.8	400.5	237.6	252.6
1958	622.6	164.9	196.5	152.7	152.4	467.8	403.6	505.7	380.0	229.5	224.2
1959	791.6	171.7	202.7	n.a.	n.a.	520.8	n.a.	n.a.	404.7	n.a.	n.a.
1960	836.6	170.9	229.0	n.a.	n.a.	540.7	n.a.	n.a.	411.2	n.a.	n.a.
1961	962.4	167.3	218.0	n.a.	n.a.	561.6	n.a.	n.a.	419.2	n.a.	n.a.
1962	1,386.0	177.0	231.9	n.a.	n.a.	856.0	570.9	660.8	426.4	281.0	163.4
1963	1,393.5	185.7	243.5	n.a.	n.a.	628.4	615.3	636.1	455.8	297.1	186.6
1964	1,617.2	196.6	260.1	n.a.	n.a.	662.5	638.3	676.8	483.3	314.0	202.1
1965	2,053.8	209.1	272.8	n.a.	n.a.	735.6	715.8	747.2	551.1	360.5	221.1
1966	2,421.5	221.5	291.6	n.a.	n.a.	721.4	n.a.	n.a.	598.7	391.1	242.3
1967	2,787.1	215.8	284.8	n.a.	n.a.	735.8	n.a.	n.a.	649.3	n.a.	n.a.

Source: Table C.1.
n.a. Not available. a. All airway and railroad transport carriers are federally regulated.

TABLE C.3. Percentage Distribution of Ton-Miles of Federally Regulated and Unregulated Intercity Freight Traffic in the United States, by Mode of Transport, 1939–67[a]

Year	Airways	Rail-roads	Inland waterways			Motor carriers			Oil pipelines		
			Total	Reg-ulated	Unreg-ulated	Total	Reg-ulated	Unreg-ulated	Total	Reg-ulated	Unreg-ulated
1939	b	62.4	17.7	n.a.	n.a.	9.7	3.6	6.1	10.2	n.a.	n.a.
1940	b	61.3	19.1	n.a.	n.a.	10.0	3.3	6.7	9.6	n.a.	n.a.
1941	b	62.4	18.2	n.a.	n.a.	10.5	3.5	7.0	8.9	n.a.	n.a.
1942	b	69.5	16.0	n.a.	n.a.	6.4	3.0	3.4	8.1	n.a.	n.a.
1943	b	71.2	13.7	n.a.	n.a.	5.5	2.8	2.8	9.5	n.a.	n.a.
1944	b	68.6	13.8	n.a.	n.a.	5.4	2.5	2.9	12.2	n.a.	n.a.
1945	b	67.3	13.9	n.a.	n.a.	6.5	2.7	3.8	12.3	n.a.	n.a.
1946	b	66.8	13.8	0.8	13.0	9.1	3.4	5.7	10.3	8.1	2.2
1947	b	65.3	14.4	0.9	13.5	10.0	3.7	6.3	10.2	8.1	2.1
1948	b	62.6	14.6	0.9	13.7	11.2	4.5	6.7	11.6	9.1	2.5
1949	b	58.4	15.2	0.9	14.3	13.8	5.2	8.6	12.5	10.0	2.5
1950	b	56.2	15.4	0.9	14.5	16.3	6.2	10.1	12.2	9.6	2.6
1951	b	55.6	15.5	0.9	14.6	16.0	6.1	9.9	12.9	10.2	2.7
1952	b	54.5	14.7	0.9	13.8	17.0	6.2	10.8	13.8	10.9	2.9
1953	b	51.0	16.8	1.0	15.8	18.0	6.4	11.6	14.1	11.1	3.0
1954	b	49.5	15.4	0.9	14.5	19.1	6.4	12.7	15.9	12.6	3.3
1955	b	49.4	16.9	1.0	15.9	17.7	6.5	11.2	15.9	12.6	3.3
1956	b	48.2	16.2	1.0	15.2	18.7	6.1	12.6	16.9	13.2	3.7
1957	b	47.2	17.5	1.0	16.5	18.5	5.9	12.6	16.8	13.1	3.7
1958	b	46.3	15.7	0.9	14.8	20.5	6.6	13.9	17.5	13.9	3.6
1959	0.1	45.6	15.3	n.a.	n.a.	21.5	n.a.	n.a.	17.6	n.a.	n.a.
1960	0.1	44.1	16.8	n.a.	n.a.	21.7	n.a.	n.a.	17.4	n.a.	n.a.
1961	0.1	43.4	16.0	n.a.	n.a.	22.7	n.a.	n.a.	17.8	n.a.	n.a.
1962	0.1	43.8	16.3	n.a.	n.a.	22.6	8.2	14.4	17.3	15.0	2.3
1963	0.1	43.4	16.2	n.a.	n.a.	22.9	8.3	14.6	17.5	15.0	2.5
1964	0.1	43.4	16.3	n.a.	n.a.	22.8	8.1	14.6	17.5	14.9	2.6
1965	0.1	42.5	15.7	n.a.	n.a.	23.3	8.4	14.9	18.4	15.8	2.6
1966	0.1	43.0	16.1	n.a.	n.a.	21.8	n.a.	n.a.	19.1	16.4	2.7
1967	0.1	41.6	15.6	n.a.	n.a.	22.1	n.a.	n.a.	20.5	n.a.	n.a.

Source: Table C.1.

n.a. Not available. a. All airway and railroad transport carriers are federally regulated. b. Less than 0.05.

TABLE C.4. Summary of Federal Program Funds in Direct Aid of Transport, Actual 1917–60, Projected 1961–75

(In billions of dollars)

Expenditure category	Program magnitude 1917 (or later) through 1960	Projected 1961–75
Corps of Engineers navigational improvements	5.08	6.58
Tennessee Valley Authority for navigation	0.22	0.09
Coast Guard expenditures for navigation	1.69	4.79
Coast and Geodetic Survey expenditures for surveys and charts in aid of navigation	0.16	0.20
Federal aid highway authorization	20.66	41.76
Federal aviation program	4.49	18.60
Merchant marine subsidies	1.28	1.84

Source: Special Study Group on Transportation Policies in the United States, *National Transportation Policy*, Preliminary Draft of a Report Prepared for the Senate Committee on Interstate and Foreign Commerce, 87 Cong. 1 sess. (1961), p. 172.

Index

Abandonments, railroad: ICC policy, 134, 140, 172–74, 179, 184; as result of competition, 142, 145
Adams, Walter A., 113n
Adelman, M. A., 49n, 150n
Agreed charges, 159–62
Agricultural Adjustment Act, 21
Agricultural producers, income maintenance, 5, 13–16, 18, 127, 165
Agricultural products: exempt from ICC regulation, 25, 57, 115, 118–19, 128–30, 179; freight rates on, 13–21, 23–26, 57–59, 74, 79, 108, 181; as ICC category, 55; and market competition, 149–52, 154–55; value-of-service pricing, 3, 10
Agriculture, Department of, 118–19
Air freight, 97, 101, 103–04, 110n, 129
Animal products, 55–57, 148
Arkansas River project, 107n, 108–09
Assessment, of railroad property, 110n
Averch, Harvey, 80n

Bain, Joe, 76n, 89n, 157n
Bandeen, R. A., 137n
Barber, Richard J., 90n, 91n
Barge transport, 1, 4–5; costs, 44–47, 110, 128, 135n, 142–43; grain, 92–93; low-value freight, 60; rail competition, 49–50, 55–57, 125, 143, 172n; regulation of, 22–23; under transportation companies, 155, 157, 166–67, 185. See also Water transport.
Benishay, H., 51n, 74
Benson, Lee, 2n
Big John freight cars, 48, 92–94, 97, 120, 125, 172, 178
Borts, George H., 79n, 82n, 83n, 86n
Brokers, transport, 185–86
Buck, Solon Justus, 2n
Bulk commodities, transport of, 101; costs, 43–51, 55, 61, 125–26, 149–50, 152; deregulation proposals, 160n, 163; effects of deregulation, 141–44, 149–55, 165; freight rates on, 4, 10, 22–26, 131, 141–44, 149–55, 181; ICC policy, 23–26, 127–28, 130, 173; under transportation companies, 167; West-East movement, 2–3, 17, 57, 59, 151, 181
Burch, Phillip H., Jr., 106n

Capacity, in freight transport. See Excess capacity.
Capital expenses, railroad, 33–34
Carriers: Common (see Common carrier); contract, 117; exempt, 1, 6, 111, 115, 117–20, 128, 148, 186; private, 111, 114–18, 122, 128–29, 143, 158, 169, 171; unregulated, 1, 115–20, 169

209

Demand: for manufactured goods, 127; for rail services, 17; for transport services, 50–65, 136; for trucking services, 118. *See also* Elasticity of demand.
Density: as aspect of transport costs, 54–55, 68–69; in rail traffic, 85–86, 124
Depression of *1930s*, 20–21
Deregulation, of freight transport, 141–56, 159, 160*n*, 163–68, 182–87
Doyle Report (*1961*), 1*n*, 45*n*, 104*n*, 107*n*, 108, 110*n*, 138*n*
Dunlop, John T., 96*n*
Dynamic costs, 78–99, 175–79, 186

East-West freight movements, 17–18
Economic efficiency, in transport, 164, 166, 179; and the ICC, 173–74; of rail traffic, 86, 140; and rate regulation, 7, 16, 130, 138, 159–60, 175; and traffic allocation, 65–69
EHV (extra-high-voltage) transmission, 120, 125, 149
Elasticity of demand; for rail services, 4, 9–15, 26, 95, 133, 135, 141–42, 147, 149; for transport services, 51–63, 72; for trucking services, 74, 147–48
Engineers, railroad, 96
Equilibrium: economic, 69–70, 87, 183; rates, 142
Excess capacity, 1, 5, 78–88, 99, 129–30, 136, 177, 185–86; in railroading, 78–86, 99, 130, 133–34, 138–40, 152, 162, 181; in trucking, 20, 86–88, 99, 111, 118, 152–153, 179; in water transport, 143, 162. *See also* Abandonments, railroad.
Exempt carriers, 1, 6, 111, 115, 117–20, 128, 148, 186

Farm income, effect of freight rates on, 13–15, 17, 21
Farm (rural) subsidy, 26, 165–66
Farmers. *See* Agricultural producers.
Fertilizers, freight rates on, 19*n*
Firemen, railroad, 96
Flood, Kenneth, 117*n*
Forwarders, freight, 120, 123–25, 169–71, 173–74, 186–87
Fragility, as aspect of transport costs, 54–55
Freight transport: alternatives to present policies, 127–62, 168–74, 180–87; decline of common carrier, 100–26; demand for services, 50–64; deregulation of, 141–56, 159, 160*n*, 163–68, 182–87; present policies re, 65–99, 163–64, 175–79; problem of, 1–6; rationale of regulation, 7–27; supply of services, 28–50
Friendly, Henry J., 26*n*, 87*n*, 94*n*
Fulda, Carl H., 113*n*, 114*n*

Goodrich, Carter, 8*n*
Graaf, J. deV., 76*n*
Grain: freight rates on, 18, 79, 92–93, 151*n*, 154*n*; handling of, 44, 47–48, 50*n*
"Grandfather" rights (motor carriers), 112
Granite, transport of, 114
Great Northern merger, 139–40, 167
Greiner, William R., 16*n*, 19*n*, 21*n*, 23*n*, 131*n*
Griliches, Zvi, 83–84
Gross national product, and transport revenues, 101–02

Harberger, Arnold C., 69*n*, 71*n*
Healy, Kent, 85*n*, 140*n*
High-value traffic, 144–48, 152, 154, 172–73, 176. *See also* Manufactured goods.
Highway Research Board, 117, 117*n*
Highway transport. *See* Trucking.
Highways: cost of, 37–38; government investment in, 103–07, 110, 179
Hoch-Smith Resolution (*1925*), 18–19
Holcomb, Robert, 160*n*

rates, 131; discriminatory rates, 3, 15–16, 25, 59–60, 77–78, 125, 127–28; inelasticity of transport demand, 4, 10, 17, 55n; pricing of, 75–76; shipping costs, 51, 66–68. *See also* High-value traffic.
Marginal costs. *See* Out-of-pocket costs.
Market competition, 61, 149–52, 154, 172
McKenzie, Lionel W., 76n
Medallions, in trucking industry, 183–84, 187
Mergers, 138–41, 157n, 167–68, 173, 184–85, 187
Meyer, John R., 7n, 24n, 45n, 49n, 65n, 66, 82n, 83n, 106n, 110n, 128n, 137n, 149n
Middleton, P. Harvey, 9n
Miller-Wadsworth Amendment, 22–23, 131n
Minimum rate regulation, 23–27, 131, 135–37, 172–74, 182
Mining, and transport services, 52, 53n, 55, 77
Misallocation: of commodities in transit, 68, 98, 176; of transport resources, 65–99, 159n, 174, 177, 179–80, 186
Monopoly: equilibrium under, 87; of freight forwarders, 170; and government regulation, 7, 13; and transportation companies, 157–59, 167–68, 187
Monopoly power of railroads, 127, 155, 182; effect of mergers on, 140–41; effects of, 10, 61, 72n, 147–48, 151; need to curtail, 2–4
Motor carriers. *See* Trucking.
Motor Carriers Act (*1935*), 21, 111
Mueller Report (*1960*), 1n
Multiple-car shipments, 125, 129, 154n, 168. *See also* Unit trains.
Murphy, Rupert L., 129n

Nathan (Robert R.) Associates, 50
National Industrial Recovery Act, 21
National Transportation Committee, 138
Nelson, James C., 112n, 113n, 119n, 147n
Nelson, Robert A., 16n, 19n, 21n, 23n, 131n
Netzer, Dick, 110n
New York Central system, 40n, 122, 140
Norfolk and Western R. Co., 25n, 140
North-South freight movements, 17–18

Oi, Walter Y., 61, 71n, 101n, 115n, 116, 147n, 161n
Oil (petroleum), 44–49, 57, 61, 109, 113, 149, 150n
Oligopolistic transport structure, 157–58, 167
Operating expenses, railroad, 32–33
Out-of-pocket (marginal) costs, 51, 75, 180–82; defined, 28–31, 48, 131–32; ICC commodity categories, 55–60, 151n; ICC estimates of, 32–34, 55n, 141; ICC's policy re, 24–25, 135–37, 172n; in rail transport, 49, 63, 72, 93–94, 116, 128n, 141–42, 148–49

Passenger service, 32, 37, 101n
Peck, Merton J., 24n, 65n
Penn-Central merger, 140, 167–68
"Percent variable": defined, 32–33; estimates of, 80–84
Perle, Eugene D., 51n, 72, 74
Petroleum. *See* Oil.
Piggybacking, 38–43, 91, 120–25, 129–30, 147; economies of, 50–51, 158n; effects of, 68, 97, 168–74
Pipelines, 4–5, 49–51, 57, 97, 100–01; for bulk commodities, 43, 61, 125; competition with water transport, 47, 109
Political pressures, 99, 108